GOVERNMENT IN THE MODERN WORLD

GENERAL EDITORS: *Paul Y. Hammond   Nelson W. Polsby*

An
Introduction
to
American
Government

OPEN UNIVERSITY SET BOOK

SOCIAL SCIENCES FOUNDATION COURSE

An Introduction to American Government

SECOND EDITION

ERWIN L. LEVINE

Skidmore College

ELMER E. CORNWELL, JR.

Brown University

The Macmillan Company, New York
Collier-Macmillan Limited, London

COLLIER-MACMILLAN PUBLISHERS
A Division of Crowell Collier and Macmillan Publishers Limited
London

The Macmillan Company
Collier-Macmillan Canada, Ltd., Toronto

The Macmillan Company
866 Third Avenue, New York, 10022

Collier-Macmillan Canada, Ltd., Toronto, Ontario

Library of Congress catalog card number: 77–156982

First Printing 1972

Second Printing 1973

SBN 02 976870 5

Printed in Great Britain by
Redwood Press Limited
Trowbridge, Wiltshire

For Cathy, who makes it all possible.

E. L. L.

Preface

Gratified by the general response to their book in the United States and Great Britain, the authors of *An Introduction to American Government* decided to prepare a second edition. We adhered to our original intent of presenting a description of the major institutions that have shaped and characterized American national government. Only when we deemed it necessary did we supplement description with interpretative analysis in the body of the text. Each chapter has been brought up to date wherever possible, although it must be borne in mind that American political events sometimes move so quickly that they tend to outdistance their own reporting. In addition, we have added a chapter on civilian-military relationships as an illustration of policy and administration. The reader will also find the full text of the Constitution appended to the end of the text.

To solve the political problems related to our urban crises, our racial conflicts, and the stresses in American society so closely tied to our political and military involvement with other nations, it is first necessary to understand clearly the background and operation of our governmental structure. Some things simply cannot be done, no matter how much we might want them done, because of the nature of our constitutional arrangements. It is our feeling that basic United States institutions must be fully comprehended, not merely accepted or rejected out of hand, before reforms are recommended.

This book, therefore, is designed to be read as a basic text. The reader, it is hoped, will then have the tools to explore the more sophisticated aspects of American politics, both domestic and foreign. We begin where all must begin, with the Constitution and its setting.

E.L.L.

E.E.C.

Contents

An
Introduction
to
American
Government

One

Constitution and Setting

T H E A M E R I C A N political system encompasses far more than the simple concept "American government." The term *government* means a set of constitutionally derived *formal* institutions such as executives, legislatures, and courts. A political system includes these, and much more besides. The extraconstitutional, less formal institutions, like the political parties and the myriad of interest groups, are also part of the political system, as, indeed, are student radical activists who disclaim the "system." Even the informal, personalized relationships that exist *within* the executive, legislative, and judicial branches of governments are smaller "political systems" within themselves. "Political systems," in fact, tend to develop within the administrative agencies and departments, the legislatively authorized offshoots of the executive branch, and among them as well. For politics, after all, is a never-ending process whereby individuals and/or groups attempt to control other individuals and/or groups.

But the United States Constitution itself is the core of the over-all American political system. For the Constitution, written and explicit, lays out the basic structural and functional arrangements that determine the operations of the executive, legislative, and judicial branches. It also attempts to divide power between the national and state governments. But because the Constitution is in part ambiguous and omits much (American society in 1789 after all was far different from that of 1972), it has acquired layered encrustations of tradition

1

and precedent, which themselves become integral parts of the total political system even without benefit of a formal amendment. In other words, there is an informal apparatus, necessary in any governmental process, which depends in large measure on the content of the constitution. The legal document called the Constitution often determines the direction the extraconstitutional and less formal developments will take.

Actually, the formally prescribed functions and procedures and the less formal, unwritten ones are mutually dependent. It is hardly possible to separate them for analytical purposes. To take only one example, the constitutionally ordained requirements for the electoral college are still very much operative. Political parties, not even mentioned in the Constitution, have developed since 1789 and have unofficially transformed presidential elections into popular contests. Yet, to a great extent, the technique of presidential campaigning is tied to the search for a majority of *electoral* votes, a constitutional requirement, using the party apparatus as a vehicle. Thus the states with a greater number of electoral votes, derived from the fact that those states have the greatest population, are catered to more than the states with fewer electoral votes, and fewer people. Add the ingredients of urban expansion and the population explosion, and the result is the interpenetration of the formal requirements (rooted in the Constitution) and the development of the informal institutions of an organic society. One feeds the other. The changes in and expansion of American society in this century, not to mention the growth of the importance of party organization, have caused many people to doubt the wisdom of continuing the present electoral college system. Several amendments have been proposed to alter this constitutional requirement, although none has been accepted by the Congress thus far. The 1968 Wallace candidacy aroused a new wave of reform agitation.

The Constitution determines the number of electoral votes each state has for the purpose of electing a President—two for both United States senators and one for each congressman, the number of the latter increasing as the population of a state increases. But as the nation has grown in size, population, and technology, the patterns in obtaining a majority of electoral votes using the party system have also changed, causing some to seek alteration of the Constitution.

Understanding the complexities of the American political system, therefore, requires first the identification of certain key features of the society at large. The importance of these becomes unmistakably clear if one but glances at other political systems. The Soviet Union, for example, is basically not much different from the United States in constitutional structure. The Russians too have a federal system, a bicameral legislature, executive departments whose heads form a cabinet, a court system with a Supreme Court, and so forth.

Hence the really basic differences would remain unaccounted for if one merely catalogued terms and structures. Instead one must penetrate more deeply. For one thing, there is a vast difference in Russian and American national values—the proper role of government, the relationship of the citizen to the state, individual rights of citizens—which are dependent on historical factors. In addition there are differences in the way Russians and Americans visualize political authority in general, their attachments to family and church, their economic institutions and other elements, which are often currently referred to under the heading of *political culture*.

In the American political culture, value is placed on *limited* government, which plays only an instrumental role as facilitator of individual self-development, not the role of interpreter of values themselves. Americans believe that one of the most important ways of ensuring that government will remain limited and nontyrannical is to separate the power of government into three branches—executive, legislative, and judicial. The Constitution requires that no person can be in more than one branch at the same time. Furthermore, each branch in theory is coequal with the others and performs specific functions within the confines of its own jurisdiction. There are, of course, overlapping jurisdictions, particularly between the executive and legislative branches, but this is one of the features of limited government. One branch checks the other so that hopefully none of them predominates for long over the other. The result is a form of limited government congenial to the values in the political culture of this country.

The federal system, whereby power is divided between as well as shared by the national and state governments, is another component of limited government stemming from the American culture and heritage. Americans by and large look askance not only at the national government, but at state and local government as well. Americans suspect people who want and go after political power as potential lords and masters. The Russians have never known limited government, have not been taught by their national experience to value it, and doubtless visualize political authority in monolithic terms. Even the Bolshevik solution to their complaints of tyranny was more governmental authority, only in Bolshevik hands. The Russians, then, despite a structure not dissimilar to America's, do not have limited government because of other factors, historical, sociological, economic, and cultural.

The British, on the other hand, who have a unitary, as opposed to the federal, form of government, whose political executives are also Members of Parliament, and whose judicial system is not "blessed" with judicial review by a Supreme Court, enjoy the benefits of limited government much as Americans do. It is hoped, then, that the reader will have a finer appreciation for the need to know more than a mere recitation of constitutional requirements. There are many determinants for the way a political system operates more basic than the formal institutions.

Before delving into the framing of the Constitution and its principles, it might be well to mention something of the existence of interests in the American political system. The pattern of interests in a national community includes the whole range of groupings, formal and informal, permanent and temporary, organized and unorganized, self-conscious or otherwise, to which direct or indirect political importance can be attributed. It includes geographic entities (such as the South, New England, the Midwest, and Farwest); cultural and subcultural groups; racial, religious, and ethnic minorities; social and economic interests; and marginal elements in the population, like the isolated elderly, the youthful "drop-outs," and the very poor, to name but some of the obvious categories.

Just as the clearly articulated demands of well-organized

and well-heeled interest groups (such as business, labor, medicine, and agriculture) become prime ingredients in the process of making public policy, so this broader pattern of interests plays a crucial, formative, and operational role in the political system. Government responds to the cues and demands emanating from classes and regions, as well as the stridently specific demands of politically sophisticated lobbyists. And furthermore, this broad pattern of interests, like the pattern of values and cultural beliefs, implicit in the national community, shapes the very system itself.

The American political system is an interlocking network of stresses and strains, centripetal and centrifugal forces, traditional and radical cultures. The Constitution holds this complicated web together. The American people look to the Constitution for their source of authority. It is by no mere chance that today's proponents and opponents of minority and radical rights groups both point to the Constitution to substantiate their claims. Some segregationists, in fact, argue that the Fourteenth Amendment, the interpretation of which by the Supreme Court has been used as the medium for the advance of civil rights, has been unconstitutionally employed. They do not argue for doing away with the Constitution, but militantly disagree with its interpretation. It is the wide acceptance of the efficacy of the Constitution, its application to contemporary problems, and its flexibility allowing it to deal with a changing society in a world of conflict and revolution that have enabled the Constitution to become the oldest written constitution still in operation. That is no small accomplishment.

THE FRAMING OF THE CONSTITUTION

In the nature of things, a close relationship—though not perhaps a simple one—exists between the political culture of a society and its constitution. Both in the framing of a constitutional scheme and even more importantly in its evolution over time, the imprint of the pattern of interests is clear and continuous. In this era of ferment in state constitutional arrangements, induced by Supreme Court apportionment decisions since 1962, the question as to just what kind of animal a constitutional convention or constitution framing process is, forces itself on the public's attention even more insistently than usual. One might assert rather dogmatically what it is *not;* it is not a copybook political science exercise carried out in a political vacuum. It is part and parcel of the over-all political process existing at the time of its framing. It is linked, in other words, to the basic configurations of attitude and interest of the community at large, and to the particular political forces of the moment.

A constitution once framed is a kind of distillation and embodiment of the values held in the community about how government ought to function and of cultural assumptions or beliefs as to how this can best be managed. The writers of a constitution have all been subjected to the hauling and pulling of groups and interests in the community as they sought either protection or advantages. Their values will emerge—if they happen to be, for example, those of popular and limited government—in structural arrangements providing for electoral participation by the citizenry (or a good portion thereof), for checks and limitations on government, and for safeguarding local initiative and autonomy. Often their values will also emerge in an explicit bill of rights.

The political culture will play a definite role in determining which among various possible institutional arrangements will appeal to, or come naturally to, the community doing the framing. The essence of the anthropologists' concept of culture is that people born and reared in a particular society become creatures of the society, its beliefs, attitudes, and values, and find it difficult to conceive of thinking or behaving in ways other than those they have already absorbed. So it was with the framers of the Constitution in 1787. They were culturally conditioned to rule out all but the familiar notions to which they had become accustomed.

The Philadelphia convention was remarkably successful, as it turned out, in both reflecting current attitudes and objectives sufficiently to gain acceptance of its work and providing a scheme that has been enduring and flexible. Historical scholarship on the convention and its membership has, over the years, offered a variety of explanations for this remarkable success. During the first century or more of this country's history under the Constitution, the tendency was to ascribe demigod status to the framers and hence ulitmate perfection to what was clearly, in these terms, a unique and inspired performance. In 1913, Professor Charles Beard published a volume entitled *An Economic Interpretation of the Constitution of the United States,* in which he veered to the opposite extreme: that the document had been drawn up in near-conspiratorial fashion by a group of men whom one would call today the Establishment—that is, the possessors of wealth and hence beneficiaries of a scheme that protected and fostered economic activity.[1]

In recent years this "revisionist" school has been displaced by a "neo-revisionist" point of view which specifically attacks the Beardian economic thesis. The thrust of the argument has not been a return to the demigod theory, but rather, a denial of the conspiracy hypothesis and some of its related assumptions. Beard had claimed to find a direct relationship between national economic interests and the work of the convention. Beard's critics Brown and McDonald compiled a considerable list of localized economic interests in the states that stood to gain and lose from the adoption or failure of the new scheme. However, they found no broad correlations between property holding and support of the work of the convention, nor any neat pattern of national economic groups involved in the process.[2]

These disputations among the historians are not of immediate concern to us in their specific terms. One can, however, distill from them some broad conclusions about what kind of process the convention did represent. In the first place, its success no doubt hinged to a considerable degree on its size. Only fifty-five of the seventy-four delegates from the states

[1] Charles A. Beard, *An Economic Interpretation of the United States* (New York: The Macmillan Company, 1913).

[2] See Robert E. Brown, *Charles Beard and the Constitution: A Critical Analysis of 'An Economic Interpretation'* (Princeton: Princeton University Press, 1956), and Forrest McDonald, *We The People: The Economic Origins of the Constitution* (Chicago: The University of Chicago Press, 1958).

who were appointed to serve put in any appearance; an average of no more than thirty attended the sessions, and but thirty-nine signed the completed document. By contemporary standards—both here and abroad—this was a tiny group. It was also a quite unrepresentative one in terms of any detailed reflection of geographical, ideological, or group interests in the country.

Geographically, the delegates were not elected by district within the states. Rhode Island never sent any at all; and the other state delegations fluctuated considerably in number actually attending. Inasmuch as most of the anti-Federalists appointed to serve either never appeared at all or shortly withdrew, this point of view was heard only indirectly, and the remaining convention group was considerably more homogeneous than the community at large. It has also been argued that important economic interests like the frontier farmer were largely unrepresented. Yet this smallness of size and relative similarity of outlook was doubtless an asset in the deliberations. Discussion could be genuine, informal, and thorough, and still agreement could be reached among a less complex array of interests and views than it might have been necessary to reconcile.

This matter of size lends some color to the conspiratorial theory, as does another matter: the fact that the body deliberated in secret. This sounds undemocratic, but all serious, responsible negotiation must be first conducted in secrecy. Grandstanding is minimized, the impact of outside interests made less direct, and public attention ultimately focused on the total product rather than on the process by which it was put together. Precautions were taken against leaks and sentries were posted at the doors of the convention hall in Philadelphia. It is said "they even had a discreet colleague accompany the aged Franklin to his convivial dinners with a view to checking that amiable gentleman, whenever, in unguarded moments, he threatened to divulge secrets of state."[3]

And then, there were the qualities of the individual delegates themselves. Professor Beard left the implication that they

[3] John H. Ferguson and Dean E. McHenry, *The American System of Government*, 6th ed. (New York: McGraw-Hill Book Company, 1963), 35.

were, overwhelmingly, men of conservative bent and who had a property stake in the outcome. If one carefully defines one's terms these conclusions can be justified. It does not follow, however, that the framing process was necessarily a conspiratorial one in which these characteristics of the framers were transmuted into prime motivating forces. Conspiracy aside, and whatever their motives, these were able, well-read, and realistic men, for the most part. They knew—or at least many of them did—the appropriate historical and theoretical literature. They were men of no little sophistication in their awareness of human nature and how it must be taken into account in government. When Madison wrote in the fifty-first Federalist Paper concerning the checks and balances that "ambition must be made to counteract ambition," he showed insight not often displayed by modern reformers.

It may well be, as some commentators on the convention have argued, that the crucial differences between the absent anti-Federalists like Patrick Henry and Sam Adams and the Federalists who provided the real leadership must be sought in different directions from those Beard followed. Madison and Hamilton, for example, were relatively young men, whose careers did not predate the Revolution but rather developed during it. They, and others like them, had become persuaded by their experiences during the war to devote their great talents and energy toward creating national organs that could do what the Continental Congresses had done ineffectively. Thus, perhaps the line dividing the Federalists dominant in the convention from the anti-Federalists who remained outside was not so much one between grasping conservatives and Jeffersonian liberals as something else. More likely it was between relatively young, nationalist-minded men with broad perspectives and the more parochially oriented and older leadership whose careers were rooted in the pre-Revolutionary era of colonial autonomy.

Hence it was probably fortunate that the convention was rather small and heavily weighted in the Federalist direction. In reality its task was a dual one: that of framing a new government scheme, but even prior to that in a sense, the job of creating a nation out of geographic and group fragments that were by no means sold on the idea of nationhood and all of its implications. Were it not for the presence in force of a group of delegates whose experiences weakened their parochial ties and oriented them toward the emerging nation as a whole it is hard to see how a national government could have emerged.

If, then, the delegates themselves displayed less of the kind of direct interest representation in their personal concerns than Beard argued, is one justified in denying that economic and similar interests were represented at all? Clearly not. There were alignments among the states as states, both regional and otherwise, on the issue of replacing the Articles with something stronger; and there were also clusters of economic interests which though tied to states and regions to some degree transcended them.

At the outset, the feelings of the states about the national union and stronger organs for its governance depended on such matters as the viability of the state's economy to go it alone, specific anticipated benefits or disadvantages from a stronger government, and the sheer matter of communication in an age of primitive technology. New Jersey and Connecticut, for instance, were in economic difficulty, knew they could *not* go it alone, and yearned for a strong central authority. New York, at the other extreme, was doing very well on her own and viewed closer national ties with skepticism. The isolation of North Carolinians from main currents in the nation and their obvious prosperity dampened their enthusiasm; the much more cosmopolitan South Carolinians, however, though with hardly more to gain, took a broader view of the world and wanted a stronger union. Rhode Island, which never sent any delegates at all, found in her autonomy the freedom necessary for her traditional habits of living by her wits.

Professor McDonald offers another way of slicing the interest array represented directly or indirectly in the convention, which supplements this state-related analysis.[4] He writes that "four sets of interests contended for special favors." One

---

[4] Forrest McDonald, *E Pluribus Unum* (Boston: Houghton Mifflin Company, 1965), 174 ff.

was that of the landless states"—which brings us back to the states again, but this time to a more specific issue. Connecticut, New Jersey, Delaware, Maryland, and New Hampshire were much concerned with the disposition of the western lands, cramped as they were within their existing borders. "The second general interest," McDonald writes, "was the carrying trade." The Massachusetts and Pennsylvania delegations figured here. Outside the convention, the artisans and mechanics strongly supported the shippers. Third, there was the interest of the Southern planters. They wanted, variously, insurance against export duties and protection of the slave trade. They had quite opposite interests from the Yankee shippers in the future shape of navigation legislation. An American monopoly of the carrying trade would have hurt them as much as it would have helped the latter, or so they assumed.

Finally, McDonald points out, there was the moneyed interest, "which meant, in effect, public creditors and stockholders in the Bank of North America." (This bank had been chartered by Congress at the behest of Robert Morris while he was serving as Superintendent of Finance under the Articles and trying to stabilize the finances of the Confederation.) These interests were rarely voiced in discussions but hovered in the background nevertheless. Taken all in all, the prevailing pattern of interests in the emerging national community was very much a part of the deliberations of the convention. "Almost every delegate participated, at one time or another, in private discussions in behalf of some interest or another." Nothing as seemingly sinister as the Beardian conspiracy theory of constitutional framing is necessarily implicit in this finding of interest involvement. Any political system is inseparable from the pattern of interests, economic and otherwise, in the community involved; and this is hardly less true of the framing and evolution of the constitutional framework than of any other part of the system. The *continuing* impact of the evolving and changing pattern of interests on the shape of the constitutional scheme will come in for attention later.

It is more difficult and more speculative to attempt to see the relationship of what can be called *ideology* or values in the community to the work of the Philadelphia convention, and even more difficult with other aspects of political culture. A few illustrations, however, will suggest the relationship. There were, for example, some rather generalized political value assumptions floating around at the time. The reader must bear in mind that nothing resembling what one would today recognize as a full-blown notion of liberal-democracy had yet been developed. The colonists were, it is true, conscious of certain rights and privileges as freeborn Englishmen. The English constitution was almost universally revered at that period as the most enlightened framework for governance ever devised. On the other hand, however, the Glorious Revolution, which had (finally) nailed down the rights of Parliament over royal absolutist pretensions, had taken place a scant hundred years earlier. The Great Reform Act, with its hesitant first step toward manhood suffrage and fair representation in Britain, was nearly a half century in the future.

In other words, notions of what was proper and desirable in governmental arrangements were still pretty rudimentary. Clearly, as already noted, limited government was valued. People felt that there were relatively few things the government should or needed to do. In the back-country areas in many of the states, almost complete autonomy and at times virtual anarchy reigned. Thus this preference for limited government was as much an instinct, perhaps, as it was a consciously held value. On the other hand, the idea of a citizen voice through elections, representative bodies, and so forth, was well and firmly established.

One of the areas of conflict had to do with the notion of localized government, close to the people. The anti-Federalists made a near-fetish of this. The Federalists, on the contrary, fought these extreme notions in the name of effective central handling of key policy areas like trade, defense, foreign affairs, and finance. It is probably safe to say, however, that no one seriously considered the total disestablishment of local organs in favor of rule via a national bureaucracy. Local responsibility was another value inherited from Britain, and the debate was over the degree to which this should be modified.

Property rights and other individual rights were clearly

uppermost in the minds of Americans at the time, and to an extent, of their representatives. What people today associate with the First Amendment freedoms were, doubtless, far less broadly defined or deeply cherished in those days than they have become since. The Constitutional Convention of 1787 indeed rejected a Bill of Rights and this fact was used often as an argument against ratification. Yet, when one of the amendments offered to the states would have guaranteed free speech, a free press, and the right of trial by jury in criminal cases against infringement by the states, the latter summarily rejected the amendment. These, after all, had not been the rights that the British had infringed. Rather, the more elemental rights to bear arms, to resist the quartering of troops in homes, to be secure against unauthorized searches or unfair trial procedures—all outgrowths of recent and painful experience—bulked the largest in current thinking. Seven of the first eight amendments in the Bill of Rights deal with these, and only the first with the fundamental freedoms of speech, press, religion, and assembly. And these freedoms related only to the national government at the time.

This is a sampling of the kinds of value assumptions that found their way into the process of framing. A central government of enumerated powers clearly left areas of concern for the state and local levels, and for the people themselves. The right of the governed to a voice in that government was ensured via election procedures, both provided for and implied. At the same time, nothing approaching modern concepts of mass participation democracy with complete faith that the voice of the people is the voice of God was provided. The framers and their generation had been brought up in an age of rule by elites and distrust of the mob. This was as true of the anti-Federalists as of the Nationalists. As has been suggested, the chief difference between these two groups "had little to do with 'democracy' (George Clinton and Patrick Henry were no more willing than Gouverneur Morris to trust the innate virtue of the people)."[5]

Property rights were safeguarded in the body of the Con-

[5] Stanley Elkins and Eric McKitrick, "The Founding Fathers," *Political Science Quarterly* (June, 1961), 201.

stitution indirectly, in various ways, besides the provision for strong government itself. Perhaps the clearest example of political values having a direct impact on the shape of the document and the system is to be found in the clamor, during the campaign for ratification, for a Bill of Rights. This was promised and supplied shortly after the Constitution went into effect, in the first ten amendments touched on previously. Quite clearly this can be interpreted as a case in which the community, or segments of it, forced explicit recognition of certain values, albeit against the national and not state government, which had not been incorporated in the original document. Thus the national ideology, or set of values, can play an explicit and major role in constitution-making.

Perhaps the most elusive factors of all to find reflected in the Constitution are some of the other matters we list under the heading American political culture. It may well be that they were some of the most fluid and uncrystallized elements of all in the situation at this early date. One can safely theorize that some political values and cultural patterns in the new nation had been acquired from the period of British rule. Among these were a permanent and inflexible aversion to monarchy, royal pretensions, aristocratic trappings, and the like; and in the same vein, a distinct aversion to unchecked executive power because it reminded people of the detested George III. This particular cluster of assumptions was reflected in the problem of the framers in securing a sufficiently strong executive to do the job at hand, but not so strong as to become an absolute ruler.

Devotion to a tripartite division of powers with an accompanying system of checks and balances has become an equally firmly implanted American cultural belief. Distrusting governmental power as they do, Americans almost never construct a set of governing institutions at whatever level— or, indeed, in their private associations—without some kind of compartmentalization of power. Whence this fixation, which is by no means universal in the democratic world? Doubtless the ultimate root, this time, *is* British experience. The United States emerged as a nation detesting monarchy but heartily approving balanced government. This is what admirers of the British constitution thought they saw in it: an equipoise among King, Lords, and Commons. This is what Montesquieu—correctly or otherwise—had extracted from study of the British system. Madison, in the forty-seventh *Federalist Paper,* quotes the great French thinker thus: " 'There can be no liberty where the legislative and executive powers are united in the same person, or body of magistrates,' or, 'if the power of judging be not separated from the legislative and executive powers.' " (Exactly what was balanced against what, which components formed the elements, differed depending on the viewer, but the notion of division and balance predominated.)

The system based on the Articles of Confederation was not tripartite. In part this was the case because no national court system had been provided for. More important, the Articles system implied only the weakest of executive organs. On the other hand, the framers of the Articles probably did not view it as a *government* at all, in the strict sense of that term. In any event, even here American cultural beliefs were evidently somewhat fluid. Immediate post-Revolutionary experience both with the Articles and at the state level, where weak governors and strong legislatures had often been the pattern, allied traditional belief in balance and equipoise.

Once the notion of three coequal branches was written into the federal Constitution, however devoted the community had been to it before, it now became unquestioned dogma. The Constitution had as much to do with setting the American political style, with solidifying political patterns, as the other way around. The Constitution itself, one might argue, both as an entity and symbol, and in terms of many of its provisions, became a major element in the American political culture. Not only can Americans not conceive of any other set of constitutional arrangements for themselves, but they often find it hard to imagine how other peoples can be so unenlightened as to choose systems other than the American to govern themselves.

We have been briefly examining the process of the framing of the American Constitution with an eye to the *impact* of the pattern of interests, the political and cultural values and beliefs of the American national community on that process. We have by no means exhausted this subject, but other problems call us. We must make certain we are clear about the major principles upon which the constitutional system was built by the framers; and look at the process of evolution and adaptation through which the Constitution has passed in the years since 1787. These things we turn to in the chapter to follow.

Two

Constitutional Principles and Their Evolution

HE CONSTITUTIONAL SYSTEM is part of the over-all political system and also the framework within which the actual operating institutions of government have their being. The nature of a given constitutional system—whether it provides, broadly speaking, for presidential-congressional government based on separation of powers as in the United States, or whether it provides for Cabinet government with a fusion of powers as in Britain, or some combination of the two as in Fifth Republic France—is an important factor in channeling the process of policy-making in the particular nation. These structural arrangements determine in part where the points of access will be located at which interests and groups can bring pressures to bear and make their demands known. Thus the shape of the constitutional system is a vital element in the political process. At the same time, when, as in the United States, astounding advancements in the nation's population, technology, and communications network are coupled with a long-standing Constitution whose sanctity has become a traditional adjunct to the culture, one can expect acute tensions from time to time. Tension is inevitable between the irresistible force of social and economic change and the unyielding object of deified and sanctified constitutional provisions. Indeed there have been such collisions, which in the long run have compelled constitutional adaptations causing the original scheme to bend considerably but not to break.

In a word, not only does the constitutional system shape and channel the governing process, but the governing process itself over time can gradually remold the constitution. Changes through time in the pattern of interests will generate new and different—and indeed a new level of—demands upon government services, assistance, and regulation. Contemporary urban society, for example, is far more politically, sociologically, and economically complex than that of 1787. So too the role of government, which is not only more complicated but far greater as well. Changes must be met within the existing constitutional framework, or the framework itself must be changed. Adapting the changes within the structure represents acceptance of the rule of law and the Constitution as the source of authority. The latter alternative is a manifestation of the notion of revolution.

As we look at the historic principles of the constitutional system—Federalism, Separation of Powers, Checks and Balances, Judicial Review, and the Bill of Rights—we shall note some of the ways in which these principles have been bent into new shapes to accommodate vast changes in the national community. Let us begin with *federalism*.

FEDERALISM

A confederation is an alliance of semiautonomous units that have come together voluntarily for certain purposes, each unit of which is relatively free from subservience to any controlling agency outside its own borders. A unitary form of government (like Great Britain) is one in which the central government has all power and the subdivisions, mere creatures of the central government, have certain powers delegated by the central government which, therefore, can be withdrawn. A federation is a system wherein power is divided between a central government and its constituent parts or subdivisions each having its own area of substantive jurisdiction. Besides the United States, other countries that are federal in character are Switzerland, Australia, Canada, India, and West Germany. In a federal system the central government deals both with its subdivisions (the states in the Amer-

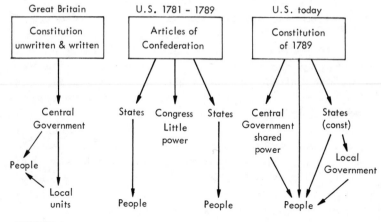

FIGURE 1

ican system) and the people at large. Indeed, the people in the United States are governed both by the United States Constitution and the constitution of the state in which they reside. In addition, the people are subject to laws passed by Congress, state legislatures, and local legislative bodies (such as city or town councils, county boards, etc.).

The framers in 1787 acted more on pragmatic considerations than according to any theoretical concept of federalism. In fact, none existed in those days for them to follow. Thus federalism can almost be called an American invention, which other countries have copied and adapted to their own cultures. The writers of the Constitution, on the one hand, collected a bundle of powers which they had come to feel must be exercised centrally, and gave them to the national government. On the other hand, they were *forced* to recognize the corporate existence of the states in various ways; for example, in the equal representation of the states in the Senate, the allocation of seats in the House, in the ratification process itself, and also in the distribution of electoral votes for the President. Thus, the result was a more or less accidental compromise, to which no one ascribed any particular sanctity at the time.

Not until later was this pragmatic compromise transmuted into a kind of sacred compact. And the *idea* of federalism as a key ingredient in constitutional government also developed later, as political party and interest group expansion developed along the federal structural lines. Today business, professional, labor, and other national interest groups are also formulated along federal lines. The Constitution, then, and one of its basic principles, federalism, have been followed by nongovernmental institutions, themselves very much part of the over-all political process in the United States. As time went on this "federal" compromise and a whole cluster of notions about "states' rights" (and as a corollary, the authority of a national organization and its locally aligned groups) became implanted in the national political structure.

If one can say, then, that the federal system as a structural arrangement began as a product of a compromise among the various interests present in the 1780's, it must also be said that it came to shape the functioning of the system in important ways later. And, in turn, federalism itself was reshaped under the impact of major changes in the nineteenth and twentieth centuries in the national community and its pattern of interests.

Under American federalism as organized in 1787, both the national and state governments were to have legislative, executive, and judicial powers, with the people subject to both authorities. What the national government could do within its area is found in enumerated powers, whereas what the states could do fell in the domain of residual or reserved powers. The latter were further clarified (or muddied) by passage of the Tenth Amendment in 1791. Some things were forbidden to the national government and others granted exclusively to it or its specific branches; many things were forbidden to the states; and several things are shared by both the national and state governments, in what is called concurrent jurisdiction. In a word, the states could do what had not been specifically granted to the national government nor forbidden to the states.

But the Constitution is a brief document and more often than not fails to define explicitly particular terms that it uses.

Even though the Constitution says, therefore, that the Constitution and the laws passed by the Congress are supreme over state constitutions and state laws (Article VI, Clause 2, known as the Supremacy Clause), there can often be doubt whether this clause is applicable when something that a state does involves concurrent jurisdiction or, according to that state, exclusive jurisdiction. The power relationship between the national and state governments is quite clear on matters of war and coining money. These are exclusive powers of the national government as stated in the Constitution. But the relationship between the national and state governments in such areas as political parties and education, civil rights, civil liberties, and economic issues is rather hazy. National supremacy in some areas of conflict between the national and state governments was early and clearly established by the Supreme Court. In 1819, for example, the Court ruled in *McCulloch v. Maryland* that a state may not use its taxing power (a shared power with the national government) against the national government. Again in 1824 the Court said in *Gibbons v. Ogden* that a law of Congress regulating interstate

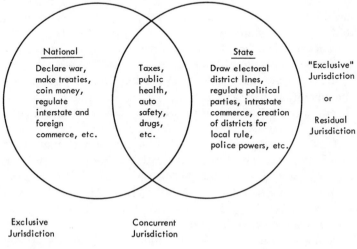

FIGURE 2

commerce (a delegated power), if in conflict with a state regulation ostensibly affecting only intrastate commerce (which is a state prerogative), must prevail over such state law. The difficulty comes in judging the existence and extent of conflict.

The federal principle has affected the operation of the whole political system. Federalism meant that there would be two levels of government at which interest demands could be voiced and policy-making processes would take place. Interest groups had in effect a choice of approaching the state governments with their requests for either aid or protection (or both), or the national government, or of playing one off against the other. The two levels of government have at times bounced problems from one to the other, or taken matters out of each other's hands, or both refused to deal with something. This can happen because, even though powers are defined, they never can be defined precisely enough to avoid ambiguity or fix absolute responsibility.

The federal division of power even had its impact in structuring extraconstitutional institutions themselves. American political parties are a case in point. Because of the existence of the federal system, with its emphasis on state constituency and district representation in the Congress, as well as the electoral college system, the national parties are decentralized, and weak nationally, yet stronger and more unified at the state level. This, in turn, affects greatly the role of the party system in over-all terms and particularly at the national level.

In these ways, then, federalism has imprinted its outline on the operation of the whole system. How, in turn, has the federal scheme itself been altered over time by the changing pattern of interests?

The evolving national economy is one of the best places to look for this. The Congress, recall, was given the power to regulate interstate and foreign commerce (Article I, Section 8, Clause 3). In general what the framers had in mind in this provision is obvious. They wanted to get the states out of the business of charging each other customs duties and obstructing the internal flow of commerce, and to provide for the protection of foreign commerce. But, beyond that, precisely *what* do the words of this clause mean? What does commerce include? Did the framers mean by the word *commerce* in 1787 what is meant today? Where does the jurisdiction of the states end and that of the national government begin? Questions of this sort arose very early in the new nation.

In 1827, in the case of *Brown v. Maryland*, the Supreme Court decided one of these questions in the so-called "original package doctrine." This stated that goods imported into a state from abroad but remaining in their original packages remained under federal jurisdiction and could not be taxed by the state. They passed to state jurisdiction only when the packages were broken open. On the other hand, in the case of *Woodruff v. Parham* in 1869, the Court ruled that if goods in interstate commerce are not imported from abroad, then the Constitution does not specifically forbid a state from taxing them, even if they remain in their original packages. Over the course of time the Court has had an impact in determining just where the line between exclusive national jurisdiction and concurrent state jurisdiction is drawn.

As for the meaning of the term *commerce* itself, it was early established that the word meant *only* the carriage of goods, trade itself, *not* mining, manufacturing, farming, selling insurance, and so forth. Then, in the period around and following the Civil War, the industrial revolution remade the national economy. The pattern of national interests changed gradually but drastically as manufacturing became a key part of the economy and state lines became crisscrossed by progress in transportation. Larger and larger corporate enterprises developed and spilled over state lines. Business became more and more national and even international in scope.

The revolution, however, went further. Labor organizations also grew up and eventually in the twentieth century business-labor strife became a national problem. Farmers organized themselves into national associations to fight for their rights in the changing economy and against the growing corporations and expanding railroads. State lines became less and less relevant to the national economy, yet under the interpretation of the commerce clause, only the states could regulate in the areas of manufacturing, labor resolutions, and agriculture. For practical purposes, however, these entities and problems became far too big for the states even to begin to regulate individually and effectively. The national government was constitutionally barred from intervening, and the states were unable to act. Federalism had become a straitjacket within which pressures steadily built up.

The great depression of the 1930's finally brought most of this to a judicial head. After some hesitation, and with much pain, the Supreme Court finally ruled that in fact *commerce* could be interpreted to include manufacturing enterprise when it really flowed, or affected the flow of goods, across the state lines. This decision came, significantly, in *NLRB v. Jones and Laughlin* in 1937, a case involving the steel industry and organized labor. Indeed, within the past few years, the commerce clause has been the basis for congressional action guaranteeing certain civil rights to people in lunchrooms, restaurants, and, indirectly, other places linked to interstate transportation, such as bus stops and railroad stations.

Since the late 1930's the national government has been in the lawfully recognized position of passing more and more legislation under the aegis of the commerce clause, while the states have had less and less exclusive (or residual) jurisdiction in intrastate commerce. As intrastate commerce became more closely associated with interstate commerce, the states at first had to share *their* commerce power with the national government and then eventually give way to Washington when a state law clashed with a congressional statute. Thus a state law regulating a minimum wage that is higher than a federal rate, as established by Congress in some industry, is enforceable in the state, but one that is lower than its federal counterpart is not.

Another changing pattern of interest that has caused more flexibility in the application of federalism to contemporary political problems is in the area of determination of electoral districts. The drawing of electoral district lines was long considered to be in the jurisdiction of the states. Indeed, in 1946 the Supreme Court refused to enter the field in spite of many complaints of gross malapportionment of both congressional and state legislative districts. The Court justified its position in *Colegrove v. Green* on the grounds that for the federal courts to decide such a political question was beyond its judicial function. Entering the "political thicket" of apportionment would be constitutionally improper. Population shifts and urban growth in the twentieth century had resulted in severe malapportionment as nonurban-controlled state legislatures did nothing to keep state and congressional district lines apace with a changing society. If citizens felt their electoral districts were malapportioned and they were thus underrepresented in the Congress and state houses, the proper way to direct their petition for a redress of their grievances was via the ballot box. Of course, in a malapportioned electoral system, there would be little chance indeed to change the nature of the state legislature in the first place. Thus the Court's decision in *Colegrove v. Green* was really no solution to the problem. True enough the United States Constitution nowhere directly enumerated the authority of the federal courts to act in such an oversight function, and the control of drawing electoral district lines was thus considered part of the residual power of the states.

In 1962, however, a differently composed Supreme Court, led by Chief Justice Earl Warren, ruled that the issue of malapportionment was now reviewable by the federal courts. The Fourteenth Amendment, said the Warren Court, justified such judicial consideration. The *Baker v. Carr* decision in 1962 in a very real sense was the culmination of social and political pressures on a sympathetic Court to do something about an increasingly desperate situation in our highly urban society. How could we justify ourselves as a democracy if our legislatures were so badly apportioned that the majority of the people in states were under-represented? In 1962 the Fourteenth Amendment, with its equal protection of the laws clause, became paramount, in the eyes of the Court, over the Tenth Amendment's reserved powers clause. Once the Court in *Baker v. Carr* said yes, we can look at this question, it *is* a constitutional question and not solely a political one for which redress can be found only in the state legislatures, the way was open for the application of the federal constitution to an area that had been solely a state

prerogative. Within a few years other decisions of the Court
—*Wesberry v. Sanders* (1964), *Reynolds v. Sims* (1964), and
*Hadley v. Junior College District of Metropolitan Kansas
City* (1970)—required a majority of the states and localities
to redraw their congressional, state, and local legislative district lines according to the concept of one-man, one-vote,
the edict which emerged from the judicial branch of the
federal government after the Supreme Court had ruled that
such an issue was indeed justiciable. Everyone's vote, under
the new rules, was to count as much as everyone else's. By
1972, a decade after *Baker v. Carr*, malapportionment was
becoming a thing of the past.

In the issue of apportionment, then, the federal courts had
in effect altered the balance in the federal system in order
to keep the balance of citizen representation (or actually to
restore it). It was anticipated that the House of Representatives would in due time more accurately reflect demographic
changes in the society, although each state regardless of the
size of its population would remain equal in representation
in the United States Senate (because of the requirement
clearly articulated in the Constitution). And, it was hoped,
the legislatures of the fifty states would also be fairer reflections of the population distribution in each of them. For
the Court to play such a role would have been unthinkable
in 1800, but by the 1960's it had become a political necessity.

In these and other ways, the whole concept of federalism
has been reinterpreted under the pressure of a changing panorama of interests making new and different demands upon
government.

Reinterpretation was not always necessary. For example,
the framers were farsighted enough to realize that they could
not—and doubtless they felt they should not—attempt to
deprive the states of all rights in dealing with their neighboring states, or with foreign powers. When they provided in
Article I, Section 10, that "No state shall, without the consent
of Congress . . . enter into any agreement or compact with
another state, or with a foreign power . . . ," their paramount
purpose was to channel the foreign intercourse of the new
union through its new national offices. But at the same time,

they left the door ajar for bilateral and multilateral arrangements to which the national government was not a direct party.

Relations between individual states under this circumscribed permission dealt almost entirely with the settlement of boundary disputes until the turn of the twentieth century. Following 1900 the range of problems of policy and interest accommodation rapidly reached such a level of complexity that any simplification that could be found or contrived became increasingly used. The so-called interstate compact was one of these. One of the earliest examples well illustrates both the problem trends and solutions involved. The states of New York and New Jersey share one of the best natural harbors in the world. As this great urban area grew in size and complexity, the need for unified control and development of key port facilities became imperative. In response in 1921 the Port of New York Authority was established via this interstate compact route, with the approval of Congress. Through the years the Authority has built or acquired a wide range of facilities, from docks and piers to jet airports. The Authority is beyond the reach of the citizens of the parent states and represents a new political entity crossing state lines but controlled by Congress.

Every year sees new developments of the interstate compact concept as new problems of an urban society demand solutions that can be brought about only by cooperation between the states and between the federal government and the states. The need for more and more water, the creation of more economic opportunities for every future generation, the crying necessity for more and better schools and colleges, the demand for increased police and fire protection, to mention but a few, all mean a changing view of federalism and what the idea of federalism can accomplish.

Federalism has come to mean more than a sharing of reciprocal governmental power between two entities, national and state government. Contemporary society now interprets the word as meaning a shared responsibility for the improvement of society. The federal, or national, government in the past few years has placed itself, or been placed by circumstances, in the position of providing the funds for development of state-oriented programs of highway, school, and public housing construction. Federally guaranteed loans, grants-in-aid to states, and outright grants of money to federally impacted areas have all brought the federal government into private lives more than ever. Indeed, the establishment of a Department of Housing and Urban Development, at Cabinet level, is but a manifestation of this new "partnership in growth" between the federal government and the states. In fact, such a department really means that the federal government has begun to deal directly with the cities and their problems rather than through the respective states. Health, education, welfare, and economic opportunity programs are all examples of this new concept of federal-state cooperation.

Both the executive and legislative branches of the federal government maintain ongoing organizations to study the federal-state relationship and to make recommendations for its improvement. The Eighty-Sixth Congress (1959–1960) established an executive body, the Advisory Commission on Intergovernmental Relations (ACIR), to give its attention to all ramifications of federalism as well as to interstate and interlocal relations. Composed of a group of private citizens, senators, congressmen, governors, mayors, state and county legislators, and federal executive officials, the ACIR issues yearly reports and recommendations for strengthening legislative and administrative roles at both federal and state levels in the federal relationship. Its professional and highly qualified staff is located in Washington and both executive and legislative branches have come to depend upon the ACIR and its staff for data, statistics, and ideas to improve the vitality of federalism.

The Senate, too, showed its awareness of the need for continual evaluation of the federal system by the establishment of a legislative subcommittee for this purpose in 1962. Thus the executive and legislative branches of the federal government have continued to maintain an active study and investigation of federal-state relations.

There is more than a kernel of truth to the opinion that

American federalism is not dead, nor is it withering on the vine. True enough, the states have often become administrators of congressionally passed national programs. But it is also true that the states have a definite hand in the establishment of these programs in the first place through their representation in the Congress, and in the administering of the law state-level administrators influence policy and the making of new rules through the over-all political process.

Not only has the power of the national government increased with more significant legislative enactments, but so has that of the states. State and local communities are doing more than ever in the fields of health, education, welfare, highway and housing construction, the attempt to control the sprawling growth of urban society and do away with the blight of the slums. Between 1946 and 1966 there was an increase of some 4 million employees of state and local government as compared to an increase of about 200,000 for the national government. In short, as the government in Washington has grown, the state governments have grown even more. But those who deplore the increase of federal power contend that Washington now controls more than ever what states do with their authority and power. The vehicle for this control, it is argued, is money. For without federal financial aid, many states simply could not carry out programs in fields of dire need. And with federal money, it is contended, comes federal control. This is the central issue in federal-state relations today.

Where do federal support and financial supplements leave off and federal policy direction and dictation begin? There is no cut and dried answer to this question. But it is true that the federal government often requires states to adhere to standards and specifications as established by the federal government in order to qualify for the various aid programs. This is true in the broad field of highway construction and the more complicated and highly controversial field of education. But it must be realized that all financial aid programs are authorized and the money appropriated by the Congress, and the congressmen are cognizant of their role as representatives of their states. As we shall see later, the Congress is not the kowtowing handmaiden of the Executive.

It is true of course that cooperation between the national and state governments in financial and other matters is historically rooted in the early days when the national government granted land for state educational purposes, helped erect railroads, and constructed roads. Federal aid to the states indeed goes back to 1787. Today's programs are merely expansions of early decisions and acts, accentuated by the complexities of modern society but within the framework of the federal system itself.

A continual process of give and take goes on between the national and state governments. The states, if they measure up to their responsibilities as they were admonished to do by Madison in the forty-sixth *Federalist Paper,* can influence the decision-makers in Washington and will check encroachments upon them by the national government. But it takes good state and local government and highly qualified and dedicated personnel to keep the states at a high level of competency in the federal system. The citizens of the states and their officials must be willing to deal with Washington, rather than sit back and complain that the national government is getting too powerful, if they are to maintain their rightful place in the federal system. Here is where the great difficulty lies in contemporary politics.

The national government can and does supply money for state programs. Between 1961 and 1964, the national government granted the states 35 billion dollars for programs in all fields. About 15 billion went for health, education, and welfare matters and 12 billion for highway construction. From President Kennedy's inauguration in 1961 to the end of the Ninety-first Congress in 1970, federal grant-in-aid programs increased from 45 to 103 in number. The grant-in-aid is a device whereby both the national and state governments each put up a specified amount of money, usually on a matching basis, for some federally approved project. According to a congressional committee, it "strengthens federalism by promoting national goals within a cooperative framework. The grant device has, in effect, prevented the nationalization of functions by strengthening and preserving State and local government."[1]

Some idea of the extent of the financial support of state programs by the federal government can be seen in Tables 1 and 2, showing federal financial aid to the states in fiscal 1969. Because the amount of federal aid is dependent on the ability of the state to put up a share of the costs of a program or project, the poorer states (which obviously need federal financial aid to a greater degree than the wealthier states) do not fare as well as they feel they should. On the other hand, the residents of the wealthy states pay a greater proportion of federal taxes from which comes the federal financial aid to the states than those of the poorer states. Yet often the per capita return of federal aid to the wealthy states is less than that to the poorer states. Thus senators and congressmen from the wealthy states are more reluctant to approve a system of grants-in-aid that does not, at least to some degree, "force" the poorer states to expend every possible effort to improve their own internal fiscal structure and broaden their own tax base. The states, therefore, do not share equally in the grant-in-aid program, nor do they receive federal financial aid according to their real needs. The political process of adjusting this conflict between state self-interest and national priorities remains ongoing, still in the throes of adjustment and accommodation.

The flow of funds going from the national government to the states and their citizens takes more than the form of a direct grant-in-aid to the states themselves. For example, there are the categories of direct federal aid to individuals in the form of grants, and to institutions for conservation, subsistence, and scientific research; second, federal civilian and military wages and salaries; third, federal transfer of payments, which take the form of railroad retirement and unemployment benefits, veterans' compensation and pensions; military retirement benefits, and, most important, payments of benefits from the old age, survivors, and disability trust funds under the

1 Senate Committee on Government Operations. *The Federal System as Seen by Federal Aid Officials.* Committee Print, 89th Cong., 1st Sess. 15 December 1965, p. 5. See also *Congressional Quarterly,* 14 August 1970, p. 2069.

TABLE 1 Federal Aid for Fiscal 1969 . . . State Breakdown of 14 Largest Programs*

	Public Assistance 1	Highways 2	Education 3	Antipoverty 4	Food Distribution 5	Public Health 6	Urban Development and Public Works 7
Alabama	$ 110,505,576	$ 73,223,621	$ 71,832,141	$ 52,077,568	$ 41,003,319	$ 19,157,982	$ 11,181,405
Alaska	5,210,423	42,280,656	17,302,913	7,071,115	1,563,963	2,331,236	10,123,925
Arizona	27,299,894	57,366,803	34,131,594	33,595,358	10,228,041	11,949,971	4,439,287
Arkansas	66,094,730	43,070,249	44,219,102	22,403,813	18,887,949	11,220,288	7,733,850
California	1,110,965,790	307,045,944	223,718,843	155,936,945	62,104,939	85,079,032	108,784,004
Colorado	66,291,665	67,662,344	37,556,281	20,396,764	10,927,123	14,120,427	4,224,682
Connecticut	74,949,708	60,498,467	27,118,565	25,196,504	9,192,462	11,219,535	34,230,375
Delaware	10,058,853	9,651,555	7,387,280	3,468,360	2,643,551	3,063,008	308,462
District of Columbia	24,701,112	31,949,879	10,323,725	51,169,772	4,599,817	8,990,649	12,871,976
Florida	113,738,824	72,277,078	73,608,802	45,981,774	36,675,442	30,542,608	12,538,861
Georgia	156,703,636	74,559,598	75,869,993	52,725,745	43,408,091	24,605,882	17,525,104
Hawaii	14,450,333	29,097,171	13,361,162	7,843,736	4,163,379	5,291,152	3,606,519
Idaho	14,985,342	31,870,778	16,399,673	3,634,227	2,841,519	3,074,569	701,824
Illinois	255,180,396	230,410,001	88,805,680	101,468,350	35,119,411	42,239,136	70,694,276
Indiana	39,902,071	141,801,135	39,779,447	21,678,801	19,004,771	17,589,748	14,145,214

Iowa	57,791,511	52,136,764	38,757,533	11,549,323	14,402,820	13,012,814	12,506,381
Kansas	52,289,480	49,156,617	33,151,679	8,513,866	9,394,818	9,420,062	5,623,369
Kentucky	126,070,230	101,443,198	60,253,294	79,100,064	29,994,715	18,730,484	8,964,143
Louisiana	181,349,661	105,972,314	58,137,012	38,438,390	31,679,894	18,704,766	3,626,318
Maine	27,012,348	18,967,697	15,418,797	7,873,971	6,211,567	5,523,186	2,690,145
Maryland	92,058,900	49,869,233	48,548,209	20,864,688	13,029,455	16,120,125	11,075,566
Massachusetts	220,395,122	106,699,713	55,456,181	50,318,547	17,608,955	21,794,578	59,672,194
Michigan	223,947,332	152,442,930	90,623,795	45,964,163	30,538,070	35,679,531	29,702,257
Minnesota	104,434,107	96,737,547	48,209,855	29,113,702	19,335,700	18,637,329	15,009,445
Mississippi	55,024,705	45,058,769	63,083,975	59,781,713	45,750,335	13,630,038	2,454,921
Missouri	149,591,176	83,705,503	62,946,037	41,192,253	24,452,454	28,915,094	17,664,953
Montana	13,187,736	52,768,124	16,250,469	7,494,029	2,803,510	3,369,562	2,223,853
Nebraska	31,349,911	30,288,180	21,681,149	11,565,969	5,913,043	8,337,079	2,590,160
Nevada	8,627,050	27,004,131	5,155,839	5,985,744	1,048,079	2,237,761	1,421,115
New Hampshire	9,915,551	20,219,299	7,665,270	5,398,956	2,436,083	3,592,619	3,052,280
New Jersey	102,219,331	119,035,339	60,040,143	65,587,993	16,703,721	24,365,461	68,393,294
New Mexico	40,610,119	48,342,859	32,000,369	16,127,047	11,414,337	7,352,070	4,184,969
New York	1,107,441,690	238,801,200	150,864,339	206,597,653	64,719,595	65,210,793	82,458,832
North Carolina	95,101,502	53,822,066	101,005,995	59,605,915	43,023,946	31,151,032	13,268,740
North Dakota	17,403,790	21,374,268	11,559,997	5,358,172	4,359,620	4,322,541	1,233,800
Ohio	184,318,968	241,533,772	99,271,098	73,722,040	44,466,336	47,863,861	39,058,019
Oklahoma	154,531,599	51,017,879	50,372,753	22,729,505	25,957,303	12,777,746	23,319,375
Oregon	38,809,481	55,398,557	26,932,923	15,687,342	11,054,748	13,013,080	4,114,129
Pennsylvania	288,129,924	227,608,215	112,766,273	100,243,679	48,979,366	56,850,736	66,585,596
Rhode Island	33,141,991	21,023,417	11,311,491	9,716,702	3,246,851	4,716,137	6,015,662

TABLE 1   Federal Aid for Fiscal 1969 . . . State Breakdown of 14 Largest Programs* (cont.)

	Public Assistance 1	Highways 2	Education 3	Antipoverty 4	Food Distribution 5	Public Health 6	Urban Development and Public Works 7
South Carolina	37,298,874	35,164,995	56,505,090	27,657,031	26,283,407	14,243,123	4,294,743
South Dakota	18,456,754	33,492,231	14,606,571	5,945,456	4,710,380	4,513,687	1,088,142
Tennessee	85,149,812	89,634,865	61,142,036	50,181,165	31,371,337	23,623,551	12,182,356
Texas	281,885,299	197,472,126	176,466,919	77,988,675	54,039,081	56,410,304	17,122,075
Utah	25,484,292	53,469,081	16,172,239	6,069,247	5,995,365	9,637,479	1,594,241
Vermont	17,431,614	34,431,108	5,788,943	3,166,081	2,110,431	5,172,822	796,144
Virginia	37,029,267	120,834,186	82,724,089	44,438,387	24,391,538	21,186,507	9,008,348
Washington	88,336,368	83,317,620	40,761,005	22,876,509	14,801,795	21,465,504	9,395,806
West Virginia	50,593,842	78,977,263	33,042,539	41,145,822	18,340,477	8,878,158	2,213,249
Wisconsin	123,154,426	41,717,046	46,807,937	21,115,218	18,119,302	17,799,042	9,654,906
Wyoming	4,497,072	42,729,468	6,245,176	2,065,257	1,491,040	3,009,107	1,046,674
Puerto Rico	44,887,990	6,357,997	29,053,168	35,411,181	32,946,658	13,096,896	8,589,210
Virgin Islands	1,350,007	0	289,974	1,277,990	552,536	567,123	553,750
Other Territories†	416,585	0	4,223,997	2,121,722	1,797,120	567,955	0
Undistributed		0	6,665,556	1,346,478	112,258,669	12,865,789	− 310,505
TOTAL	$6,321,763,766	$4,161,789,853	$2,643,319,957	$1,946,097,862	$1,180,098,234	$988,840,753	$877,248,440

TABLE 1 Federal Aid for Fiscal 1969 . . . State Breakdown of 14 Largest Programs* (cont.)

	Unemployment Insurance 8	Vocational Rehabilitation 9	Conservation Practices 10	Child Care 11	Business Development and Area Redevelopment 12	Agricultural Conservation; Extension Work and Research 13	Veterans Benefits 14
Alabama	$ 7,162,849	$ 12,658,231	$ 7,883,690	$ 4,887,305	$ 2,203,391	$ 4,255,921	$ 0
Alaska	2,805,243	858,481	11,061,629	412,125	2,612,653	657,785	0
Arizona	7,316,057	3,356,589	3,450,883	1,867,558	1,508,061	1,328,406	0
Arkansas	5,198,729	7,466,282	5,493,993	2,682,857	5,814,841	3,276,485	0
California	69,240,456	24,030,434	19,469,888	11,020,905	12,127,342	4,147,830	1,862,455
Colorado	5,770,902	4,043,104	6,164,681	4,305,838	2,324,493	1,820,087	102,613
Connecticut	9,599,351	3,501,508	1,930,354	2,067,985	691,138	1,219,656	995,211
Delaware	1,351,193	1,045,163	1,054,304	728,711	48,581	755,530	0
D.C.	5,019,512	3,517,331	443,771	4,527,893	768,822	72,000	0
Florida	11,398,910	14,350,264	3,027,425	7,747,854	71,192	2,191,896	0
Georgia	8,202,044	15,371,137	6,002,442	4,711,311	3,276,265	4,534,884	809,235
Hawaii	2,304,230	1,315,756	1,682,457	1,354,150	267,686	959,646	0
Idaho	3,396,814	791,230	4,138,754	1,155,765	349,655	1,366,372	72,878
Illinois	25,714,181	16,087,943	3,651,610	11,309,262	8,226,281	4,723,597	869,590
Indiana	9,243,689	2,598,995	4,292,841	3,446,036	1,141,284	3,677,259	333,000

TABLE 1 Federal Aid for Fiscal 1969 . . . State Breakdown of 14 Largest Programs* (cont.)

	Unemployment Insurance 8	Vocational Rehabilitation 9	Conservation Practices 10	Child Care 11	Business Development and Area Redevelopment 12	Agricultural Conservation: Extension Work and Research 13	Veterans Benefits 14
Iowa	5,306,869	5,455,086	3,741,806	2,609,381	83,614	4,024,698	820,362
Kansas	4,523,049	1,917,365	4,727,284	1,765,779	239,196	2,753,823	206,696
Kentucky	5,761,265	5,147,611	5,933,731	3,074,860	7,928,108	4,333,802	0
Louisiana	9,020,743	7,784,144	5,856,906	3,418,462	2,902,060	3,158,650	105,510
Maine	2,902,347	1,175,501	3,003,790	1,044,399	538,922	1,339,233	0
Maryland	9,076,819	6,546,568	3,030,989	6,882,403	444,247	1,674,279	0
Massachusetts	19,142,819	6,698,333	1,931,513	5,796,330	5,210,639	1,540,302	987,692
Michigan	25,837,255	13,196,755	4,485,408	10,290,794	3,271,857	3,901,709	1,048,438
Minnesota	8,792,329	7,171,266	4,287,734	4,290,917	4,721,901	3,615,836	345,244
Mississippi	5,455,811	6,471,336	9,293,649	2,961,174	5,589,384	4,570,424	0
Missouri	11,575,456	7,494,566	3,544,061	3,408,770	3,158,537	3,675,597	135,068
Montana	2,683,242	1,134,258	7,749,975	966,895	1,825,039	1,423,969	57,357
Nebraska	3,051,310	1,658,569	2,862,100	1,992,018	87,045	2,298,605	361,828
Nevada	3,393,928	993,397	2,771,615	807,988	122,805	720,385	0
New Hampshire	2,159,160	656,057	1,761,153	754,566	1,589,429	909,761	81,778
New Jersey	26,489,207	8,123,738	1,713,693	3,232,826	2,373,168	1,489,056	511,798
New Mexico	3,698,030	934,095	13,606,240	1,376,573	1,657,747	1,264,658	0
New York	76,611,579	24,408,626	5,459,395	13,560,021	2,119,686	4,074,043	74,386
North Carolina	10,125,387	11,722,313	5,176,924	6,058,171	3,195,678	6,061,875	16,200
North Dakota	2,139,494	1,230,166	2,470,703	764,368	528,334	1,725,671	86,485

Ohio	22,687,952	8,451,226	2,545,566	9,262,754	4,577,043	4,645,726	659,347
Oklahoma	7,437,154	5,959,788	10,287,643	1,987,810	4,653,432	2,735,360	850,004
Oregon	7,387,001	4,005,172	53,906,252	1,712,159	1,612,770	1,908,080	0
Pennsylvania	33,369,190	26,410,359	4,857,951	9,495,808	6,369,430	4,982,362	273,369
Rhode Island	5,201,208	1,718,048	856,772	1,245,827	4,731,747	662,305	644,193
South Carolina	5,232,365	9,088,414	3,079,424	3,789,588	1,155,403	3,785,524	0
South Dakota	1,787,100	1,088,502	2,393,507	569,115	344,815	1,658,795	164,878
Tennessee	7,103,494	5,952,889	12,045,054	3,761,710	4,279,291	4,377,983	0
Texas	23,976,172	19,436,502	14,442,071	8,474,599	7,567,965	6,498,533	0
Utah	5,324,368	1,840,970	5,247,985	977,609	651,110	1,190,918	0
Vermont	1,840,780	1,220,726	1,428,339	573,943	128,356	976,854	82,994
Virginia	6,490,730	9,088,076	5,683,850	3,781,094	704,299	3,805,393	0
Washington	11,456,715	5,745,166	12,371,091	2,614,597	5,664,288	2,402,675	548,225
West Virginia	4,362,340	6,114,211	4,045,614	2,394,803	11,710,652	2,400,844	0
Wisconsin	9,840,714	9,178,049	3,960,337	2,906,916	2,534,264	3,916,304	1,342,570
Wyoming	1,684,967	832,654	18,505,675	511,169	120,114	966,748	39,079
Puerto Rico	6,104,574	4,050,071	1,573,386	6,615,481	712,580	3,951,554	0
Virgin Islands	315,000	132,548	12,719,094	1,080,076	14,894	45,000	0
Other Territories†	45,626	334,698	167,927	168,000	25,500	10,600	0
Undistributed	14,944,327	0	−277,879	0	276,370	4,099	0
TOTAL	$588,061,976	$351,510,267	$342,947,552	$199,155,308	$146,853,404	$140,469,387	$14,488,483

Reprinted from *Congressional Quarterly*, 14 August 1970, pp. 2070–2071.

* The figures presented in each column are the totals of numerous separate programs.

† Includes American Samoa, Canal Zone, Trust Territory of the Pacific, and certain foreign countries.

TABLE 2   State Allocations of Federal Aid

States	1969 Total Grants	1969 Est. Population	1969 Per Capita Grants
Alabama	$ 419,207,000	3,531,000	$119
Alaska	106,429,000	282,000	377
Arizona	203,645,000	1,693,000	120
Arkansas	244,448,000	1,995,000	123
California	2,223,312,000	19,443,000	114
Colorado	246,765,000	2,100,000	118
Connecticut	263,274,000	3,000,000	88
Delaware	42,065,000	540,000	78
District of Columbia	251,359,000	798,000	315
Florida	427,427,000	6,354,000	67
Georgia	490,011,000	4,641,000	106
Hawaii	92,435,000	794,000	116
Idaho	85,784,000	718,000	119
Illinois	897,119,000	11,047,000	81
Indiana	319,621,000	5,118,000	62
Iowa	223,364,000	2,781,000	80
Kansas	184,630,000	2,321,000	80
Kentucky	457,832,000	3,232.000	142
Louisiana	472,281,000	3,745,000	126
Maine	94,492,000	978,000	97
Maryland	280,362,000	3,765,000	74
Massachusetts	575,201,000	5,467,000	105
Michigan	673,613,000	8,766,000	77
Minnesota	367,217,000	3,700,000	99
Mississippi	321,150,000	2,360,000	136
Missouri	443,275,000	4,651,000	95
Montana	114,675,000	694,000	165
Nebraska	124,864,000	1,449,000	86
Nevada	61,200,000	457,000	134
New Hampshire	60,477,000	717,000	84
New Jersey	502,286,000	7,148,000	70
New Mexico	189,182,000	994,000	190
New York	2,047,620,000	18,321,000	112
North Carolina	440,913,000	5,205,000	85
North Dakota	75,675,000	615,000	123

Ohio	785,045,000	10,740,000	73
Oklahoma	376,400,000	2,568,000	147
Oregon	236,303,000	2,032,000	116
Pennsylvania	989,562,000	11,803,000	84
Rhode Island	104,671,000	911,000	115
South Carolina	228,532,000	2,692,000	85
South Dakota	92,794,000	659,000	141
Tennessee	393,452,000	3,985,000	99
Texas	944,867,000	11,187,000	84
Utah	134,472,000	1,045,000	129
Vermont	75,451,000	439,000	172
Virginia	370,223,000	4,669,000	79
Washington	324,093,000	3,402,000	95
West Virginia	264,849,000	1,819,000	146
Wisconsin	314,187,000	4,233,000	74
Wyoming	84,086,000	320,000	263
Territories	397,251,000		
Undistributed	147,952,000		
TOTAL	**$20,287,399,000**	201,921,000	$100

Reprinted from *Congressional Quarterly,* 14 August 1970, pp. 2070–2072.

Department of Health, Education, and Welfare; fourth, procurement expenditures by the Department of Defense and the National Aeronautics and Space Administration, which include research and development contracts between business and defense agencies; and, last, there are the Civil Works of the Department of Defense and military reserves expenditures. Figures 3 and 4 speak for themselves.

The recipients of federal money, on the other hand, are concerned that the national government is playing too great a role in the federal-state relationship. The states often complain that federal officials do not really understand their local needs, suspect the motives of state and local officials, and tend to complicate what to them are relatively simple problems. Yet, a study by the staff of the Subcommittee on Intergovernmental Relations of the Senate Committee on Government Operations in 1963 reported that by and large state and local governments do maintain their separate identity, continue to

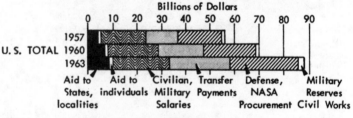

CONSTITUENTS OF ALLOCATED FEDERAL EXPENDITURES
U. S. TOTAL AND BY REGIONS, 1957, 1960, AND 1963

Billions of Dollars

0   10   20   30   40   50   60   70   80   90

1957
U. S. TOTAL   1960
1963

Aid to   Aid to   Civilian,   Transfer   Defense,   Military
States,   individuals Military   Payments   NASA   Reserves
localities   Salaries   Procurement Civil Works

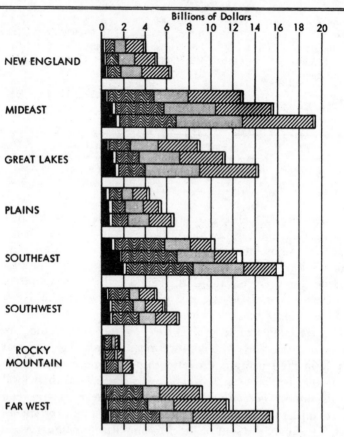

Billions of Dollars

0   2   4   6   8   10   12   14   16   18   20

NEW ENGLAND

MIDEAST

GREAT LAKES

PLAINS

SOUTHEAST

SOUTHWEST

ROCKY
MOUNTAIN

FAR WEST

FIGURE 3 Subcommittee on Intergovernmental Relations. Senate Committee on Government Operations. *Federal Expenditures to States and Regions* (June 29, 1966), p. 11.

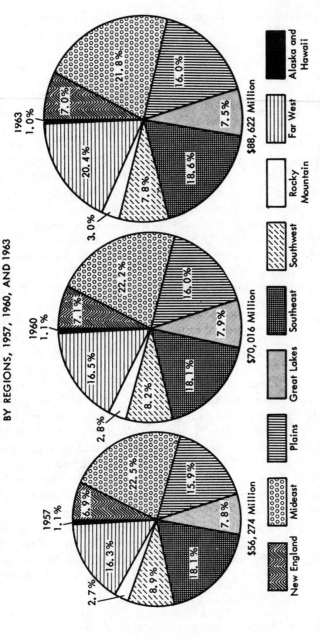

PERCENT DISTRIBUTION OF TOTAL ALLOCATED FEDERAL EXPENDITURES WITHIN THE STATES
BY REGIONS, 1957, 1960, AND 1963

1957
$56,274 Million
1.1%
2.7%
16.3%
22.5%
6.9%
15.9%
7.8%
18.1%
8.9%

1960
$70,016 Million
1.1%
2.8%
16.5%
22.2%
7.1%
16.0%
7.9%
18.1%
8.2%

1963
$88,622 Million
1.0%
3.0%
20.4%
21.8%
7.0%
16.0%
7.5%
18.6%
7.8%

New England   Plains   Great Lakes   Southeast   Rocky Mountain   Alaska and Hawaii

Mideast   Southwest   Far West

FIGURE 4 Subcommittee on Intergovernmental Relations. Senate Committee on Government Operations. *Federal Expenditures to State and Regions* (June 29, 1966), p. 31.

41

have freedom of action in the making of policy, and share decision-making on all issues, thus "preserving a cardinal principle of traditional federalism."[2]

In the mid-1960's, a new term, *creative federalism*, crept into our political vocabulary. The concept of *creative federalism* emerged as a concomitant of another slogan, President Lyndon B. Johnson's "Great Society," borrowed from Graham Wallas and Walter Lippmann for the presidential campaign of 1964. In an early speech in that campaign, President Johnson envisioned what he stated was a great society in America's future. Well aware of America's needs in areas of health, education, welfare, poverty, economic and manpower development, crime prevention, and civil rights enforcement, the Johnson Administration presented to the Congress numerous programs for raising the nation's living standards. These programs, many of them enacted into law by the Eighty-ninth Congress in 1965 and 1966, cost a great deal of money, require much detailed planning, and need qualified administrators in new agencies and bureaus. Thus, in the past few years, demands for joint action between the national and state governments became ever more prominent articulations from the Office of the President and the halls of Congress. Senator Edmund S. Muskie of Maine described *creative federalism* as "merely a response to the staggering fiscal burdens under which [the states and their localities] labor" and as fundamentally "based on the traditional habit of sharing responsibility." In the 1960's, *creative federalism* indeed made allowances for the "expanding role of state and local governments to take on greater political and administrative responsibilities." At the same time, *creative federalism* relied on a "strengthened federal role to provide new ideas, incentives, and resources to the states and localities to meet common goals." Better coordination between federal and state governments, more careful planning, and more effectively directed programs for the states were required if *creative federalism* was to work. *Creative federalism,* it was hoped, would involve

[2] Subcommittee on Intergovernmental Affairs, Senate Committee on Government Operations. *The Federal System as Seen by State and Local Officials.* Committee Print, 88th Cong., 1st Sess., 1963, p. 206.

a "matrix of independent powers and differing methods of achieving the common objective of building our country and improving the lives of our citizens."[3]

In the last two years of the Johnson Administration, however, the uncertainties and national turmoil caused by our continued involvement in the Vietnam conflict tended to depress the ambitious programs contemplated by Johnson's Great Society in partnership with *creative federalism*. Our military commitments in Vietnam were siphoning off billions of dollars, much of which might well have been used to advance the new shared programs. Too, much of the Great Society program bogged down in administrative inefficiency at both federal and state levels, and often suffered from a lack of careful planning. State and local politics, as well, sometimes presented powerful obstacles to innovations recommended by federal officials and locally participating groups of citizens. By the time of the 1968 election, *creative federalism* appeared more of a forgotten slogan than a national actuality.

When Richard M. Nixon became President in 1969, following his close victory over Hubert H. Humphrey in November, 1968, he soon took up a new description of federalism that had been expounded upon by the ACIR in its January, 1969, report. *New federalism* became Nixon's attempt to keep the federal-state relationship viable. As described by the ACIR, the search for a *new federalism* was as follows:

> While 1968 commenced and coursed with developments that endangered American federalism and its political system, both appear less threatened today. The ultimate futility of violence, divisiveness, and racial strife coupled with the turmoil and razor-thin results of several hard fought National, State, and local elections have produced a sober realization that our pluralistic, pragmatic system of government and politics has great intrinsic worth. Its traditional traits—mutual forebearance, compromise, and moderation—now are viewed as more relevant than ever. Above all, the essentiality to national unity of ameliorating the many social and economic problems facing urban and rural America is widely acknowledged.
>
> Yet, there is also widespread awareness that our governmental

[3] *Congressional Record,* 25 March 1966, p. 6501.

and political system needs new and more secure bridges to the future, that the gap between government and citizens must be filled by reciprocal responsiveness, reliance, and trust. In a very real sense, this is the prime domestic assignment of the new Administration, which, as a recent *Wall Street Journal* editorial counselled, "must somehow restore the faith of the American people in their institutions and their society." Realism and fairness, however, dictate that concerned citizens in every region, every State, and every community as well as all officeholders from the White House to City Hall must make this their paramount public purpose.

From the standpoint of intergovernmental relations, 1968 witnessed a growing acceptance of the need for a New Federalism:

- One theme involved a recognition that narrowly designed programs and specialist middle managers, legislators, and interest groups at all levels comprise the core of the old Federalism —the Federalism of balkanized bureaucracies, segmented legislative committees, and the fragmented program administration.
- A related theme involved efforts to bolster the discretion, and staff authority of top policymakers at all levels of government, for the New Federalism requires that a balance be struck between the limited perspective of program specialists and the broad perspective of general political leaders in elected and high administrative posts.
- A third basic motif in the emerging New Federalism was the struggle to achieve a better balanced and thus more effective system via decentralization. Greater flexibility, greater discretion and greater decision-making authority by Federal field offices, and by State and local governments are the hallmarks of this continuing drive. Devolution of administrative power, grant packaging, consolidation, and revenue sharing are the reforms most commonly called for.

So, at the beginning of 1969, the Nation continues its search for a New Federalism—dedicated to balance; designed to correct structural, functional, and fiscal weaknesses; and rooted in a vital partnership of strong localities, strong States, and a strong National Government. Federalism, after all, seeks to enhance national unity while sustaining social and political diversity. The partnership approach is the only viable formula for applying this constitutional doctrine to late Twentieth Century America. Yet, this approach can succeed only if all of the partners are powerful, resourceful, and responsive to the needs of the people. The alternative is a further pulverizing of State and local power, and the consequent strengthening of the forces of centralization.[4]

Federal financial aid is greater for public assistance programs than for any other type of federal aid to the states. In fiscal 1969 welfare benefits to the aged, handicapped, blind, and families of dependent children totaled almost one third of the $20 billion appropriated as the federal share of all grants-in-aid to the states during that year. From fiscal 1960 through fiscal 1969, federal grants to the states increased 189 per cent. By fiscal 1969, 11 per cent of federal revenues was returned to the states in the form of grants.[5] If the states were to be able to maintain their own fiscal integrity and political stability in an era of inflationary tendencies it was clear that the President and the Congress would have to devise a better method of sharing the costs of increasing state and local governmental services. The concept of *new federalism* placed the responsibility on the federal government for providing the wherewithal and the advice for state and local programs and projects, while it charged the states themselves with administering the programs and projects according to their own views of administrative necessity within their own states. Such a notion of decentralization fit into the Nixon Administration's idea of easing the sort of strong federal control (some of course called it dictation) that had emerged from previous Democratic administrations. To reverse the trend to centralization in the federal system, Nixon proposed that Congress approve a revenue-sharing program and block-grant approach to grants-in-aid.

The concept of revenue (or tax)-sharing was not new with Nixon. Walter Heller of the University of Minnesota proposed in 1960 that the federal government begin to give serious consideration to distributing federal revenues directly to the states in block grants with few or no strings attached. Joseph Pechman of the Brookings Institution made a similar proposal,

[4] *Tenth Annual Report,* Advisory Commission on Intergovernmental Relations, Washington, D.C., 31 January 1969, p. 10.
[5] *Congressional Quarterly,* 14 August 1970, p. 2069.

and since then all variations of such block grants of money to the states, beyond the traditional grant-in-aid system, have been rooted in the so-called Heller-Pechman revenue-sharing plan. In 1964, when Heller was President Johnson's Chairman of the Council of Economic Advisors, he pressed hard for implementation of the plan in conjunction with the grants-in-aid program. Although Johnson established a Presidential Commission to study the issue further, the President did not put the influence and prestige of the executive branch behind the idea. Some congressional Republicans, whose party was in the minority in the Congress, did propose several bills of varying types, all of which were based in the concept of direct grants. Indeed, one of the most ardent supporters of revenue-sharing was Republican Congressman Melvin Laird of Wisconsin, who was to become Nixon's Secretary of Defense.

The major elements of the revenue-sharing idea are (1) each year the federal government would set aside a flat percentage of federal revenues (say, 2 per cent) culled from federal income taxes; (2) the money thus obtained would be placed in a trust fund, similar to social security revenue the federal government receives from the FICA tax system; (3) the states would share the proceeds of the trust on a per capita basis. If such a sharing still did not result in enough income for an extremely poor state, an equalization rate would then be established to raise the level; (4) some money would be granted directly to localities without being granted to the states. This "pass-through" system is itself controversial; and, (5) very few, if any, restrictions on the way the states or localities spent the proceeds would be imposed.

Revenue-sharing is designed to strengthen the power of the states to deal with specific problems each might have—educational, health, and welfare needs, pollution control, economic programs, etc. The concept of "pass-through," however, hamstrung progress on revenue-sharing in the 1960's. Urban-oriented congressmen and senators pressed for such a method, but Congress (except for the years 1965 and 1966) was not (and is not now) controlled by urban-oriented legislators. In August, 1969, President Nixon, in line with his commitment to strengthen the states in the federal system, urged a Democratically controlled, but nonurban-led, Ninety-first Congress to pass revenue-sharing legislation. Nixon wanted

> to restore to the states their proper rights and roles in the Federal system with a new emphasis on and help for local responsiveness; to provide both the encouragement and the necessary resources for local and state officials to exercise leadership in solving their own problems; to narrow the distance between people and the government agencies dealing with their problems; to restore strength and vigor to local and state governments; to shift the balance of political power away from Washington and back to the country and the people.[6]

But the Ninety-first Congress was in no rush to support Nixon's *new federalism*. Fearful that urban America, where civil unrest and racial conflict are focused, would have too much money without congressional or state controls and wary that state and local governments might let their own sources of taxation decay even further, the Congress in 1969–1970 did little to further revenue-sharing, despite a few attempts on the part of some to press for it.[7] Although the Congress strongly supports the federal system, with a legitimate and rightful place for the states, the Ninety-first Congress could not bring itself to accept the concept of revenue-sharing.

The issue of revenue-sharing shows that federalism is by no means a dead issue. It only remains to modernize it further in order to keep pace with contemporary problems of the states.[8]

SEPARATION OF POWERS AND
CHECKS AND BALANCES

The two principles of separation of powers and checks and balances can be usefully dealt with together because they are

[6] *Congressional Digest* Vol. 48, No. 10, October, 1969, p. 225

[7] See *Congressional Record*, 30 June 1970, pp. H6282-H6284; 14 July 1970, pp. S11260-S11262; 4 August 1970, pp. S12703-S12704; and 9 September 1970, pp. H8473-H8474.

[8] For a concise review of modern concepts of federalism, see the illuminating report by the Subcommittee on Intergovernmental Relations, Senate Committee on Government Operations. *The Condition of American Federalism*, 89th Cong., 2nd Sess., 15 October 1966.

so closely linked. As noted previously, the framers of the Constitution adopted a notion set forth by the French political thinker Montesquieu, who had modeled a scheme on what he thought he saw in the British system of his day. The framers believed that the making of laws, carrying them into execution, and adjudicating disputes evolving from them were the three major functions of government. The end of civil society and government was justice, as the *Federalist Paper* No. 51 pointed out, and justice would be served in a society with a number of diversified interests if the functions of government were spread out among three branches, each of which would be separately manned. Thus tyranny would be avoided because there would be no accumulation of all these powers in the same hands, "whether of one, a few, or many, and whether hereditary, self-appointed, or elective." Separating government into three branches in this way permitted the constitution-makers to allay the fears of those who did not want too powerful a central government, dreaded a new tyranny, or feared the establishment of a strong executive authority.

Such a separation of powers also enabled them to avoid the practice of legislative dominance that had developed in the immediate post-Revolutionary period in the states as an outgrowth of colonial distaste for the power of the Royal Governors and George III. Recognizing the need for a national court system with judicial power over the citizens of the new nation, the framers also made a major contribution to the development of political theory, the concept of judicial review of government acts. The tripartite idea struck a balance congenial to the preferences of the interests and groups who were involved in and committed to the new society.

The principle of separation of powers contains four basic elements. The first is that no person may serve in more than one of the three branches at the same time. Had there ever been an inclination to develop parliamentary forms in American resembling the British model, this provision would have prevented it. At Westminster, the Prime Minister and the other ministers who make up his Cabinet are chosen from the House of Commons (and a few from the House of Lords) and *remain* members of the Parliament while at the same time they constitute the executive.

The second element is that the powers, duties, and responsibilities of the three branches are delineated in a written constitution. The substitution of three theoretically coequal branches for the principle of parliamentary supremacy that underlies the British scheme makes it necessary to have such a written constitutional power allocation. In America one might say that "constitutional supremacy" had replaced parliamentary supremacy. Since the Constitution is a brief document, however, to the point of being almost cryptic in some passages, the delineation of the functions for the three branches is by no means free of ambiguity. Article I, for instance, enumerates the powers of Congress, but then provides that all laws may be enacted which are "necessary and proper for carrying into execution the foregoing powers." This left the door open to frequent controversy over the precise extent of congressional power. Likewise, Article II, dealing with the executive, is even less exhaustive and detailed about presidential powers than Article I is about Congress, and hence invited at least as much confusion and dispute.

In actuality, as the system has developed over the years, the relation between the legislative and executive branches has become one of enforced and often reluctant cooperation in spite of the theory of separation. In the course of this uneasy partnership, at times one branch has dominated the other in the realm of policy-making, only to have the pendulum swing in the opposite direction a few years later. In the last four decades, there has been a consistent tendency for the executive to attempt to dominate the legislative branch, not always successfully. As the legislative initiative has been passed (or thrust) into the hands of the executive, the Congress has attempted to assert more strongly its legislative oversight and appropriations roles. Ultimately, of course, the process of legislating, especially in the domestic sphere, requires agreement between the executive and legislative branches. The process of achieving such agreement is at times very slow and painful, but this is one price that must be paid for separation of powers.

The third element in the American system of separation of powers, which also differentiates it from the British scheme, is the power of judicial review lodged in the Supreme Court. This principle, which has been firmly embedded in American constitutional practice since the case of *Marbury v. Madison* (1803), makes the Court a formidable third partner in the governmental system. Under it the Court not only interprets the law, but in effect *makes* law through its right to review congressional and state statutes, and state constitutional provisions, for conformity with the national constitution. Striking down a law obviously involves the Court in "legislating," at least in a negative sense. Many recent decisions, however, like those already cited relating to legislative apportionment, by affirmatively prescribing new policies to replace those invalidated, find the Court legislating in a much more direct way.

The fourth element in the concept of separation of powers is what Madison in his forty-seventh *Federalist Paper* called "partial agency," which gives each branch enough power over the others to be able to check them when they appear to be going beyond the limits of their own jurisdiction. More familiarly, this is the principle of checks and balances, designed to enable the three branches to protect themselves from each other's encroachments. No one branch could therefore hope to act completely independently or to arrogate to itself dominant power. The framers thus sought to achieve a balance that would at the same time promote interbranch cooperation when necessary, and yet maintain branch equality and autonomy. In practice, stalemate has also resulted from time to time.

Separation of powers with its corollary principle checks and balances is thus a complex framework for government that reflects the preoccupations of the men of the eighteenth century who put it together. Uppermost in their minds was a fear of government power in an age when men expected relatively little of government in the way of the myriad positive programs we take for granted today. From our vantage point, the crucial problem is often the unresponsiveness of government to felt needs, rather than incipient tyranny. Thus, in practice, the system has come to operate in ways that the framers could hardly have dreamed of.

Presidential supremacy in policy initiation versus the intended role of Congress as the seedbed of legislation represents one of these adaptive patterns of operation. The role of the Supreme Court as champion of the certain groups and interests in the society—often groups that have failed to win a voice through other branches—suggests another. In short, each branch has developed its own constituency, a pattern of interests to which it is especially attentive, and hence its own special role in the policy-making process. Policy development remains what the framers intended it to be: the result of interaction (and friction) among the three branches. But the dynamics of that interaction and the rich variety of political involvements of all three branches go far beyond anything the men of the eighteenth century could have imagined, or intended. The pressing question raised for the 1970's and 1980's by the structural principle of separation of powers is whether still further adaptation to meet ever more pressing problems of the city, the environment, minority groups, and the rest will be possible. Only time will tell.

Before leaving this crucial structural principle of separation of powers to deal with the Bill of Rights as the final constitutional principle in our catalog, we might take a concrete look first at the presidential veto as an illustrative "check and balance" and then at that unique American contribution: judicial review.

The presidential veto power has many ramifications. Because the framers believed there was a tendency in a republic for a legislature to be predominant, the legislature was divided into two houses, one to represent the states equally on a geographic basis, the other, the people in the system according to the population within the states. The executive could check this divided legislature with his veto power. The latter could override his veto by a two-thirds vote of each house, one theoretically representing state sovereignty and legitimacy, or in John Adams' view, the aristocratic, and the other standing for the mass of people, the so-called "radical element," or the democratic.

But the simple veto power of the President is itself subject to many sophisticated checks and balances, some of which the framers were doubtless unaware of or could not foresee. The President cannot veto specific sections of a bill enacted by Congress, but must reject the entire bill if he wants some objectionable part negated. Thus a built-in system of compromise exists between the executive and the legislature within the process of writing the legislation in the first place. Sometimes a President must accept some one thing he believes unworthy of enactment into law in order to obtain in the bill the essential thing he might have wanted in the first place as good and proper. Then too, because the President executes the laws, it is up to him to decide just what level of enforcement will be applied, if any, to that section of the bill he deems improper.

The Congress can pass laws, the President can sign them, but it is almost an impossibility for the Congress constitutionally to compel the President to act. They can withhold legislation or block appropriations he wants, but they cannot compel. True enough, the House can impeach and the Senate can convict a President if they want to press their constitutional privileges. But this device is rarely even threatened. If the extraconstitutional checks and balances are coupled with the constitutional ones, it can be readily seen that the political system interlocks in countless ways. Many of these checks and balances are explicitly built into the constitutional system, and others are implicit because of the separation of powers and federal principle. This will become more apparent as we delve more deeply into the pressure group and political party aspects of the American political system.

Judicial review was an auxiliary precaution to ensure free government and facilitate harmony between the national and state governments. For judicial review is not only the right of the courts (with the United States Supreme Court having the final say) to declare an act of the Congress unconstitutional, but it is also their right to declare an act of any state as contrary to the United States Constitution. The latter is tied to Article VI, Clause 2, of the Constitution, which states unambiguously that the Constitution is the supreme law of the land; "and the judges in every state shall be bound thereby, anything in the constitution or laws of any state to the contrary notwithstanding." The question of course is to determine when a state law is in conflict with the Constitution. Historically, the Supreme Court, in the final analysis, does this determination. This was firmly established early in the country's history in the cases of *Fletcher v. Peck* in 1810 and *McCulloch v. Maryland* in 1819. These and other cases are long-standing precedents.

With the addition of the Fourteenth Amendment following the Civil War and the judicial interpretations of the due process and equal protection of the laws clauses of the Fourteenth Amendment (to be discussed later in the chapter on the courts), the Supreme Court of the United States has seen a substantial share of its annual business devoted to questions of constitutional validity of various state statutes. This has been particularly true since 1954, when a unanimous Court ruled that segregation in the public school system of Topeka, Kansas, enforced by state law, violated the United States Constitution. The host of cases arising from this historic landmark of constitutional law in the United States showed again that the Supreme Court has the power to declare any state law contrary to the Constitution, even in so sensitive an area. The only recourse the states have in such an event is to attempt to have the Constitution itself amended or have the Congress legislatively negate such decisions whenever constitutionally possible. This is a difficult task indeed.

But this right to declare congressional and state enactments unconstitutional was not easily established. After Thomas Jefferson was inaugurated as President in 1801, he instructed his Secretary of State, James Madison, not to deliver the commissions of appointment as justices of the peace in the District of Columbia to one William Marbury and three others, who had been so appointed by President John Adams and confirmed by the Senate. John Marshall, Adams' Secretary of State, had failed to deliver them before he left office. The appointees brought suit in the United States Supreme Court seeking a writ of mandamus (court order to an official to carry out the functions of his office) to Secretary of State Madison demanding he deliver their commissions to them. They did so under the Judiciary Act of 1789, passed by Congress, which gave the Supreme Court original jurisdiction to issue such writs "in cases warranted by the principles and usages of law, to any courts appointed, or persons holding office, under the authority of the United States."

The Supreme Court, however, under its new Chief Justice, the same John Marshall, took a dim view of this procedure. Yes, said the Court, Marbury and his three colleagues should have those commissions and Madison had no right to withhold them. But, at the same time, the Congress had no right to grant the Supreme Court original jurisdiction in such things under Article III, Section 2. Granting writs of mandamus was clearly not an area of original jurisdiction for the Supreme Court. Accordingly, this provision of the act was unconstitutional, and, Marshall wrote, the Supreme Court has the legitimate right to declare such an act unconstitutional. Marshall then went on to say, "It is emphatically the province and duty of the judicial department to say what the law is . . . if two laws conflict with each other, the courts must decide on the operation of each." In this famous case, *Marbury v. Madison,* in 1803, the Supreme Court paradoxically took onto itself the *great* power of declaring laws unconstitutional using a *minor* issue of this kind.

Even though judicial review is not explicitly mentioned in the Constitution, it must be included as a constitutional principle. For one thing, Marshall's decision in *Marbury v. Madison* became firmly established in American constitutional law. Second, most students of constitutional law and its history believe that the founding fathers felt judicial review to be a natural part of the Constitution. Indeed, Hamilton himself says as much in the seventy-eighth *Federalist Paper.*

The interpretation of the laws is the proper and peculiar province of the courts. A constitution is, in fact, and must be regarded by the judges, as a fundamental law. It therefore belongs to them to ascertain its meaning, as well as the meaning of any particular act proceeding from the legislative body. If there should happen to be an irreconcilable variance between the two, that which has the superior obligation and validity, ought, of course, to be preferred; or, in other words, the Constitution ought to be preferred to the statute, the intention of the people to the intention of their agents. Nor does this conclusion by any means suppose a superiority of the judicial to the legislative power. It only supposes that the power of the people is superior to both; and that where the will of the legislature, declared in its statutes, stands in opposition to that of the people, declared in the Constitution, the judges ought to be governed by the latter rather than by the former. They ought to regulate their decisions by the fundamental laws, rather than by those which are not fundamental.

Hamilton's words, in 1788, and Marshall's dictum in 1803 have firmly established the doctrine of judicial review. But not until 1857, in the famous Dred Scott case, was another congressional law declared unconstitutional. And, indeed, as Professor Edmund Cahn has pointed out, between 1865 and 1936, the Court invalidated an average of only one act a year, and between 1937 and 1956, only one every six or seven years. In fact, since the Franklin D. Roosevelt days, not one important congressional act has been declared unconstitutional.

Why is it that so many federal laws pass the test of judicial review when and if they are before the Court on some constitutional issue? The executive and legislative branches of the national government, in light of the New Deal laws declared invalid by the Court prior to 1937, have been very much aware of this ever-present power of the Court. Indeed, the independent agencies of the federal government (about which we shall have more to say in the chapter on the bureaucracy), the committees and subcommittees of the Congress itself, and the Executive Office of the President try to be as certain as they can that legislation actually enacted will stand the scrutiny of Supreme Court examination. Every office in the executive branch, every agency and bureau, and every congressional committee has its legal counsel and advice. The Attorney-General's office gives constitutional advice to both the President and the Congress. No wonder then, in the final analysis, that very few federal laws have been declared unconstitutional by the Court. This is not true with state laws. Between 1950 and 1963, 102 state laws were invalidated.

Indeed, if and when an act does come before the Supreme Court of the United States on an issue of constitutionality, and the Court does declare such act *constitutional,* that legislation becomes even more firmly rooted in the American political system than ever. Contrariwise, when a state law is declared *unconstitutional* by the Supreme Court, practically nothing can be done by the state other than to comply with the edict of the Court, however slowly and reluctantly compliance may come. The Constitution is looked upon by most Americans as a sacrosanct document, and the concept of judicial review has become a part of that constitution.

THE BILL OF RIGHTS

The Bill of Rights can be included as the last of the constitutional principles because without Washington's promise that such a bill would be added to the original constitution in the form of amendments, the Constitution would probably not have been ratified by the states at all. It followed closely on the heels of ratification and became a traditional part of the Constitution, and the formal statement of the civil liberties and, now, civil rights of Americans. The Bill of Rights is the first ten amendments to the Constitution, although some have argued that actually one can consider only the first eight as a Bill of Rights. Be that as it may, the important thing to bear in mind is that the Bill of Rights applied originally only to the national government, and not the states. The First Amendment begins "Congress shall make no law . . ." and the succeeding amendments are protections of the people and the state against encroachment on their lives by the national government. Extending this set of prohibitions into rights of the people against the state has taken much time and pain, and it could not have been accomplished without the passage of the Fourteenth Amendment, an outgrowth of the Civil War.

Behind the Bill of Rights lay the action by the Congress of the Confederation in 1787 adopting a set of rules governing the Northwest Territory. These contained a rudimentary form of a bill of rights. *Habeas corpus* was protected, no cruel and unusual punishments could be used, and so forth. But in September, 1787, in Philadelphia, the Constitutional Convention failed to adopt a bill of rights for the new constitution. There was the belief on the part of some, Hamilton for example, that the Constitution itself was a bill of rights and there was no need to define rights because the people themselves were the authors of the Constitution. Another argument advanced was that if some rights are written down, it might be inferred by some that those not included were not rights at all. In any event, shortly after the ratification of the Constitution, some 127 amendments were proposed by the states as various forms of bills of rights against the national government. After extended debate in the Congress, these were boiled down to twelve, which were proposed to the states. The states rejected two of them (including a guarantee of civil liberties against the states) and ratified the remaining ten.

John Marshall affirmed the doctrine that the Bill of Rights was applicable only against the national government in the Supreme Court case of *Barron v. Baltimore,* in 1833. The doctrine was confirmed again and again over the years by the Court. When the Fourteenth Amendment was adopted in 1868, it was used as a means of extending the Bill of Rights, piece by piece, against the states. The Fourteenth Amendment says, in part, that no state shall ". . . deprive any person of life, liberty, or property without due process of law [a phrase that occurs in the Fifth Amendment]; nor deny to any person within its jurisdiction the equal protection of the laws." The two phrases, *due process of law* and *equal protection of the laws,* have been the key phrases in this process. The Constitution of the United States now protects all people against encroachment on their rights by both the national and the state governments. This is not to say that there is no difficulty for the courts to decide *when* such rights have been denied by either sovereignty. Nor can one say that *all* the amendments of the Bill of Rights *now* apply *in toto.*

The civil rights cases of recent years have leaned on the "equal protection of the laws" clause. Understanding this is not difficult. It is a question of the Court deciding when something a state does is or is not within the confines of this clause. It applies to civil rights of Negroes, but it can also apply to questions of reapportionment, and freedom of speech, press, and religion (as it has). It is also significant to note that recent civil rights laws passed by Congress, however, have leaned on the interstate commerce clause rather than the Fourteenth Amendment.

In short, the Supreme Court plays a major role as policy-making organ of government through the exercise of its power of judicial review in areas of economic and social policy, and here, too, in the realm of fundamental rights the policy process is a dynamic one. The most spectacular examples of Court-made policy are to be found in this area—certainly the most spectacular of recent decades, and perhaps of the entire national history. Further demonstration could hardly be required of the importance of the Bill of Rights plus its more recent additions like the Fourteenth Amendment.

Three

Pressure Groups

HE UNITED STATES is a nation of great diversification, widespread heterogeneity, and a multiplicity of interests. This point has been belabored time and time again, but it is worth repeating. Madison recognized this truism in 1788 when the country contained but 4 million people and consisted of only 13 Atlantic coastal states. Indeed, Madison contended this diversity would ameliorate some of the evils inherent in democracy. Of course, other institutional checks and balances had to be structured as well. And, Madison had the faith that in such a well-ordered republic ambition would counter ambition, and thus the less savory aide of human nature would not lead to abuses in government. Since 1788 the United States has grown along the lines earlier suggested by Madison. The nation, now composed of over 200 million people and embracing 50 states from the East Coast across the continent and 2,500 miles of Pacific Ocean to Hawaii, has become one vast "mixing bowl" of cultures, religions, classes, races, ethnic and, to a great extent, economic groups. No matter how one dissects the United States, a variety of groups reflecting countless interests can be found.

Individuals belong to various groups, consciously or otherwise. To some degree, everyone is part of a family, culture, race, region, association of friends, age and educational group, economic stratum, political party, and so on. Even if one professes no religion, he is indeed part of a group with the same feelings. He is then classified as an atheist or agnostic, but not as nothing. If one openly disavows kinship with any political party, he is a member of the group that thinks the same way, and is then classified as belonging to the "independents."

One could elaborate further, but the point has been made. Everyone is an object of pressure from groups to which he belongs, not to mention the ones to which he does not. Because people belong to many groups at the same time—family, economic, religious, social, cultural, and political—they experience stresses and strains causing different reactions at different times. The family may pull in one direction, friends in another, and business associates in a third. No doubt many people find themselves at odds trying to figure out exactly what they should do in any given crisis. Patterns of group interaction then become important, maybe even more important than the sets of common characteristics that hold each group together in the first place.

The United States is a multigroup society, manifested by a tremendous number of associations, groups, and organizations. Indeed, American society is so group-oriented, the rank-and-file citizen who wishes to have an impact on policy decisions of government finds he must either become part of the governmental apparatus itself or lend his support (and contribute his money) to one or more groups trying to influence government the way he wants. We are a joining society. Much research has shown, however, that most Americans do not consistently engage in the political process necessary to maximize their importance within the groups they join and, because interest groups are so numerous, large, and diversified, we often find that a small but active minority runs them. Sometimes this active minority, or elitist element, undercuts the very reasons for the existence of the groups in the first place. When that occurs, the majority of the group's members can find themselves frustrated, if not alienated, because of the slow, conservative progress the group makes and at times even by the apparent failure of the group to achieve its goals and purposes.

In recent years the nation has seen the sudden rise of many

ad hoc interest groups composed of people dissatisfied with the traditional groups who use traditional means to affect governmental decisions. These *ad hoc* groups organize to press for quick and direct action on the seat of government power, and on the people at large, rather than to work slowly and carefully through and within the existing political framework. The essential problem of the multigroup society, as R. M. MacIver points out in *The Web of Government,* is to balance all these various organizations, and the groups of people who maintain them, within the ordered yet free life of the community.[1]

We shall leave it to the sociologists, anthropologists, and psychologists to analyze why people do what they do, and will confine ourselves only to the groups that are organized to make their opinions known and to have an influence on the process of government. We shall use as our working definition of a pressure group, or interest group, *any collection of people organized to promote some objective they have in common, which somehow relates to the political process.* A ladies' garden club is not, therefore, a pressure group unless the membership decides to petition the mayor to have the local playground cleaned up, or send a representative to Washington to plead for a billboard-free interstate highway system. The American Medical Association *is* a pressure group, by our definition, even though it is ostensibly organized for professional reasons. It frequently concerns itself with public policy matters it believes fall into the sphere of interest of its members. The AMA was certainly (and negatively) involved in the political process of decision-making during the establishment of medicare and medicaid, and it continues to press for influence in administering such programs.

Most professional organizations that are national in character have as a major objective the protection of their narrow interests or the advancement of the public interest as *they* see it through *their* eyes. Accordingly, they relate to the political process as they attempt to influence the passage or defeat of pending legislation before the Congress and state

[1] R. M. MacIver, *The Web of Government,* rev. ed. (New York: The Free Press, 1965), 316–322.

legislatures. Numerous groups of this sort—business, labor, professional, trade, religious, and other types—exist in order to promote their own objectives in the political process.

Interest groups represent a part, and a key part, of the broader "pattern of interests" in American society. They do not, however, represent the whole of that pattern. They reflect the organized, more or less, articulate minorities. But because they are well organized and able to present their views in a forceful manner, they have political influence far greater than their numbers would ordinarily provide. On the other hand, many groups in the over-all system have objectives and interests in common but are not organized—such as all the mothers of draft-age boys or consumers of heating oil or gas. These people may well be quite aware, individually, of their interests, but simply lack an organized voice. Their feelings, however, can be obvious and taken into account by government. Mothers of draft-age boys, for example, do have an influence on governmental policy on military conscription, and on the activities and promises of senators and congressmen, particularly in an election year. It seems apparent that unorganized pressures from the parents in the United States forced the government to recall hundreds of thousands of troops from Europe at the very end of World War II. The 1946 election was coming and the Congress did not wish to incur the wrath of so many voters.

In 1970, relying on the constitutional authority of the Fourteenth Amendment, Congress lowered the voting age to 18, and the House approved a constitutional amendment guaranteeing equal rights to women. Both of these actions were in great measure a congressional response to over-all pressures brought to bear on the society by large numbers of previously unorganized interests who demanded and demonstrated for their goals. To some extent the amendment to guarantee women equal rights with men was a congressional action to forestall even more pressure by women's liberation groups, only recently organized as a loose coalition of heretofore powerless and apolitical associations. There are, indeed, all sorts of groups—religious, ethnic, and racial—which are noneconomic and which will often have a good many organized and articulate elements. White segregationists and black power advocates are fair examples. Then there are large segments of the community—the very poor, the migratory farm workers, and the growing number of the lonely aged—who are neither organized nor articulate, and for practical purposes may be virtually outside the pale of the entire political process, unless some major pressure group takes up their cause.

Historically, pressure groups have been present since the very beginnings of the government under the Constitution. In fact, simple functions akin to those associated with pressure groups have always been performed in any government that permits itself to be influenced at all by the wishes of the governed. By looking briefly at the history of pressure group activity in the United States, one can further document the point made in the first chapter about the changing "patterns of interest" in the community.

Pressure group activity was very much evident in the first Congress under the Constitution. One of the foremost issues was the funding of the Revolutionary debt. Apparently, members of Congress had bought up quantities of the depreciated certificates in hope that legislation would be passed (by them) making these more valuable. Thus, they themselves were interested parties, in addition to interests in the country at large. When the Treasury's funding measure was introduced, Senator Maclay of Pennsylvania, a rather abrasive and outspoken foe of special privilege, wrote in his diary:

> I do not know that pecuniary influence has actually been used, but I am certain that every kind of management has been practiced and every tool at work that could be thought of, Officers of the Government, clergy, citizens, (Order of) Cincinnati, and every person under the influence of the Treasury . . . worked for the success of the bill.[2]

A modest tariff had been enacted as part of Hamilton's financial schemes, and this was supplemented with a much more protectionist tariff in 1816. This issue of tariff protec-

[2] Edgar S. Maclay, A. M., ed., *Journal of William Maclay* (New York: A. and C. Boni, 1927), 209.

tion for a host of individual businesses became one of the major sources of pressure activity that has continued to the present. Periodic revisions would call down a swarm of industry representatives on Washington. Not until the reciprocal trade agreement policy adopted during the administration of Franklin D. Roosevelt did this kind of activity slacken off. It has by no means disappeared today. Despite recent tariff schedule revisions, businesses and industries adversely affected by the lowering of tariffs maintain their channels of influence on the Federal Tariff Commission and the Office of the Special Representative for Trade Negotiations, not to mention the congressional committees that deal with this area.

Connected with the increase in tariffs as an issue was the founding of one of the earliest national associations to enable manufacturers to bring pressure to bear at appropriate times. The National Association of Cotton Manufacturers was organized in 1854, at about the same time as the National Brewers Association. The American Medical Association was actually established somewhat earlier, in 1847. Today there are over 13,000 different trade associations, about 15 per cent of which are national in scope.

Other potent issues that brought lobbyists to the nation's capital were symptomatic of the changing nature of the economy under the twin impact of industrialization and westward expansion. Patent renewal, in an age of important inventions basic to industry and agricultural development, was a key issue and required an act of the Congress once the period of statutory protection expired. The making of princely land grants to encourage the building of transcontinental railroads offered much opportunity for activity for those skilled in getting Congress to do things.

The tactics used by Cyrus McCormick and Samuel Colt in getting patents renewed are illustrative. As Karl Schriftgiesser has noted, in his work on lobbyists, in 1855 a congressional committee showed that Samuel Colt had paid $10,000 to one congressman, who, in return, would refrain from attacking the patent extension bill. In addition, the same congressman was supposed to have several other members of Congress beholden to him. Colt's chief lobbyist, besides passing out "many handsome and beautifully decorated revolvers," also used "more attractive bait in the persons of three charming ladies who were professionally known as Spiritualists" but who moved about rather easily with members of Congress. In the last half of the nineteenth century, the tactics used were fairly typical of "interest articulation" of the day. Samuel Ward, called the King of the Lobby for some twenty years during and after the Civil War, provides a good example.

Ward operated on the theory that the shortest way to a congressman's vote was not necessarily through his pocketbook or his desire to consort with female companions, but rather through his stomach. Ward gave famous breakfasts of ham boiled in champagne, with wisps of new mown hay thrown in for flavoring.[3] Techniques of this sort were pretty general until the turn of the century for one major reason (besides the fact that congressmen often went to Washington without the sobering influence of the family in those days). Communication technology had not progressed far enough to keep the congressman in the kind of constant touch with his home district that he has today. People were also more parochial, no doubt, in an era when the national government touched their lives relatively little, and government to them for the most part meant state and local government. The great progress made in communications reshaped the nature of the political process. Once the telegraph, telephone, mass circulation newspapers, and later radio and television came on the scene, the constituent could keep far better track of his representative than before. Because the elected officials were now more responsive to their constituents, pressure groups could use the home folks to lobby the legislators on the group's behalf. In short, the people often became the brokers for pressure groups and their lobbyists, the middlemen in appeals to the legislators.

Other forces too made for change in pressure group activity. The need to mount more elaborate campaigns to influence the public as well as Congress meant the development of more elaborate forms of organization for pressure groups with a

[3] Karl Schriftgiesser, *The Lobbyists* (Boston: Little, Brown and Company, 1951), 10–15.

greater tendency to hire professional staffs. The growth of the economy and the increase in population, coupled with the development of various kinds of government regulation and intervention, also fostered the growth of interest group activity and organization. The matter of prohibition is a case in point.

Oberlin College, a Protestant-endowed school, started the prohibition movement. Established in 1833 as a college dedicated to "sound morality and religion," it became a center for abolitionist sentiment. In 1874 the Anti-Saloon League started at Oberlin. Nineteen years later the League organized Ohio on a statewide basis and in 1895, a call went out for an interstate organization dedicated to wiping out liquor traffic. The movement, spreading throughout the country, relied on a paid professional staff to give its entire time to the League's activities, a monthly subscription from those who belonged to the League, political agitation for the defeat of wet and election of dry candidates, and a concentration of public attention on the liquor question. In the Anti-Saloon League one found all the elements of a modern pressure group—financially supported, pressuring the public and the politicians, and working at election time to influence the selection of public officials.

The Anti-Saloon League concentrated on saloons in particular. Pamphlets, newspaper ads, and weekly papers to subscribers kept up a steady stream of anti-booze talk and propaganda. Innocent children were depicted as being neglected by their parents who guzzled corn mash in the local pubs. Saloon keepers and liquor dealers were represented as a vile sort of species. Facts and figures on the money passed in the liquor industry were advertised and publicized. Drinking, in the eyes of the League, was a national disgrace. In addition, when war came in 1917, the League tied its activities to the war effort and tried to make drinking unpatriotic!

The League used much the same approach as is carried out today for a national campaign. First, there was centralized authority in the organization itself. Today we call this the active minority, the elite of any organization which calls the turns. Second, there was a purpose, a precise objective, and a single one at that: to do away with liquor. Similar groups exist today. Tax associations are concerned with one thing, keeping taxes down if not doing away with most of them. The AMA attempts to protect the independence of the physician from governmental controls, and the NAACP is concerned almost solely with obtaining civil rights for the Negro. Third, the League linked its power to other groups, in this instance the Protestant churches, to further its cause. In the 1970's this particular type of liaison exists between church and non-church groups who take sides on the issue of financial aid to public and private schools. Fourth, the League avoided seeking political office for its own members in the name of the League. The leadership realized that its future rested with gaining access to government, not in winning office. This is also true today with almost all major groups. The member of a pressure group can win an office, but can lose it the next time. However, if the group has access to political officials, it can probably keep its influence all the time.

The League selected key congressmen and senators and would-be candidates and labeled them wet or dry. Women (this was in the early days of the suffragette movement) and children were urged to see that husbands and fathers voted right, or not at all. The major job was in lobbying. In 1912 the League was successful in having prohibition passed in Kentucky. As prohibition was debated at the state level, it brought pressure to bear there. Its practices were to see that temperance legislation went to friendly committees in the legislature; that bills were introduced early in the session, first in the lower house by a skilled representative; that attendance was ample at hearings; that no stand was taken on any matter other than temperance; that the countryside was aroused by letters and telegrams; and that the legislative galleries were crowded with sympathizers. These overt tactics are still used today by hundreds of pressure groups.

In the Congress, the League employed the same set of rules. In 1902 the League managed to have a prohibition bill introduced in Washington. After a bitter fight with the brewers' groups, the bill was killed. But each year, more and more bills were presented to Congress, introduced by friendly congressmen, many of whom had outright fear of what the League could do to them politically. In 1913 the League managed to lobby successfully for a bill that withdrew federal protection from the liquor trade within the states. In other words, if a state had a prohibition law on the books, freedom of interstate commerce could not be cited to permit shipping in liquor from outside the state's borders. This law was passed by a Democratic Congress over Republican President Taft's veto, and sustained by the Supreme Court in 1917 in *Clark Distilling Company v. Western Maryland Railroad*. The League then turned to national prohibition, which culminated in the passage of the Eighteenth Amendment. Here was one instance where pressure group activity was moral in tone and flavor, rather than economic—and *highly* successful.

At times the government itself has fostered the formation of trade associations to facilitate dealing with major segments of the economy. This occurred during World War I and as recently as 1962 when the late President Kennedy was instrumental in getting business to organize to pressure for passage of his tariff and trade reforms. Thus did the pattern of interests change, that is, the pattern of self-conscious interest group activity, in response to changes in the economy and the society. And these changes brought about alterations in the political process itself.

PRESSURE GROUP METHODS

Let us look briefly at what pressure groups seek to do in the political process, bearing in mind that some pressure groups emphasize one aspect, others another. First, pressure groups seek to influence public opinion. Their purpose is to present a specific kind of image to the public so that if and when some political issue is at stake, and their position on the matter is made known, they will have already conditioned, hopefully, a favorable response in the public mind. Of course, this can be overdone. When the American Medical Association went all out to convince the American people that no form of medical care to the aged through the services of the government was proper, all it really accomplished was bringing to the attention of millions of people the need for such a program. The outcome was that the AMA lost the grand fight and had to adjust to the legislation that eventually did pass the Eighty-ninth Congress. But in general the object of the pressure group is to shape the public mind about its interests, reshape it if necessary and possible, and to keep the image of the group bright and favorable.

One example of a professional interest or pressure group that has attempted to equate its own professional and economic interests with the public interest is the American Institute of Architects (AIA). Founded in 1857, the AIA has grown to 23,000 members and attempts to portray itself as a group of licensed architects who are not only concerned with advancing the architectural profession but who also seek to employ their skill and expertise in bettering the living and social conditions of the United States. In 1970 the AIA took a series of advertisements in leading national magazines to depict the plight of the poor, the dangers from air pollution, and the increasing decay of our badly planned cities. This was an attempt to show millions of readers that a national but relatively small group of dedicated architects shared with them an abiding concern for America's future. By showing its support for decent housing and air pollution and sign control laws, the AIA was trying to create an image in the minds of millions of Americans that they, the professional architects of the nation, were not responsible for poorly designed public housing, the incongruent array of highway signs, or the construction of industrial plants that polluted the air. On the contrary, the AIA was trying to create a favorable image in the minds of the public that architects, too, were trying to alter the nation's priorities and redirect Americans toward a better society.

Second, pressure groups attempt to influence other pressure groups of like-minded or, at times, dissimilar views. The more groups with comparable values and goals adhere together over issues, the better off they all will be. Some pressure groups are antithetical to others in their standards. Thus they will support different things and be on opposite sides of the same issue. On the other hand, some of them, even bitter enemies, will be on the same side at times. For example, the NAM and organized labor unions are usually on opposite sides but they can be in agreement on such matters as supporting tax cuts and opposing legislation that places the government in a position of arbitrating labor-management disputes. On the issue of medical care to the aged through the social security program many of the leading pressure groups lined up against passage. The AMA, the National Association of Manufacturers, the American Farm Bureau Federation, the United States Chamber of Commerce, and others opposed the bill. On the other side, such groups as the AFL-CIO, the National Farmer's Union, the American Nurses Association, and others supported it. It is easy enough to understand this. The interests of one group sometimes coincide with the interests of another.

After the assassination of President Kennedy and Martin Luther King, Jr., there was, at least for a short time, a public outcry for strict congressional legislation on gun control. Highly pitched emotions over the issue brought a number of prominent Americans in public life to condemn the widespread ownership of guns in the United States. Reacting to this pressure, the National Rifle Association, a formidable pressure group with a highly skilled professional staff in Washington, sought out and found allies in wildlife organizations and sportsman and gun clubs to offset publicity adverse to new special self-interest attendant to the controversy. Despite public outrage associated with the assassinations, Congress never did write strong legislation to curb current traffic in firearms. To a great extent, this was due to the success of the alliance of the NRA and like-minded national and state groups that have powerful and direct influence with key members of the Congress.

Third, it must be realized that pressure groups also pressure their own membership. A pressure group tries to keep its own support, within its own group, strong. This implies constantly educating its own membership, increasing it whenever possible, and presenting as united a front as possible. The more cohesive a group is, the more influence it can have, or appear to have. The leadership of any well-organized pressure group seeks to find ways to keep the organization together. When a congressman or state legislator has some representative of a pressure group, or lobbyist, come see him about a matter it is concerned with, there is more of an impact on the legislator when he believes that the lobbyist speaks for "all of them" rather than just a few scattered people. A group's own values can be influential in the political process only when some kind of strength is manifested by a cohesive, united front of its membership.

Labor unions are particularly cognizant of this strength in unity, as are business-oriented public service groups like the Rotary, Kiwanis, and the U.S. Chamber of Commerce. The American Institute of Architects can also serve as an example of this attempt to pressure its own members to keep their attachment to the group strong in order to enable the AIA to have a strong influence on government. In 1968 the AIA established its Legislative Minuteman Program, designed to develop a "congressional contact system." Impressing its own members with the necessity for them to maintain liaison with their own senators and congressmen required an extensive educative program of its membership by AIA leadership. The legislative staff of the AIA constantly communicated with the membership as to how important specific congressional committees and federal agencies were to the AIA. The aim of the program, of course, was to develop among the members the strong feeling that they could have an impact on the governmental and political system, if they but knew what was happening in Washington. Indeed, AIA fact sheets, guest columns, and political items in the *AIA Governmental Affairs Review,* distributed to the membership, were designed to make the membership a more cohesive body and thereby make its mark in the halls of Congress and the executive agencies. Architects need not be concerned only with architecture. They could also have an important role to play in the over-all political process as Congress and the executive branch coped with inflation, the environment, education, housing, transportation, welfare reform, and taxation problems. Only by organized effort—directed indeed by the

AIA's active minority and professional staff—could 23,000 licensed architects bring together their self-interest with the public interest.

Fourth, pressure groups often seek to influence elections. They themselves do not put up candidates for office under the label of their particular group. Pressure groups do not seek the office itself. But they do want *access* to all levels of government and accordingly they have played and continue to play an important part in the electoral process, by bringing pressure to bear for or against certain candidates. Some pressure groups even go so far as to publish the voting records of various incumbents seeking re-election in an attempt to show how they rate according to the set of values of the particular group.

Five prominent pressure groups which do this nationally with a fair amount of regularity are the Americans for Democratic Action (ADA), the AFL-CIO Committee on Political Education (COPE), the National Farmers Union (NFU), the Americans for Constitutional Action (ACA), and the National Associated Businessmen, Inc. (NAB).[4] One of the more successful rating systems for state politicians is carried out by the state bureaus of the American Farm Bureau Federation. This type of publicity is aimed at showing the members of the various farm groups where their best interests lie, and which senators and congressmen in their state can be counted on to vote favorably for their position in controversial issues. Then there are organizations such as the National Committee for an Effective Congress (NCEC), which not only tries to portray liberal members of Congress in a favorable light but also raises money to help selected liberals of either major party in their bids for election.

Pressure groups can serve three important functions for their favorite candidates. They can supply the research and publicity needed to point up the voting records of candidates favorable to their views, as well as those of the opposition; they can raise funds for specific electoral contests hoping that successful candidates kindly disposed toward them will re-

---

[4] See *Congressional Quarterly*, 20 February 1970, pp. 567–576, and 2 October 1970, p. 2421.

main loyal when the legislative votes are counted in the Capitol; and, they can supply organization to a candidate who lacks strong party support and/or a personal political organization. If a candidate for office is not wealthy enough to supply his own funds, has little access to sizable sums of money from private sources necessary to support a long and hard campaign, and lacks a grass-roots organization, it is only natural for him to reach out to those pressure groups in his constituency who can hopefully supply the missing ingredients needed to win campaigns. For every candidate for office who reaches out, there is a pressure group that is ready to extend a helping, though not always a helpful or successful, hand.

Some pressure groups, of course, do not play politics this way, but want to keep their lines open to both major parties and stay out of the election process itself. This is particularly true of the big business corporations, which themselves act as pressure groups and maintain strong lobbies in Washington and at state capitals. Indeed, they take great care to stay right in the middle. Educational programs of the American Telephone and Telegraph Company and Western Electric can serve as good examples of this. Both parties are balanced off in the programs and the companies take care to walk a straight and narrow nonpartisan path.

Last and most important, pressure groups seek to influence government specifically, as the core of the over-all political process. In order to carry out effectively its purpose and objective, the group has to have access to the key spots in the political areas of government. The key word is *access,* access to where the decisions are made or influenced. The more important within the society the group is, in prestige or possibly in voting power at election time, the easier it is for the group and its lobby to gain access and be heard. The AMA and Bar Associations have prestige, the labor unions allegedly have great voting power, as do many religious and ethnic blocs, not to mention racial groupings that tend to be clustered in urban areas. The state of Mississippi does not pay much heed to what the Knights of Columbus have to say about some matter, but the Knights would be important in the city of Boston, or even a small city in upstate New York like Saratoga Springs. The view of the Zionist Organization of America is relatively unimportant in Grand Forks, North Dakota, but it means something in New York City. Bearing in mind that congressmen are elected from districts within the states, and that senators must pay heed to the large urban blocs of their state, one can see the importance of a pressure group at the governmental level in Washington.

Pressure groups seek access to Congress at many places. The committee system, as we shall develop in a later chapter, is particularly useful to the pressure group. A pressure group represents a formalized, readable, and knowable public opinion about some matter. It is only natural that a congressman or senator should listen to what the group has to say, particularly if he is involved within that geographic area himself. A legislator on a committee dealing with labor matters will of course keep aware of organized labor's demands. If he represents a district that contains many union people, he has another valid reason for paying close attention to organized wants and desires. The same holds true for a senator from an agricultural state. He too will have a working relationship with the various farm groups, sometimes preferring one over another (if that one has more influence at home at the moment than the other). Substantial advantages, as David Truman points out, are likely to go to the group that can accentuate and exploit the preoccupations of the legislator.[5]

Furthermore, the pressure group itself is probably the best informed segment of society about the issues with which it is concerned. A congressman from a dairy district in upstate New York can seek information about some pending oil bill from the Petroleum Institute, which can provide all kinds of answers to his questions. The Institute may even supply him with good questions if he has to ask some at a congressional hearing. Pressure groups are sounding devices for the Congress and of course they often originate legislation for the Congress. Anyone who has attended committee hearings will detect a pattern in the question and answer exchange between the

[5] See David B. Truman, *The Governmental Process* (New York: Alfred A. Knopf, 1955).

members of the committee and the witnesses. The witness makes an opening statement and is then questioned about the matter. Leading questions, opening new avenues for the witness, are posed by the members favorably disposed toward him; and loaded questions, attempting to trap the witness, may be posed by members unfavorably disposed. Indeed, more often than not, questions to be asked, and the anticipated answers, are supplied to the members of the committee by the witness or his group beforehand. Pressure groups are information grounds for members of the Congress and as such they are vital, necessary parts of the political process there.

Congress has made some halfhearted attempts to regulate lobbying and the activities of pressure groups at the national level. Just after the turn of the century bills began to be introduced to this effect. In 1913 a House special committee investigating lobbying showed that the chief page of the House was in the employ of the NAM, which paid him for information about private conversations taking place on the floor and in the House cloakroom.[6] In 1938 a Foreign Agents Registration Act was passed that required merely registration of foreign agents of firms and nations with the Department of Justice. And in 1946 the Congress passed a Federal Lobbying Act, which required lobbyists, who were seeking to influence legislative action, to register with the Clerk of the House and the Secretary of the Senate. The information had to contain the name of the employer, the salary being paid, and the type of interest manifested in the Congress. Only three convictions, however, have ever resulted from failure to register in the past twenty-five years. (Many do not register because they claim they do not seek to influence legislation. The National Rifle Association did not register until December, 1968.)

Table 3 shows the 25 top spenders of the almost 300 organizations which filed spending reports in 1968 and 1967. It must be remembered that these represent only a fraction of the thousands of pressure groups which do not "register" with the Congress as lobbies seeking to "influence" legislation. Nor does this list reflect the importance of those pressure groups

6 Cited in *Congressional Record*, 4 March 1966, pp. 4763–4764.

TABLE 3

Organization	1968	1967
United Federation of Postal Clerks (AFL-CIO)	$170,784	$277,524
AFL-CIO (headquarters)	154,466	165,505
Council for a Livable World	154,022	77,470
American Farm Bureau Federation	147,379	133,777
American Legion	141,134	100,088
American Trucking Assns. Inc.	121,399	61,718
United States Savings & Loan League	119,784	108,485
Record Industry Association of America Inc.	111,394	139,919
National Federation of Independent Business Inc.	102,455	96,701
National Housing Conference Inc.	96,935	91,995
National Farmers' Union	95,639	86,994
Brotherhood of Railway, Airline & Steamship Clerks, Freight Handlers, Express and Station Employees (AFL-CIO)	93,456	53,352
Laborers' Political League*	90,214	4,175
National Education Association Division of State and Federal Relations	84,146	73,612
Association of Mutual Fund Plan Sponsors Inc.	78,608	70,402
Liberty Lobby Inc.	75,807	61,341
National Association of Home Builders of the United States	70,095	40,568
Central Arizona Project Assn.	66,542	78,867
National Association of Letter Carriers (AFL-CIO)	63,797	133,877
American Textile Manufacturers Institute Inc.	58,378	57,394
National Council of Farmer Cooperatives	57,832	21,600
National Federation of Federal Employees	57,148	49,567
American Medical Association	56,374	58,378
National Association of Electric Companies	54,182	61,382
American Hospital Association	•50,199	61,283

Reprinted from *Congressional Quarterly*, 30 June 1969, p. 1130.
* Campaign contributions reported by mistake.

which spend large sums of money to influence the outcome of elections to the Congress.

Congress has not enacted strong measures curbing lobby activity for the simple reason the Congress generally feels that lobbying is an integral part of the governing process and performs a most important informative function. Some members of the Congress feel that lobbyists are easily identifiable anyway and are not a group of people to be feared. Congress realizes that pressure groups, when all is said and done, must come to the Congress for the passage or defeat of laws favorable or unfavorable to them. The Congress, too, has the great power of investigation and appropriations. It is simple enough for a congressional committee to smoke out the interest group behind any effort by some department or agency pressuring the Congress. And the Congress likes it this way. A 1964 report of the Senate Foreign Relations Committee stated that "lobbying has always played a necessary part in our democratic form of representative government. In effect it is the institutionalization of the people's constitutional right to petition their government."[7]

In recent decades there has been much criticism of the allegedly insidious role of the lobbyists in the American political system. The rather naive assumption underlying this kind of hand wringing is that there is some kind of objective public interest in most policy areas, and that any special pleading by pressure groups is bound to distort the execution of this public interest. This, unhappily, is an oversimplification of what the public interest is. In some areas of policy, there is no public interest in the objective sense. What is good for one large group in the society is bad for another, and the public has no really identifiable interest than can be measured. Thus policy, which often is the least common denominator of pressures brought by groups, could rarely be anything else.

Hence the role that pressure groups play in the society is not as pernicious as is often asserted. In fact, a strong case can be made that pressure groups are not only useful, but necessary. Most administrative agencies would find it terribly difficult to function without interest groups to supply them with information, and on which they could try proposals for effect. Throughout our history, particularly in the last thirty years, the Congress has found that pressure groups are well nigh indispensable in the law-making process. (Indeed, the pressure groups nowadays originate about 30 to 40 per cent of all legislation introduced into the Congress.)

[7] Senate Report No. 875, to accompany S. 2136, Senate Foreign Relations Committee, 88th Cong., 2nd Sess., 21 February 1964, p. 4.

Pressure groups also have access to the administrative side of the executive branch. Lobbyists make just as sure they know who the people are at the executive level in areas close to their own as they do members of the Congress. In fact, the agencies and bureaus of the government are obvious places for pressure groups to lobby, as more and more important legislation is initiated every year by the executive branch. The bureaucracy tends to be stable in membership (as do the lobbies representing pressure groups), and they in turn have direct access to the professionals of the congressional staff system. In fact, specific political relationships go on continually between the professional staffs of the Congress, the administration, and the lobbyists, who are the *professional* representatives of the pressure groups. These people themselves belong to an interest group—the professionally oriented bureaucrats, whether they work for the legislature, the executive branch, or the pressure groups.

The courts, too, are subject to pressure activity. Some pressure groups which, because they lack electoral strength, a forceful voice at the legislative or executive levels, or both, have had to depend on their ability to know the law and pressure for changes in interpretation of that law on the behalf of their people. The National Association for the Advancement of Colored People for many years used court litigation as its means of pressuring government. Its efforts culminated in the 1954 integration decisions, but it had also won many battles before that in the courts. Today's extensive political activity of the several civil rights groups on the legislative and executive branches is rooted in the judicial pressuring done by the NAACP. The American Civil Liberties Union comes to mind as another of these. This organization attempts to protect the civil liberties of the people. Although its lawyers often appear as witnesses for or against various types of legislation before the Congress, they more often appear in court as legal representatives of some defendant involved in a civil liberties controversy or as a friend of the court, filing a brief.

Important and influential pressure groups hire attorneys, law firms, public relations experts, and former senators, congressmen, committee staff and administration officials to do their lobbying of legislative and the executive branches. It is politically wise for the American Farm Bureau Federation to have as one of its lobbyists a former congressman who served on the Agriculture Committee. His congressional experiences give him important contacts with the various agencies of the executive branch that deal with agriculture, other members of Congress on the Agricultural Committee, and the other lobbyists from allied pressure groups. The American Bankers Association finds it convenient and prudent to hire away a professional staff man of the Senate Banking and Currency Committee. The Tobacco Institute finds it almost a necessity to pick up a former governor, congressman, and U.S. senator from Kentucky for its chief lobbyist. The list of such relationships is very long indeed. In the Ninety-first Congress (1969–1970) pressure groups and their professional lobbyists clashed and collided over educational funds, tax laws, defense spending, postal employees' pay and postal reform, the Anti-Ballistics Missile system, airport development, antipoverty programs, bankholding corporations, broadcast regulations, occupational safety, urban needs, and voting rights.

Figure 5 depicts the place of the pressure group in American politics.

Adding, in the mind's eye, to this simplified diagram, the intra-pressure group political process, a diversified economic system, and the role of the Court in adjudicating disputes

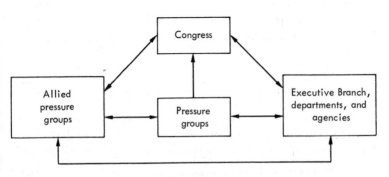

FIGURE 5

that emerge from the clash of group interests with the governmental system, one can have a fair idea of the highly complicated and integral part the pressure group plays in the over-all political process. As needs, expectations, and demands occur in society, they are reflected in pressure group expansion and increased lobbying. Permanent, well-organized, and financially stable pressure groups become more active in stressing the convergence of their interests with those of the public at large. New, temporary groups form and coalesce with older permanent groups as well as each other to depict the public interest as they see it. Usually the more established groups argue from the particular (their self-interest) to the general (the public interest), while new groups (such as Zero Population Growth, the ecologically oriented Friends of the Earth, and the Committee to End the War in Vietnam) argue from the general to the particular. It is necessary to control world population, the argument goes, so join Zero Population Growth; the environment must be improved, so join Friends of the Earth; overinvolvement in the Vietnam conflict is "wrong," so join the Committee to End the War in Vietnam. Nevertheless, both types of pressure groups in varying degrees of emphasis act the same way. They attempt to influence the Congress, the President, the administrative agencies, each other, and the public. Although it can be forcefully argued that pressure groups represent a small fraction of the people and therefore are an elitist element in the system,[8] it goes without saying that the system, as it now stands, requires that these elitist groups play an important (although not omnipotent) role in the federal system. One can quite realistically view pressure groups virtually as part of the machinery of governance.

TYPES OF PRESSURE GROUPS

Many of the organized, articulate pressure groups rest largely on an economic basis. These highly self-conscious groups can and do make a stream of specific demands on the

[8] Thomas Dye and L. Harman Ziegler, *The Irony of Democracy* (Belmont, Calif.: Wadsworth Publishing Company, 1970).

national government. To a great degree they often represent the decisive factor in the framing of public policy and are virtually an essential part of the formal political apparatus itself. Of course, at times the pressures brought to bear on the Congress are so great and so varied that public policy decisions sometimes must be put aside when Congress finds that the pressures tend to cancel each other out. This was the major problem in 1961 when President Kennedy's aid to education bill was emasculated over the issue of federal aid to private schools. In this instance, the pro and con positions of the pressure groups interested in such legislation proved too formidable, so the Congress did nothing.

Much pending legislation has an economic aspect and the thousands of pressure groups with some stake in the economy stand up and are heard. The great advances in industry, communications, science, and technology (not to mention the population explosion) have brought more and more economic interests into the process of governing. Many business firms became so elaborate in size that they have their own representatives in Washington. Thus they attempt to influence the governmental process from two vantage points, their own and that of the industrial or business association to which they belong. Firms like General Motors, American Telephone and Telegraph Company, and several of the large steel and oil companies fall into this group.

The number of business, industrial, and trade associations seems endless. A sampling will show the variety of such a long list: the National Association of Manufacturers (NAM), the American Petroleum Institute (one of the most powerful in the congressional process), the American Newspaper Publishers Association, the American Bankers Association, the United States Chamber of Commerce, the Portland Cement Association (which spends a great part of its time trying to convince the public and the government that concrete is better than asphalt), the Institute of Life Insurance (which has managed to keep the federal government from regulating the insurance companies to any great extent), the National Association of Electric Companies (which combined with other public utilities firms fights against government extension of public power), the Association of American Railroads (which feels that it has lost its fair share of federal subsidies to the other modes of transportation), the Air Transport Association (which along *with* the Association of American Railroads has led the battle for reduction of transportation taxes!), and the National Association of Broadcasters (which at times is so powerful that it appears to regulate the Federal Communications Commission, which is supposed to do the regulating in the broadcasting field).

The Department of Commerce each year publishes a Directory of National Associations of Businessmen. Each year the directory becomes fatter and now comprises nearly 100 pages of close print. One can see the broad scope of business groups by reading the *Congressional Record,* which prints the quarterly reports of pressure groups trying to influence legislation. The need to belong to business groups is exemplified by a recent statement of a prominent supplier. His company, he claimed, felt it should join no less than fifteen different business pressure groups with total annual dues of over $40,000 in order to help keep the channels of communication open to the Department of Defense and the congressional committees dealing with the military.

Labor groups, too, have as great an interest in maintaining access to government and being a strong pressure group force as their counterpart, business. And just as business groups sometimes take positions antithetical to each other, so do unions. The electrical workers' problems are not those of the teamsters or machinists or plasterers. There are more than five seagoing unions, representing some 70,000 seamen, each of which has a slightly different interest from the others. Anyone of several separate unions can keep the nation's commercial jet aircraft on the ground too. But all in all, organized labor has made great strides over the past thirty years in catching up to the influence on government that business groups had long before established. Some would argue it has not only caught up but has surpassed the power position of business. Others would claim the opposite. Be that as it may, business and labor groups represent a major share of the influence wielded on the national government.

But they are not alone. The role that farm organizations play in the American political system is a well-established fact. The American Farm Bureau Federation and the National Farmers' Union are the two most powerful of the farm groups. The AFBF, which is strongest in the Midwest, South, and up-state New York, tends to conform to business lines with its emphasis on the profit motive and the free enterprise system; opposes federal regulation and intervention in the farm economy; takes strong stands against unionization of agricultural workers; and, in general, votes Republican. Indeed, one of its spokesmen, Ezra Taft Benson, was Secretary of Agriculture throughout the Eisenhower Administration. The National Farmers Union, or NFU, is an heir of the old-fashioned, agrarian, radical, and populist movement of the nineteenth century, with strength in Oklahoma, the Dakotas, Wisconsin, Nebraska, and Colorado. The NFU leans away from the business orientation of the big farm combines; welcomes governmental regulation and price supports; and, in general, supports the Democratic Party. One of its spokesmen, Orville Freeman, former Governor of Minnesota, was the Secretary in the Kennedy and Johnson Administrations.

One of the newest agricultural pressure groups is the National Farmers Organization, a militant group of cattlemen who seek the same kind of influence already won by the national labor unions, and who often use the same tactics of striking, boycotting, and holding back products from the market. The Grange, the most important in the 1870's, started as an anti-railroad, anti-bank, and anti-monopoly organization. Somewhat less powerful today, it has become more of a social group than anything else as the AFBF took over the more conservative wing of the farmers. (Paradoxically, today the AFBF is pretty much pro-bank and pro-monopoly in its own operations.)

But a farmer can be a member of more than one group and thus be subject to the same problem of cross-pressures as anyone else. Among others there are the National Cooperative Milk Producers Federation, the National Council of Farm Coops, the National Beef Growers Association, the Cooperative Fruit and Vegetable Association, the National Potato

Growers Association (even onions are protected by an organization!), and the National Wool Growers Association. One can easily see the great difficulty the government has at times determining, or indeed establishing, a consensus of farm opinion.

There are now only some 3 million farmers in the United States, but their influence on government (on the state level as well as the federal) remains extensive. Although the farm lobby consists of the major agricultural and commodity pressure groups, farm cooperatives, and trade associations, a seemingly multi-interest body of people, "they do coalesce from time to time in shifting series of coalitions."[9] and still wield considerable political clout.

Professional associations have both an economic and a professional interest to protect. A majority of physicians (but by no means all) belong to the American Medical Association to ensure certification to a local hospital, advertise their views, and use their combined strength as a means of disseminating information to the public and the government. Agitated by what this most prestigious of all professions in the United States considered to be increasing national power in their field, the AMA took a leaf from the political book of the AFL-CIO and formed a political action committee that now plays an active role at election time in particular. The AMA contributed about $2 million to campaigns in the 1968 election.[10] There are other professional associations; several in the law enforcement field such as the National Police Chiefs Association, the National District Attorneys Association, and the Association of Attorneys-General of the United States. One of the most influential is the American Bar Association, which not only expresses great interest and concern about legislation being considered by Congress but which has also issued guide lines for presidential appointments to the federal bench. (Presidents do not always pay attention to them, however.)

Veterans groups have been particularly active and success-

9 *Congressional Quarterly*, 7 March 1969, p. 341.
10 *New York Times*, June 28, 1969.

ful in the political process. Their objective is to advance the "rights" of veterans as opposed to nonveterans and to take a patriotic stand on the issues of the day. The American Legion, with a membership of 2.7 million, is one of the largest. Others are the Veterans of Foreign War, with 1.5 million, the AMVETS (of World War II origin) with 220,000, the Disabled Veterans, the Catholic War Veterans, the Jewish War Veterans (there is no Protestant War Veterans!), and a few others. Each group has certain requirements for membership and many veterans belong to more than one veterans' organization. The American Legion takes every veteran, though! But changes in society affect these types of groups, too. As people and generations die, veterans groups lose some of their effectiveness. The Spanish-War Veterans simply do not have much influence in Congress anymore. Indeed, some of the Veterans of World War I, who make up about a third of the $2\frac{1}{2}$ million or so members of the American Legion, have formed a pressure group of their own because World War II veterans were taking over the political machine of the Legion, and they did not like it. The VFW was an elite group after World War I because to join required prior service overseas in a war. But World War II sent so many men overseas, it has ceased to have that kind of connotation. Nevertheless, rare it is for a senator or congressman to defy any veterans group with a "wrong" vote or a slur in a floor speech. (Pension grabs may be blocked quietly in committee.) For many years the American Legion alone has been one of the top ten pressure groups in expenditures of money to influence legislation. All in all, veterans groups tend to be articulate and very well organized at all political levels.

Then there are the military pressure groups who backstop the military services. The Navy League, the Air Force Association, the Marine Corps League, and the National Guard Association are good examples of the kind of group that is encouraged by government agencies to provide support for them. As the Navy vies with the Air Force for funds, these reservists and veterans apply pressure to accessible points in the Congress, and other agencies. Every military service has "its men" in Congress, and the service pressure groups reinforce the military to a remarkable extent.

There are over 260 religions and sects in the United States and most of them have some kind of political outlet in Washington. To mention but a few, there are the Federal Council of Churches, the Legion of Decency, the Holy Name Societies, the Methodist Board of Temperance. There are patriotic and internationalist-minded groups, like the old League to Enforce Peace, the Sons of the American Revolution, and the Daughters of the American Revolution, the United Daughters of the Confederacy, and a few jingoistic ones like the old America First Committee. Possibly belonging in this category are the left- and right-wing extremist groups.

Ethnic groups, like the Italo-American Society, the Hibernian Society, and the cohesive Greek and Lithuanian communities, are recognized annually with publicity in the pages of the *Congressional Record* by alert members of the Congress, or their office staffs. The list of pressure groups is endless. They run the gamut from the Association of University Women to the American League to Abolish Capital Punishment, from the Society for the Prevention of Cruelty to Animals to the Mail Order Association, from the National Reclamation Society to the National Funeral Directors Association.

Nor are domestic pressure groups all. Numerous foreign businesses and nations maintain offices and hire prominent law firms to represent them in the nation's capital. They attempt to obtain commercial and political connections, financial aid, and special favors from the government. The Eighty-seventh Congress conducted a penetrating investigation of the nondiplomatic activities of lobbyists for foreign governments and found that they could be divided into four groupings: (1) The large industrial nations that have hired public relations firms to do the same job with the American public and government as that done for any large industrial pressure group in the United States, (2) the controversial countries that are trying to influence public opinion in the United States on their side and "deal out sums of money to various individuals and firms in the United States, in a constant effort to gain and keep U.S. Government support for their regimes."[11] (3) The newly developing nations who often look to nongovernmental American firms for guidance, and (4) international disputants, particularly those involving an independence-seeking colony, who hire Americans to argue in the public communications media on one or the other side. The number of foreign interest groups seeking to have some influence in American politics grows larger every year.

As James Madison wrote in the tenth *Federalist Paper:*

> Extend the sphere and you take in a greater variety of parties and interests; you make it less probable that a majority of the whole will have a common motive to invade the rights of other citizens; or if such a common motive exists, it will be more difficult for all who feel it to discover their own strength, and to act in unison with each other. Besides other impediments, it may be remarked that, where there is a consciousness of unjust or dishonorable purposes, communication is always checked by distrust in proportion to the number whose concurrence is necessary.

This defense of the countervailing power of factions was written almost 200 years ago, but as a theory of the role of pressure groups in contemporary society, it is currently under attack. If pressure groups and their political activity are for the most part rooted in democratic values, despite their elitist system of representation, Madison's prescription holds true. If, however, they lose this dedication to democratic values (or have already lost it), then the United States will continue to have civil unrest and turmoil in increasing intensity as more and more people feel that pressure (or interest) groups have lost their legitimacy. The nation will then be in for difficult and painful times. Today there are many who argue the nation has already reached that point.

[11] Senate Committee on Foreign Relations. *Nondiplomatic Activities of Representatives of Foreign Governments.* Committee Print. 87th Cong., 2nd Sess., 1 July 1962.

Four

American Political Parties

MERICAN POLITICAL PARTIES exist in a curious kind of legal limbo. They are, as it were, somewhere between pressure groups and the other formal parts of the institutional system, like the Congress and the Presidency. For the most part, pressure groups are genuinely private, nongovernmental institutions, and only because the public recognizes their substantial impact on the policy-making process can they be included as quasi-official institutions of government.

Parties are in a rather different position. Basically and historically, they are no more official, no less private, voluntary associations than are pressure groups. They are not governed by federal laws, nor do those who consider themselves members of one party or another pay dues or fees (as do members of many pressure groups). They are not in any way mentioned in the Constitution, nor were they anticipated by the framers. In fact, Madison made it a point to warn of their serious danger to a republican, stable governmental system. Yet today no one would deny that they are so much a part of the over-all political system that it probably could not function without them. This has come to be the case for several reasons.

In the first place, it now seems clear that parties are essential elements of a system of popular government, and make possible giving the people a choice of candidates, programs, and an alternative to the existing ruling group when they desire a change. In probably no other way can democratic government on a large scale be made workable.

In the second place, parties have become essential to the political system not just in this theoretical sense, but also in a legal sense as well. Beginning with the adoption of the secret ballot in the latter part of the nineteenth century (replacing a system wherein each party supplied its own paper ballot), the states have become ever more deeply involved in the business of writing legislation regulating primaries and elections, thus officially recognizing the permanency and legitimacy of political parties. The states have come to regulate define, set limits to, and provide for the role of parties in quite a specific and comprehensive fashion. Today there are hundreds of laws on the states' books relating to political parties and their functions.

The examination of the American political party system in this book has essentially two parts: first, a look at American parties and a description of the party system and its major characteristics; second, the relation of the parties to the political system and the political process in a rather broad manner. Almost always a vast discrepancy exists between the formal structure, the organizational chart, if you please, and the actual power relations between the parts: who really makes the decisions in an organization? Either one can say, "This is the way parties appear to run, but disregard appearances and I'll give you the real scoop on how things actually are," or one can say, "Let's skip over the formalities and get down to brass tacks at once. This is how our parties really work, although according to some theory or other they are supposed to work very differently."

We shall start with things as they appear. In theory, the national convention, which meets every presidential election year, is the top governing body. This is an enormous, unwieldly body made up of delegates chosen from all the states and territories by an elaborate formula. The national convention's job is not only to nominate a presidential and vice-presidential candidate, but also to write the party platform, elect the members of the national committee, and in other respects to govern the organization of the national party.

The national committee is formally elected by the convention, but is actually previously chosen by the various state party organizations, in any way they see fit or as governed by state law. Thus the national convention merely confirms what has already taken place. The committee is composed of one man and one woman from each state, with, in the case of the Republicans, some bonus representation in the person of the Republican state chairman of each state that went Republican in the last presidential election. It acts as the substitute governing body between conventions and also elects the national chairman of the party. Lately, however, the national committee has come merely to rubberstamp the selection of the chairman made by the presidential candidate of the party.

Each state has what appear to be subordinate levels of organization: a state central committee for each party, headed by a state chairman; usually county committees; then city or town committees; ward committees; and at times, precinct captains—the privates in the party army. Sometimes the state chairman and central committee share political power with a state convention, but this is true only in some states. Indeed, in some states the chairman is chosen by the convention, in others by the state central committee. In some states the state central committee is elected in a party primary, in others it is selected by the state convention. All this goes to prove a point previously made: That the states, in their own way and as they see fit, determine the form and legality of the state parties. Because of the legal status parties have thus acquired, the United States Supreme Court has ruled that no state political party may legally practice racial discrimination. That interpretation of the Constitution is based on the Fourteenth Amendment, which applies to the states.

One would expect that in a presidential campaign, after the national convention has chosen the nominees and adopted the platform, these decisions would be binding on a unified, centralized organization all through the hierarchy. But everyone knows that although the formal structure just described does more or less exist, the party system is about as far from being highly centralized and disciplined—appearance to the contrary notwithstanding—as one could possibly imagine.

One merely has to look at the bifurcation in the Democratic Party in the 1948 election, the bitter division that took place in the Republican Party in 1964, and the straying away from the reservation on the part of both Republicans and Democrats in 1968, to see the truth in that statement. In fact the most trite and obvious statement made about the American party system is that the parties are very weak as national organizations, are highly decentralized and undisciplined, and, between presidential elections in particular, fragmented entities. What accounts for this vast discrepancy between what the organizational chart seems to imply, and the actual fact of the matter?

The governmental structure of the United States has a direct impact on the way American political parties have developed through the years. Federalism in particular is an important factor in this development. The country is constitutionally and politically divided into fifty states, each of which is represented by two United States senators elected by the people of the respective states and a number of representatives (or congressmen) dependent on the relative size of the state's population. The states are in turn subdivided by their own legislatures into congressional districts. Up to the 1960's the state legislatures had pretty free rein as to exactly how these districts would be delineated. But by the end of the decade, as we have noted, the Supreme Court of the United States had declared that all districts must be apportioned numerically equally (or close to it) and that racial determination by law of any type of district (congressional or local) was unconstitutional. Because United States senators and congressmen have no political link to a national party which *requires* their turning their primary attention to national problems and issues, and because the President is elected on an entirely different basis than they are, senators and congressmen have little or no party-ideological ties to one another, other than those dictated by economic, regional, or personal causes. *Patterns of interest* among senators and congressmen might well tie them together in many instances, but these patterns of interest are by no means permanent or national. In short, representation in the Congress in both the Democratic and

Republican parties, is usually centered on narrow, parochial interests (state and local constituencies) and only secondarily on national issues. Although American politics has to some extent become national in feeling and emotion, the federal principle keeps intact the state and local electoral system. There is very little ideological connection between the state party (of any of the individual states) and the national party. Thus the federal structure to a remarkable degree determines the kind of party system we have. Federalism has the effect of chopping up parties into fifty state segments, so that not one Republican or Democratic party but actually fifty of each exist in practice. Federalism has this impact because again the states make the rules for the governance of the state parties, and because the only officials elected nationally are the President and Vice-President (and even these elections are based on the electoral college, which is tied to the states), all the rest are elected at the state and local level. In terms of the available rewards of office, the stakes are at the state and local level, not the national.

Separation of powers, too, is another factor in the weakness of national party ties and discipline. Unlike the system employed in a parliamentary democracy, like Great Britain, the American executive branch is constitutionally separated from the legislative branch. Neither the President nor the members of the Congress are electorally dependent on the other (although they may at times lean politically on one another) and there is very little reason for party principles and national organization to be an effective cohesive element necessitating both branches of government to be continually united by party. Unlike the British system of Cabinet-Prime Minister government, the President cannot constitutionally dissolve the legislature if he is unhappy with it or is unable to maintain a favorable majority although he can try, as Nixon somewhat unsuccessfully tried in 1970, to influence the voters in the states to elect to the Congress those favoring his policies. Neither can the Congress constitutionally vote out the President because it has lost confidence in him as the executive leader of the nation, although it can impeach and remove him in a complicated constitutional manner. Federalism and the separation of powers have a collective impact on the political party system. The constitutional structural arrangements, despite the absence of any mention of parties in the Constitution, have caused a particular kind of development of the party system.

The argument is, in other words, that the mechanism and procedures of political organization are rooted in the structural framework of the Constitution. Just as the foundation and skeletal framework of a building determine the height and breadth of the final construction, so it is with the constitutional foundation. The sociological processes and socioeconomic characteristics of the society itself are so much decoration and elaboration on the original constitutionally determined structure. For example, one definitive cause of the two-party system nationally, despite the fragmentation of the individual parties, is the constitutional requirement of a majority of electoral votes for the selection of the President (and Vice-President). Each state has as many electoral votes as it has United States senators and congressmen and at election time every four years, a date that is set by federal statute solely for convenience, the voters in the states choose a slate of electors (whose names do not usually even appear on the ballot). These electors then meet in December in their state capitals to cast their votes formally and officially, in two separate ballots, for the President and Vice-President.

When a voter has cast *his* one ballot for the President and Vice-President, earlier in November, he has actually voted for as many electors as there are pledged to that "team." Furthermore, except for California and Massachusetts, no state has a law compelling the electors so chosen in November to cast their ballots for the candidates of their party. This is the reason that the electors themselves are chosen in forty-five states by either state party convention or the state central committee. In four states, the electors are chosen by a primary vote of the people registered in their respective parties, and in the Commonwealth of Pennsylvania, the presidential nominee of the party selects his own slate of electors.

The Constitution requires a *majority* of electoral votes for a candidate to be successful and consequently the parties, and thus the electorate, on the national level will divide into two and only two broad political camps. Failing this there would be no majority and the election would then be thrown into the House of Representatives, where each state has but one vote regardless of its electoral strength. To avoid this unsatisfactory condition, wherein stalemate could easily result (as in the election of 1824), a stable system dividing into two political parties has developed and persisted. Very few electoral votes indeed have been won by third candidates for the Presidency, George Wallace's candidacy in 1968 notwithstanding.

This single fact, probably more than any other, unites the various state parties in a presidential campaign and is the only mechanical link among the states. True enough, sectional and other factors may make neighboring states more alike than dissimilar in their political behavior. But it is this electoral requirement that is the basis for the loose union in the first place. Anyone seeking the Presidency as a candidate of a party must secure such an electoral majority. He must put together a combination of states sufficient to win a majority of electoral votes, which means that any third party that has any intention of making a serious attempt to win the Presidency must comply with the laws of fifty states in order to get its electors on the ballot in November of a presidential year. This takes an extensive organization and a great amount of money. No wonder then that the United States has generally had the kind of two-party system it has. For any third party to stay in business, it must successfully contend for a majority of electoral votes, or to put it another way, any third party must in reality replace one of the two other parties.

Furthermore, inasmuch as neither party in any state is very much concerned with who leads the same party in any other state, no matter where, there is no other tangible link between state parties. It takes the form of presidential support only. Because the electoral college too is an "all or nothing at all" contest, with the winner of the plurality of popular votes cast in the state taking all the electoral votes, the state itself tends to be organized along the lines of a two-party system.

States rarely have more than two parties and sometimes only one (or one and one half), as in the South for many years. The contest thus normally develops between two opposing forces seeking a state's electoral vote, to combine that vote with another state to win the Presidency.

The bipolar pattern is also reflected in the same two parties vying for control of Congress, which is based on a state and single member congressional constituency system. The national party, such as it is, is simply a presidential party, and when one speaks of the national Democratic or Republican Party, that is what is meant. Political scientists often focus their research on the presidential election and the presidential party as a means of measuring national partisan sentiment, however tenuous.

This is also a major reason for the often-cited dichotomy between the presidential party, whether Democratic or Republican, and the congressional party bearing the same label. Professor James MacGregor Burns has elaborated this theme in his *The Deadlock of Democracy: Four-Party Politics in America*.[1] The congressional party, moreover, is tied almost solely to the narrower interests of state and congressional district. The national party that does not occupy the White House usually has its leadership very much fragmented and focused by default on the congressional leadership of the party; for a party out of executive power rarely has a leader outside the Congress to channel party activity at the national level and its "presidential party" drifts off into temporary (it hopes) oblivion.

The federal system, then, results in a decentralized party system and this is, as E. E. Schattschneider rightly says, "the most important single characteristic of the American major party."[2] In no real sense, ideological or otherwise, does a national party exist other than in a presidential election year. No wonder that every four years the parties usually attempt to establish a consensus to attract votes, and strive to avoid

[1] James MacGregor Burns, *The Deadlock of Democracy: Four-Party Politics in America* (Englewood Cliffs: Prentice-Hall, 1963).

[2] E. E. Schattschneider, *Party Government* (New York: Rinehart and Company, 1942), 131–132.

a party rift that would divide the electorate. Even in a presidential election year, much depends on the political circumstances at the moment in an individual state or district. For example, a state party that controls the governorship and legislature (the in-party) may embrace or shy away from the candidate of the national party depending upon perceived advantage. If that state party's national counterpart is out of power in Washington, the former party is cast in the role of defender of itself, while the latter tends to be an attacker and challenger. And these two types of campaign do not ordinarily go together.

The separation of powers principle has much to do with the way the two-party system operates. The man who sits in the White House is the leader of the presidential wing of his party but not the leader of his party within the congressional apparatus. Furthermore, even if he and the party leaders (who are chosen by the party within the Congress) are friendly and their political beliefs, desires, and goals are the same, the congressional party may be a minority in one or the other house, and not the majority party. Since 1865, nine different Congresses had both houses of the Congress in the control of a party other than the President's; this occurred in two Congresses with the Senate only, and, in six Congresses, with the House only. Thus 34 per cent of the time the President, since the Civil War, has not had both houses in the control of his own party. Dwight D. Eisenhower had Democratic majorities in both Houses for six of his eight years as President (1955–1960), and Republican Richard M. Nixon has had the same condition in Congress in his first four years in office (1969–1972).

A President is chosen by one of two national parties, a Congress by 100 different parties, varying in outlook, composition at the state level, and in degrees of electoral security. Regardless of party orientation of the President and the Congress, cooperation on the part of either with the other is not assured. The specific power of both branches of government, as laid down in the Constitution, creates a natural feeling of separateness of the two branches, and the party system, because of its decentralized nature, could not overcome this state of affairs, even if it tried to. Actually the reverse is the case. The Constitution has produced this presidential-congressional dichotomy in our parties. Each of the two houses of the Congress has become, as will be shown later, an institution unto itself, and the parties play a much more secondary role in the minds of the members of the Congress than most people think, although the party majority-minority ratio determines the committee majority-minority ratio and the leadership patterns.

When the framers of the Constitution established the separation of powers and check and balance system between the executive and legislative bodies, whether knowingly or not, they created an institutional system that lessened the chances for tyranny by a one-party dictatorship. Even though the separation of powers is another factor, along with the federal system itself, in the creation of the kind of amorphous party system now in existence, nevertheless it is also another check against the possible abuse of government power. Party patronage and other factors have played their part, and continue to do so, in bridging the gap between the two branches of government. But the basic structural impact of this gulf on the parties remains.

Not only must one look to the constitutional framework from which the political party system has emerged, but it is also necessary to view the system in terms of the "patterns of interest" in the national community. American society can be analyzed in terms of class as well as economic and non-economic groups. The tensions and stresses in the social fabric are contributory factors to the development of the political party system. People identify, however tenuously, with the political party which appears to them to best represent their overall economic and social interests. One can have a more comprehensive idea of the forces which shape the party system by analyzing the psychology, sociology, and historical traditions of the people. We have to have an understanding of both the formal and informal framework of government *as well as* the cultural patterns and socioeconomic forces in the society in order to have a fair idea of how the party system works, and why it works the way it does.

Governmental decentralization derived from federalism, the separation of powers, and the heterogeneity of America's traditions generally force the national parties to be of a "broker type." The national party is the agent for bringing together a people divided in their loyalties to their national, state, and local constituencies, in their belief as to which branch of government at both national and state levels better represents their interests, and by the diversification of society itself. The society must focus upon something to become united as a nation. Pressure groups have a centrifugal tendency in society. It is the political party which has the centripetal tendency. As a centripetal element, political parties act as "brokers" and as a consensus-gathering force for the purpose of selecting those who govern for set terms in office. But the party is itself an authority-structure organization with distinct patterns of power distributed among groups and subgroups (just as government is an authority structure with similar division). Those who sit in places of government interreact with those who sit in places of party control. Sometimes, but not always, one who holds an elective office also holds an important party position in his state, and *he,* rather than his party, is the "broker" between government and party. On the other hand, it is not unusual to find a party leader at the state or local level (such as a state or county chairman) who is the "broker." Thus the party, with its broker concept at both national and state level, is the buckle which links the nation's constitutional framework with its structure of social forces.

The parties thus help perform the function of organizing the amorphous public will. The party, especially during an election campaign, at whatever level, is the broker of ideas, and the politician the personification of that brokerage. These ideas clarify, or confuse, systematize and explain, or confound and bewilder the voters. In organizing this public will the party is the bridge of social interests, economic interests, ethnic, religious, sectional, philosophical, and any other conceivable interests. It is the positive link that can unite—even temporarily—the diversified elements of a precinct, a village, or even a street in political action. The actual act of voting is a concerted activity whereby the people make a choice of candidates who themselves have had to appeal to those very diversifications in order to capture that vote. Put in another way, the party is the centralizing force that brings together a large segment of the society, which because of other natural factors, tends to be split apart in countless directions.

The word *party* carries with it some kind of magic which by label alone makes someone kin to someone else, even though the things that they do not have in common are far more numerous than those they do. An upstate New York Democrat in Saratoga County is as different from a South Boston Democrat as night could be from day. A Republican Senator like Javits of New York has little common ground on which to stand with a fellow Republican Senator like Goldwater of Arizona. The party is the thing that brings them together. Through inheritance or deliberate choice they share a loyalty, which may be the only tangible manifestation that unites them, as individuals, in their relation to the body politic.

The party is also the medium, at the same time, that brings together different pressure groups having vitally important though highly divergent interests. Political party organization serves the function of giving them a choice at election time. The Republican Party is generally the mode of expression for such groups as the American Farm Bureau Federation, the National Association of Manufacturers, and the American Medical Association. Here are three major pressure groups, which contain three sizable though different groupings, that can unite for political activity and pool their strength under the party aegis. The same holds true for the National Farmers Union, the AFL-CIO, and the membership of the American Political Science Association, all of whom have strong predilections toward the Democratic Party.

In a nation as diversified as the United States, the party is the only institution that can serve as a unifying force, and can create a temporary majority whereby the society can be governed. Franklin D. Roosevelt used the Democratic Party as a vehicle for constructing a majority coalition of industrial workers, farmers, and ethnic minorities, each of whom is quite different from the other. The political forces behind Eisenhower did the same thing in a different political direction in a different era. John F. Kennedy successfully tried to put together a coalition of interests to gain a narrow victory over Richard M. Nixon in 1960. After his inauguration, as is the custom with all Presidents, he shifted his emphasis from that as leader of his party to that as leader of the nation. Yet, to maintain his position as national party leader, he continued to expand his appeal to those groups which had supported him in 1960. In 1964, the Barry Goldwater campaign for the Republican nomination and presidency was geared to a different sort of "pattern of interests," while Lyndon B. Johnson based his campaign on the concept of consensus among the nation's antithetical groups.

In 1968, the candidacies of both Eugene McCarthy for the Democratic nomination and George S. Wallace for President under a third-party banner were directed at completely opposite segments of society. Neither was able to accomplish victory but the 1968 presidential campaign can well serve as an example of the interrelationships of constitutional and social forces at work in society. A substantial number of people supported Eugene McCarthy, then Senator from Minnesota, for the Democratic nomination. Although he failed to win the nomination, his candidacy, as well as that of the late Senator Robert F. Kennedy of New York, served to focus attention on the need for bringing America's youth onto the political scene. McCarthy's anti-Vietnam war stand and his appeal of understatement and calm rhetoric injected a different tone into politics in early 1968. The candidacy of George S. Wallace, the Governor of Alabama, was ultra-conservative in direction and oriented against the centralizing tendencies of the federal government.

Republican Richard Nixon and Democrat Hubert Humphrey vied for the electoral college majority, mindful of the potential impact of Wallace on the outcome in the event of a close election. If Wallace had managed to win enough states to keep either Nixon or Humphrey from obtaining the electoral college majority, the election would then have been thrown into the House of Representatives, where anything might have happened. A majority of the states would then have been needed for the election of the President. Constituencies in the United States in 1968 were very unsettled and indeed the election was close. But Nixon managed to win the electoral college majority, thought not the popular majority. The election of 1968 set in motion once again the often-made attempt to change the presidential system to some form of direct election. Many pressure groups and, from what public opinion polls tell us, a majority of the people, wanted to eliminate the electoral college system. In 1969 and 1970 the Ninety-first Congress wrestled with many reforms of the electoral college system and almost cleared a form of direct election as an amendment to the Constitution. The patterns of interest in the nation had changed almost to the point of scrapping a deeply rooted constitutional method for electing the President.

We have contended here that the search for the electoral college majority is a most important constitutional factor in maintaining a two-party system. The question arises, if the electoral college majority becomes a thing of the past, would the pattern of interests themselves change under the new pressures generated by a search for a simple plurality of popular votes to elect a President rather than a majority of electoral votes? The answer, of course, is yes, but in exactly what manner, only time would tell.

The party, then, channels the desire, frustrations, and goals of millions of people and thousands of groups that compose the public. Given the federal system, the party indeed is the only vehicle that could accomplish this in such a heterogeneous society. In short, the political party is a most important pillar supporting the stability of the over-all political system. Almost everyone, except the extreme fringes, thus has a place to go politically.

Another function of the party system, besides serving in an organizational capacity for the diversified society, is that of education. During election years, tons of printed matter are distributed by every available means, giving the public reasons to vote for or against something or someone. Of course, there is no guarantee that the citizens will read the material carefully, if at all. But because of this function, this channeling of information to the people, a basis is created for the biennial or quadrennial political dialogue upon which the parties compete for the people's favor and their votes. Thus they offer alternatives in personality if not in actual program at election time. This is true at all levels of government. Knowing that this is true, realizing that his opposition will make public his mistakes, an elected official will take that much more care to see to it that he does a better job than otherwise might be the case. If no opposition party existed to begin with, there would be less need to pay such attention. But the possibility always exists that some group might unite behind a political leader in opposition. Even such a venerable and long-serving Congressman as Howard Smith of Virginia and his Senate colleague A. Willis Robertson were defeated in primaries in an area not exactly noted for organized opposition. The political parties are the clearinghouses for ideas and the seedbeds for opposition.

In short, the party is the means for disseminating political ideas and offering alternatives so that the voters may have a choice of programs or candidates. Even choosing the lesser of two evils is better than having no choice at all. Furthermore, because the party system is a relatively open one, if anyone does not like what his party does, he can always actively join in campaigning for his own point of view within the confines of his own small segment of the party. In part through its sponsorship of this educational process, unorganized though it might be, political parties help give the citizen a sense of belonging, of being integrated into a group with some common goal. The lower down the socioeconomic ladder one goes, research has shown, the less the tendency to belong to interest groups and therefore the more important a sense of belonging may be to the person who aligns himself with a political party. The party can then become more significant in his political education and participation. Even at the top of the socioeconomic ladder this sense of political identification is important, though perhaps the industrialist or banker who considers himself a staunch Republican educates the party as much as it does him. For different reasons, all classes in a society can feel the effects of the educational process in politics. The party system is a two-way street.

The political party also has the function of providing the

connecting link between the government and public opinion. In a democracy, public opinion has an impact on government policies. Anyone who knows how important public opinion polls are to the politician in or out of office can attest to this. Always aware of the fact that at the next election the party in power may be turned out of office, that party has to be aware of public opinion, or at least its leaders do. The party organization itself is an excellent mechanism for communicating the opinions of the citizenry, and their intent, to the government, that is, to the party in control at that moment. This too is true at all levels. The President wants to know what the people are thinking in the cities and on the farms. The governor wants to know what the party chances are in the counties this year, and the mayor wants to know why he and his party are losing favor in some ward.

The American democracy has a broad base of public support, consisting of millions of people who are not involved to any great extent in either pressure groups or political parties. These are the followers or nonactivists who have a vague political attachment to one or the other party, or who swing from one to another. The job of the political party and its organization is to keep the channels of communication to those people open and clear. Political parties, in varying degrees, are the controlling agencies of government in a representative democracy. They are by no means the only links that bind the body politic together, but they are absolutely essential. Under the best of conditions the leaders of the nation will be selected by an enlightened public. But this will only be true if there is freedom for the functioning of all political parties that contribute to society. In democracies governmental leaders are elected by the people, but the political party is the vehicle for this mechanical, though vital, activity.

Nowadays a good deal is said about the necessity of having to establish a consensus in the nation in order to have governance that is stable and unified, and a peaceful, progressive society. If the society, despite its heterogeneity, is not deeply divided on fundamental social issues, the parties will tend to be different only in degree and not in kind. If society is deeply divided, the system will tend to be more and more fragmented, or else bitterly divided along some ideological line. The theory goes that in the United States the people have a high degree of agreement, or consensus, about the constitutional basis as well as the policy content of their politics. This consensus is not always clearly articulated or even perceived by all the people; in fact, it rarely is. But the manifestations of such a consensus, subconscious or otherwise, are present.

America's vertical social mobility (arduous for some groups in comparison to others); a lack of class consciousness (although objective class divisions are obvious); devotion to the principle of equality (although severe differences of opinion exist as to just what the concept of equality itself means), and acceptance of the modified free enterprise capitalistic system are reasons for and reflections of this consensus. In addition, there is a surprising lack of church-state conflict. A major basis for this consensus is the near-universal acceptance of the rule of law and of the Supreme Court as arbiter in matters of great controversy. The federal system also permits fringe groups to have a political outlet and the chance to experiment at the state level, while not allowing them to force their extreme attitudes on a major segment of the population. Thus the broad center of the political mainstream tends to be fairly stable and unexcitable (some would argue, apathetic!).

Diversification and heterogeneity, in a large republic—just as the Founding Fathers saw—are important reasons why the two parties in the United States usually support rather than attack this notion of consensus in the electoral system itself. Political ideology or absolute political principles do not play a permanent or continual role in American politics. When the 1964 presidential campaign of the Republican party took on this kind of dogmatic tone, the results were disastrous, to say the least. The American party system, as Frank Sorauf has said, "reflects the absence of both the unifying solidarity of the one-party societies and the persistent divisions on which multi-partyism thrives. Its politics grows out of a fluid social pluralism."[3]

The United States is a large, continental, exceedingly di-

[3] Frank Sorauf, *Political Parties in the American System* (Boston: Little, Brown and Company, 1964), 31.

verse nation, with an enormous variety of economic interests, important regional-cultural differences long rooted in its history, and racial, religious, ethnic, and similar noneconomic interests. It is probably true that no party could at one and the same time, bring together a national majority of so diverse an electorate and group pattern behind one candidate, and run that candidate on a clear, consistent, specific national program. Or to put it another way, under such difficult circumstances, no party could be both broad and all-inclusive, but still remain centralized and disciplined. Furthermore, these very same reasons account for the fact that no unifying ideological creed has ever held sway over one or the other of the two major parties for very long, although differences in policy tendency have been persistent.

As a matter of fact, a recent study in the *American Political Science Review* documents the point that the electorate is relatively innocent of ideological orientation, although the activist minority that works in the political system and runs the machinery is more ideological.[4] As a result, it *can* be argued that consensus exists among most of the people and any differences are found among those who run or work in campaigns. But even among the latter ideology is not very clearly defined. Hence the basis for the often-stated assumption that a harmonious and stable society permits a lack of ideology. But, given a serious calamity—war, depression, or some grand catastrophe—there is always the possibility of triggering ideological extremism that seems to be latent within the community. The nation had its sad experiences in both world wars, the Korean and Vietnam conflicts, and in some large-scale depressions.

Generally speaking, the stuff of ideological two-party politics does not exist in the Amercian system. Party activists do tend to have strong ideological commitments, but most of the electorate is not thus polarized. Differences stem from *issues,* at times based on socioeconomic class, and loyalties of one group to another. But the American major parties *are* committed, usually, to a constellation of *interests,* broadbased sup-

4 Herbert McCloskey, "Consensus and Ideology in American Politics," *American Political Science Review,* Vol. 58 (June, 1964), 361–382.

port from different interest groups, which fluctuate and alternate as conditions change. Under this state of affairs, with the continuing search for a majority in presidential election years, which in itself is a search for consensus, the two major political parties have not often been deeply divided on an ideological basis. This is still true today. They have different views of methods to achieve more or less the same sort of goals. Sometimes this consensus type of politics tends to obscure, rather than clarify, issues.

The American political party rests upon three columns—the organization, the candidates, and the electorate. The organization is interested in maintaining itself and winning elections, in putting together a combination of forces that can win. Only thus can the leaders of the political organization, those who are in the background and who do the work of the party, remain in their positions of prestige and power. The candidates want political power in the public realm, and thus share the goal of the behind-the-scenes activists. The electorate seeks good, honest, and at times imaginative government, which solves their problems. None of the three is concerned with ideology. Therefore, keeping or trying to keep a permanent, continual ideology as the basis for a political party has proven impossible. American politics are the politics of pragmatism.

Carry this a step or two further for more detailed illustration. It is generally taken for granted that the United States does not have serious class divisions. As a result, so the argument goes, this country does not have class parties, as is so often the case in Europe. But this analysis has become more difficult to understand as improved research has made socioeconomic groups more identifiable. Patterns of class behavior, unconscious though they may be, do appear on the graphs and charts of the social scientist. The higher the individual's position, socially and economically, the greater the chances are that he will vote Republican, for example; and the lower, the more the likelihood he will vote Democratic. From what has been stated earlier, however, the two major parties do not really differ very much on public issues because each party nationally has to appeal to the entire electorate in the two-party system, and, therefore, cannot really appeal to narrow interests of a particular class grouping in order to gain its vote. In spite of identifiable class voting patterns, parties must act as if classes do not exist. This, in a nutshell, is the consensus theory.

Heinz Eulau argued, in his *Class and Party in the Eisenhower Years,* that when the parties were beginning to evolve out of the early political system, a mutual adjustment between class and party was taking place at the same time.[5] This has continued; that is to say, there is a relationship between class and party identification, which can be evaluated and determined empirically. It is obvious that both major parties do not overtly emphasize one class to the exclusion of the other.

Eulau's assumption is that the class structure is a social confirmation of the consensus, a symbol and at the same time an institutionalization of the social consensus. And so is the political party. Political parties, however, paradoxically tend to cause cleavages in society, but, at the same time bring about consensus. In other words, class and party function as catalysts of division *and* consensus. What keeps the party system in the United States within manageable limits is the integrative function of the American class system. Although it can be cogently argued that the nation does not have class parties in a true sense, it does have a party system whose manageability depends on the class system itself.

Political parties, when they present alternatives in candidates or issues to the electorate, *must* operate *within* the values that have become ingrained in the class system. The parties cannot go beyond the boundaries set by classes and the values which the classes place on things. Therefore, the present kind of two-party system is the result not only of constitutional roots like the electoral college, but also of the fluid, mobile class system, which helps in great measure to resist minor or fringe parties. The diverse needs of the nation are such that both parties in the two-party system *have* to appeal to the whole electorate to win office. The class system helps bring

[5] Heinz Eulau, *Class and Party in the Eisenhower Years* (New York: The Free Press, 1962).

about and continue the two-party system; the two-party system helps to keep the class system from being a divisive force in the United States. The open-class system provides the party system with a broad rather than a narrow social base. And, Eulau rightly points out, wherever social differentiation and the class system break down, the society is most vulnerable at that point to complete political fragmentation. It is no accident that just prior to the Civil War, the Democratic Party was the very last large-scale institution crossing North-South lines to break down. Classes, then, can have a significant and legitimate function to perform in supporting the party system rather than in contributing to its disintegration.

Eulau's conclusions are worth noting. First, he argues, there is no *consistent* pattern of identification of class and party with individuals. "The structure of the relationship between class and party is not monolithic, but the boundaries between class and party interpenetrate in a flexible and fluid fashion, very much as do geographical boundaries determined by the course of a river."[6] Second, he suggests that when class restricts freedom of movement, that is, when it acts as a cause for cleavage in society, the role of party can offset this because the party system itself is consensual, that is, it cuts across class lines. Class and party can thus be said to function as mutually limiting elements in the political process. And, last, the structure of relationship, therefore, between class and party, although fluid and diffuse, is stable enough through time so that the structure itself seems to serve as an element of stabilization rather than disruption in the political system. Class and party buttress each other in keeping a stable society and democracy. "While American parties are not class parties, the structure of the relationship between class and party is such that cleavage is minimized and consensus is maximized."[7]

It must be recognized, however, that the American society is now in the throes of great change. The expectations of sizable groups of racial and ethnic blocs have become greater since the end of World War II. The increasing population that has resulted in the vast growth of America's urban areas,

6 Ibid., p. 141.
7 Ibid., p. 144.

the more and more widespread use of the automobile that has permitted such a constant migration of people from one section of the nation to another, and the interpretations of the Supreme Court relative to civil rights and liberties as well as legislative innovations are all pressures that are seething and bubbling in the American "mixing bowl." The political party system itself must continue to be a reflection of these changes. The political party system is very much indeed part of the changing pattern of interests of which American society is composed. Just as the rest of the parts, it must not be static, but a constantly fluctuating, changing dynamic organism.

In retrospect it may well become clear that the events surrounding the 1968 presidential election presented to the party system its severest test and the most insistent demands for its revitalization that have been voiced since the 1930's. The Vietnam war and the urban and racial crises at home spawned the most vigorous third-party candidacy in many years in George Wallace, and also the most precedent-upsetting major party challenger in Eugene McCarthy. Furthermore, no candidacy since that of Adlai Stevenson in 1952 drew as many of the college-trained youth into the political wars as the siren call of Gene McCarthy. Finally, no national convention in decades triggered such vociferous demands for reform of the nominating processes as did the 1968 Democratic conclave in Chicago.

What the precise impact of all these legacies from 1968 will be on presidential and party politics in 1972 is not yet wholly clear. Probably the major parties, as they have so often in the past, will broaden their appeals, both toward the right and the left, to embrace dissidents, and herd them back into the fold. It is possible, too, that many on the right and the left will veer toward the center to make certain that they are not counted out in American politics. Past events suggest that the two-party system will be able to renew itself enough to stem the tide of alienation provoked by its performance in the recent past.

Five

The American Presidency

HE EXECUTIVE POWER and superintendence of the executive branch are vested in the President of the United States. That the nation has a one-man executive, rather than a collective one, is highly significant for a variety of reasons. The very existence of a one-man executive means that even as he is being chosen by the national convention of his party, in America's complex and decentralized party system, he comes to represent certain broad accomodations and compromises among the interests in the society. At the same time and for the same reason, the office of the President is highly pliable. Each new occupant of the White House begins his administration virtually with a clean slate and to a great extent, although not completely, can operate the office more or less as he defines it. The office has thus fluctuated in mode of operation far more than either the Congress or the Court. This has been particularly true in the twentieth century.

However, the President is not wholly free from past precedent and practice. When the people have come to accept certain institutional changes brought about by the preceding President, the new incumbent sometimes finds it easier and more practical to work within the limitations thus imposed upon him. Some things a new President may do, therefore, alter only in degree, but not in kind. This is essentially true in matters affecting the public. All Presidents since the days of Wilson have had to engage in some sort of press conference or meeting with reporters, for example. Each President has had his own method, establishing his own innovations, or variations on the theme. On the other hand, a President is relatively free to reorganize his own immediate executive family, within the boundaries previously laid out by the Congress. Thus, when a President comes into office for the first time, the entire Cabinet resigns (this may also be true in the event of his re-election) and he is free to select a brand new set of heads of departments, or secretaries. On the other hand, no custom exists for the heads of the regulatory agencies, boards, commissions, and authorities to hand in their resignations. Their appointments by previous Presidents are for a set number of years and it takes from one to four years of the new President's administration before he can fill this kind of administrative position. Thus, although the President in effect has a Cabinet that serves at his pleasure, this is not true of a couple of hundred other high-ranking people in the executive branch. The new President must use other political and budgetary weapons to bring about changes in policy direction in any or all of these agencies.

When President Kennedy took office in 1961, with one executive order he abolished the Operations Coordinating Board of the National Security Council, an Eisenhower addition to the Presidency to coordinate agendas and decision-making in the field of national security at a high Cabinet and Sub-Cabinet level. Kennedy had to bide his time, however, to change the "system" in such agencies as the Federal Communications Commission and Federal Trade Commission, to mention but two. In 1970, President Nixon was able to reorganize the budgetary planning system of the executive branch, consolidate major programs to combat pollution in a single new Environmental Protection Agency, and consolidate several oceanic and atmospheric research projects in the Commerce Department.

In conducting foreign relations, a President is also free to alter policy, *but* previous Presidents have made foreign commitments on behalf of the United States to which a new President often finds it absolutely necessary to commit himself immediately on taking office, if not even before. This is doubly true when a new President takes over following the death of the incumbent, as was obvious in President Johnson's foreign policy statements shortly after President Kennedy's assassination in 1963. When Richard M. Nixon became President in 1969 he found it necessary to associate himself with the same kind of determined resolution and purpose displayed by his predecessor regarding the Vietnam war, even though he was attempting to disengage the nation from the war at the same time.

The President also functions within the separation of powers principle, which has the effect of isolating and insulating him from the currents of political machination, negotiation, and personal relationship in the legislative branch as compared with continental Cabinet executives. The President is elected nationally through the electoral college. Congress on the other hand, is elected by the states and congressional districts. The respective powers of the President and Congress are thus reinforced within each of the branches by virtue of their separate constituencies. As President Kennedy noted in a television interview after the first year of his administration, the Congress looks different from the White House than from Capitol Hill. It is a large, formidable group, with its own prerogatives, powers, and principles operating quite independently of the President. Even such congressionally rooted Presidents as Lyndon Johnson and Richard Nixon have had to keep their public distance from the Congress for fear of seeming to encroach on the congressional system by imposing themselves on it.

Lack of party cohesiveness in Congress and its factional divisions also present roadblocks to presidential leadership. Even when a Democratic President has a Democratically controlled Congress, he must always remember that a sizable number of Southern Democrats within that Congress would just as soon vote with the Republican minority on key legislation vitally affecting their area as not. Thus, his "presidential Democrats" can find themselves a voting minority. Franklin D. Roosevelt, Harry S Truman, John F. Kennedy, and Lyndon B. Johnson had this serious problem and many a time were defeated by the noted Republican-Southern Democratic coalition. The Johnson Administration had such a whopping Democratic majority in the Eighty-ninth Congress (1965–1966), stemming from the landslide Democratic victory in the 1964 Goldwater debacle, that most of the President's legislative requests managed to pass. But several times it took a handful of *Republican* Northern liberals to put the measures over. In the last two years of his administration, however, there was a resurgence of the "conservative coalition" in Congress and Johnson found his legislative leadership further stymied. When Republican Dwight D. Eisenhower was President, the leadership of the Republican majority in the Congress in 1953 and 1954 was so antagonistic to him and his legislative program that Eisenhower was stalemated at that time. Indeed, he found it easier to work with the Democratic majority following the 1954 election. Richard Nixon, on the other hand, did not enjoy as friendly a relationship with the Democratic majorities in both Houses in the Ninety-first Congress (1969–1970). When a few Republican senators strayed from his leadership upon his nomination of Clement Haynesworth and G. Harrold Carswell to the Supreme Court, the Republican-Southern Democratic coalition broke down, and both nominees were rejected by the Senate. This, more than likely, would not have been the case if a Republican majority had organizational control of the Senate. Presidents do not act alone, nor can they dictate to the Congress. That body has its own institutional autonomy and identity, to which we shall come in the next chapter.

Although fraught with political difficulty in his relationships with the Congress, isolation is also a kind of protection for the President. The fact that he has a fixed four-year term which, short of impeachment, the Congress cannot alter, further enhances his role as a focal point for accommodating and compromising major interests in society. Furthermore, the presidential office has become a *de facto* popularly elective one. The framers had apparently visualized it as nonpartisan in character and above the political factions in the nation, a kind of arbiter of the system and a brake on the passions of the popular body in Congress. But, with the tight party alignments and the pledging of electoral college members (as well as their careful selection by state party leaders) that emerged from the election of 1801, the office has become one of popular election, despite the constitutional requirement of an electoral college majority.

The coupling of this development of popular election with the acceptance by Jefferson of the role of party leader, both in the country and the Congress, meant that the early Presidents, particularly after Jackson, generally could, if they chose, become the champion and tribune for the groups in their electoral majority, specifically helping to pave the way for the President's role in the making of public policy. The large states with their growing urban populations and problems are also the ones to which White House aspirants must appeal. Thus the electoral college requirements have reinforced the Presidency as a focal point for popular appeal. Without this popular following, and without the advantages that party leadership gives him, interest groups—both articulate and nonarticulate ones—would pay little attention to him and fight their battles in Congress and elsewhere. (Indeed Black groups were forced to use the Courts very often as an outlet for their search for identification in the political process until they had gained the legal right to be heard in the political and social sphere.)

One final point needs to be made along this same line: the evolving role of the office as it was molded by those coming after Jefferson and Jackson. Following Jackson, there were few really noteworthy Presidents who left much imprint on history by comparison to "Old Hickory." Then came the slavery controversy and the Civil War. The towering figure of Lincoln more than any other President is a reminder of the enormous leadership potential to be found in the office. Lincoln really set the pattern for another facet of its development—as a focus for crisis and wartime leadership. Since Lincoln's time the country has engaged in two world wars, two minor ones of national importance (Spanish-American and Korean), and now is involved in a military commitment in Southeast Asia.

With fine disregard for constitutional and legal niceties, Lincoln raised armies, spent money Congress had not appropriated, blockaded the South, suspended the writ of *habeas corpus* (by the time the Supreme Court caught up with him there, it did not matter anyway), and did a variety of things that collectively made possible the winning of the war for the North and the saving of the Union. Building on the positive, activist role which Jefferson and Jackson had pioneered, Lincoln became the virtual embodiment, as President, of the national war effort and the national will to save the Union and free the slaves, pushing Congress (which bitterly resented it) into a secondary and background role. This pattern of crisis leadership, like the Jeffersonian-Jacksonian pattern of political-partisan presidential leadership, joined the array of available precedents for the future.

Theodore Roosevelt, Woodrow Wilson, Franklin D. Roosevelt, and Harry Truman fully developed the model for the current Presidency. The keynote of the office since 1933 has been the fact that the President has taken over (seemingly once and for all) virtually full responsibility for the total shaping of national policy, both domestic and foreign. Congress, in many periods going all the way to Jefferson, has looked to the President for leadership from time to time. But, now, presidential responsibility for *continually* taking the widest initiative in national policy is both acknowledged and accepted, even by the Congress. The great depression of the 1930's and the total commitment to internationalism following World War II are the major causes of the strong leadership patterns of the contemporary office of the President. This is nowhere better symbolized than in the present-day State of the Union messages, which are delivered by Presidents usually in person (and now at prime television time), and followed by a series of special messages on special topics to the Congress. Collectively these represent the major legislative projects that Congress is likely to deal with during the session. It is significant that the Taft-Hartley law, passed over President Truman's veto, and perhaps the McCarran Act, are the only major pieces of legislation initiated by the Congress, and not the executive, that have been passed since World War II.

This last point, particularly, raises the question as to just what kind of powers the President has that can be exercised in the discharge of these growing responsibilities. The opening sentence of Article II—"The executive power shall be vested in a President of the United States of America"—gives little clue. It neither indicates nor implies what exactly the executive power is, and is less explicit, more vague, and less imaginative than Article I, which deals with the legislative power.

A series of specific powers or prerogatives, however, can be extracted from Article I. A somewhat miscellaneous collection, they hardly provide an adequate schematic basis for the present giant role marked out for the President. One category can be quickly disposed of: routine functions of little political importance, which are part of the executive role in most governmental systems: (1) Granting pardons and reprieves in cases under federal jurisdiction; (2) Convening a special congressional session on extraordinary occasions, and adjourning Congress when both houses disagree as to the time for adjournment; and (3) Commissioning all officers of the United States.

The second group of prerogatives include the several powers or statements of function that have acquired evolutionary significance and which underpin some of the key roles which the President is called on to fill, though appearing insignificant on the surface. For instance, the wartime emergency powers which Lincoln (and Wilson and Franklin D. Roosevelt) exercised rest largely on the statement in Article II that (4) "The President shall be commander in chief of the army and navy. . . ." This is a particularly good example of how meaning has been poured into phraseology that could have remained merely ceremonial in import. The British monarch is also commander in chief, but the role *is* purely ceremonial.

The President actually has become far *more* than merely commanding official of the military forces, by virtue of the meaning that has come to be attached to this clause. Even in peacetime, the President has assumed the challenged role of number one military man in the nation. He can order shifts in command of the various armed forces and, in general, deploy troops, ships, and planes anywhere he sees fit, even without a declaration of war by the Congress. Recent examples of the use of this power are the landings in Lebanon in 1958, the Cuban blockade in 1962, the action in the Dominican Republic in 1965, and the presence of American forces in South Vietnam. All these actions are derived from this power as commander in chief just as was Theodore Roosevelt's dispatching of the great white fleet around the world to show the flag. The United States involvement in Vietnam can well serve as an example of the use of the President's military powers in opposition to and/or in cooperation with the Congress. Once again the principle of the separation of powers has a profound impact on the nation's commitments.

One of the objects of the powers conferred on the Congress by the Constitution, said Madison in the *Forty-first Federalist Paper,* is "security against foreign danger." Within this broad classification are the congressional powers "to declare war, grant letters of marque and reprisal, make rules concerning captures on land and water . . . to raise and support armies . . . to provide and maintain a navy . . . to make rules for the government and regulation of the land and naval forces . . . to provide for calling forth the militia to execute the laws of the Union, suppress insurrections and repel invasions . . . [and] . . . to provide for organizing, arming, and disciplining the militia, and for governing such part of them as may be employed in the service of the United States, reserving to the States respectively the appointment of the officers, and the authority of training the militia according to the discipline prescribed by Congress." This broad authority is contained in Article I, Section 8, Clauses 11 through 16. The framers of the Constitution were careful to ensure that the executive branch did not have the power to declare war. It would seem that a reading of this section of the Constitution makes clear that the United States could go to war only when authorized by the Congress. But the concept of shared power between the executive and legislative branches immediately comes into play. The United States has been in five declared wars (War of 1812, Mexican War, Spanish-American War, and World Wars I and II) in which declarations of war were made by the Congress in the form of legislative enactments and signed by the Presidents then in office.

By the same token, the President must also depend on Congressional cooperation when he exerts *his* constitutional power *related* to the war powers of the Congress. Besides Article II, Section 2 which provides that the "President shall be commander in chief of the army and navy of the United States," the President also has the authority granted by Article II, Section 3, to "take care that the laws be faithfully executed." Now the United States has been involved in six "undeclared" wars or "conflicts" (Naval War with France, 1798–1800; the First and Second Barbary Wars, 1801–1805 and 1815; the Mexican-American clashes of 1914–1917; and the Korean and Vietnam wars). There have been at least 125 instances in which the President has ordered the armed forces to take action or maintain positions abroad without obtaining prior congressional authorization, starting with the undeclared war with France in 1798. The Congress has in the past, as in the Vietnam involvement, authorized and appropriated money as well as raised and maintained military forces, knowing full well that the money, personnel, and equipment were being or would be used in an armed conflict. If the Congress authorizes and appropriates money for the armed forces, and the President has military powers as commander in chief, it can be argued that he can indeed order the armed forces into action under both Article II, Section 2 and Section 3. The President, then, does not act alone when, under his power as commander in chief, he authorizes military action. For to act, he must have the manpower and funds, and this the Congress provides. If the Congress failed to provide for the manpower and funds, or formally withdrew such provisions, the President would be limited in carrying out the full extent of his military-constitutional powers.

A formal declaration of war by Congress would today immediately call into play several standby laws already provided by Congress. These laws are serious restrictions on the normal course of American society. Severe penalties and restrictions associated with broad definitions of treason, subversion, and curtailment of such civil liberties as free speech would go into effect. Detention of suspected security risks, regulation of movement of enemy aliens (who might indeed be loyal to the United States), and a take-over by government of a major portion of the economy all could be easily ordered within hours of such a declaration of war. Neither the President nor the Congress, nor for that matter the people, would be anxious to place the nation in such a state. But the nation can, *in effect,* "carry on" or "make" war even without formally having such a war "declared."

We can delve further into the military and war-making related powers of the President. In 1936, a conservative Supreme Court stated that "the powers of external sovereignty did not depend upon the affirmative grants of the Constitution." In *U.S. v. Curtiss-Wright Export Corp.* the Court tried to show that the "law of nations" (or international law) also provided authority to the national government for actions in the international politics. The Court then went on to expand on the power of the President as representative of the national government:

> we are here dealing not alone with an authority vested in the President by an exertion of legislative power, but with such an authority plus the very delicate, plenary and exclusive power of the President as the sole organ of the federal government in the field of international relations—a power which does not require as a basis for its exercise an act of Congress, but which, of course, like every other governmental power, must be exercised in subordination to the applicable provisions of the Constitution.

If we depend upon the Court's *dicta* in 1936, therefore, the President has inherent power in the field of international politics to do what he thinks he ought to, provided he does not violate the Constitution. Thus the President could order troops to take up a defensive position (or offensive for that matter) on foreign soil but could not under the same reasoning suspend freedom of speech. But if Congress should declare war, he could indeed curtail free speech in such an emergency because Congress, under its powers, would have provided for such a restriction. The sending of armed forces abroad is within the authority of the President as commander in chief of the armed services, pragmatically bolstered by the raising, maintaining and supporting of those services by the Congress, and within the broad but controversial view of the 1936 Court that the President can act without congressional approval or constitutional sanction because of the "law of nations."

Does that mean that the Congress is thus powerless? No indeed. The Congress, exercising its powers under Article I, Section 8, Clauses 11 through 16, can formally restrict the use, size, and even deployment of the armed forces, *provided that Congress wants to do so.* Congress has the statutory power to limit the exercise of presidential power if it so wills. In the absence of such limitation, the President's power to act under his own authority as defined by Article II, Sections 2 and 3, is very extensive. But with such limitations placed upon him by the Congress, and this is clearly within the constitutional jurisdiction of the Congress, the President cannot roam at will in the field of military policy. The Congress also has the political pressures inherent in its legislative oversight power to investigate policies of the executive branch. The focus of publicity can, at times, cause a President to alter his policies by spotlighting public attention on the President's allegedly unwise actions. In fact, the Congress has, if it wishes to employ it, the power to impeach, convict, and thus remove the President from office.

The political reaction that eventually emerged from the military involvement in the Korean conflict beginning in 1950 has caused Presidents since then, despite the powers inherent in the President as commander in chief, to go to the Congress in advance of any possible military activity overseas to try to extract some kind of loosely worded resolution, supporting presidential action in the event of need for it. Excellent examples are the Formosa Resolution in 1955, the Middle East Resolution (known as the Eisenhower Doctrine) passed by Congress in 1957, the Berlin and Cuban Resolutions in 1962, the Resolution on Communist Subversion in the Western Hemisphere in 1965, and the Tonkin Resolution in 1964. Thus, the Congress, in its desire to show the country and the world that the nation was united behind its commitments in the field of foreign policy, has granted the President a certain amount of political leverage he lacked before as commander in chief of the armed scervices. He can point to expressions of support in the past for presidential policy in some specific area and strongly request further legislative action to help him carry out the commitments which he himself or past Presidents have made. The power as commander in chief, then, has been coupled with another—the President's crucial role as chief maker of foreign policy—to place the office of the President in a most powerful position in this day of international commitments.

Nothing in Article II explicitly confers this foreign policy power on the President either. One does find the statements that he shall (5) "make treaties," though with two thirds of the Senate concurring and (6) "receive ambassadors and other public ministers." These two taken together, plus the President's position as head of state, have become the basis for the giant structure of foreign policy responsibility over which he presides. For instance, the receiving of ambassadors has come to mean the right of the President alone to decide when a foreign government shall be recognized. The Supreme Court has ruled that the President as head of state, has the right to enter into executive agreements with the heads of other states. And even though these agreements are not treaties in theory, in fact they have the force of treaties (without the consent of two thirds of the Senate) and thus confer on the President any other powers that might have been derived from his treaty-making power.

The President is also regarded as the chief administrator of the government, who presides over the vast administrative establishment of departments and agencies. Again, this role hinges on nothing explicit in the Constitution. There is the statement that (7) he "may require the opinion in writing of the principal officer in each of the executive departments." This, by the way, is the only mention of executive departments in the Constitution and constitutes merely an assumption that there will be some. The whole concept of the Cabinet is outside the Constitution and depends in large measure on just what the President wants to make of his department secretaries; an important collective force in his Administration as President Eisenhower did, or merely a collection of individual departmental heads, as Kennedy and Johnson have done. But, requiring the opinion in writing of his departmental heads is a heavy personal weapon of the President in the day to day running of his over-all administrative establishment. As the nation has grown in size and complexity, the Congress has established by legislation numerous non-Cabinet agencies further expanding the bureaucracy and thus has conferred on the President even more power in the running of the executive branch.

Again (8) there is the famous elastic clause: "he shall take care that the laws be faithfully executed." This statement gives the President an inordinate amount of authority in ordering things to be done to put into operation the broad legislation passed by Congress. Thus executive orders are issued by the White House at opportune times, putting into effect what the Congress may have given as discretionary authority to the President within limits set by the Congress. It is then up to him to decide when and how to put into motion what the legislature has deemed proper. Of course, the corollary is that the President has the "right" not to put into motion what he considers to be improper and many an appropriation passed by the Congress has gone unspent or impounded because the President did not personally approve of the expenditure.

Finally, there is (9) the prerogative to nominate, and with the consent of the Senate, appoint, government officials, domestic, foreign, and judicial. Here is where patronage plays a not insignificant role. Even though the civil service laws have made career positions of many jobs that used to be on the patronage list, the prestige appointments in the foreign service, the courts, and the upper echelons of the departments and agencies fall into the category of political appointment. Lesser but more numerous jobs throughout the nation also have remained part of the patronage list. There has been some tendency in the past several years to draw on the career people, the professionals, to fill some of the higher positions, but it is still safe to say that political choice is the rule rather than the exception. Clearly, in executing the laws of the land, the President must act through administrative branch officials and agencies. He cannot do it himself.

Most of the nine items of presidential power or prerogative

listed so far clearly relate to the executive function as narrowly defined: the first three rather formal powers, the military function, the formation and execution of foreign policy, and the superintendence of the administrative establishment and carrying out of laws.

What about the relationship of the President to the over-all process of making policy? Or, to put it in another, less understandable way, what about the role the President clearly plays in the aggregation and accommodation of interests? Now obviously, in making foreign policy and in the whole management of the executive establishment, the President is constantly in the business of accommodating and balancing interests. Take foreign policy alone. All sorts of foreign problems, like that of competing American industrial groups versus aspects of the foreign trade policy, affect adjustments at home which the President must often mediate.

But what about policy-making in the more basic legislative sense? This is where many of the most difficult problems of interest accommodation and aggregation arise, and in which neither American political parties, nor the Congress, can do the full job that needs to be done, especially in relation to broad national groups and the over-all-direction of national policy. The President has become, so to speak, the last resort in finding a focal point for this kind of ultimate policy responsibility. The budget has become the President's budget, the annual legislative program has become the President's program, America's foreign policy has become the President's foreign policy (Congress uses this expression in particular when it becomes uncertain of foreign policy), and the party in control of the White House has become the President's party.

But what powers can be found in the Constitution for him to use in the extensive broadening of the presidential role in the political process? The answer is, precious few. The framers did not really envision any such continuing policy responsibility for the chief executive. Actually, a series of Presidents ranging from Jefferson to Franklin D. Roosevelt, who viewed the office as that of a place for innovation, forcefulness, and dynamic direction, carved out this area of concern for the White House occupant, and not the framers at all. Theodore Roosevelt viewed the Presidency as a "bully pulpit" and indeed it has been.

In essence, the President has only one power in dealing with Congress and legislative policy-making: the veto. This is, of course, important, but it is inherently negative and if this were all he could rely on, he would have little influence indeed. The only statement in Article II about the relationship of the President to the Congress is "He shall from time to time give to the Congress information of the state of the Union, and recommend to their consideration such measures as he shall judge necessary and expedient." But this it not a *power, per se*. Any individual can make recommendations to the Congress in the form of petitions! Nor does the article say that Congress must consider, much less enact, the President's suggestions and recommendations. Indeed, calling the Congress into special session, as President Truman did in 1948, to enact what he termed essential legislation (much of which he based on the Republican Platform of 1948!), is no guarantee that anything will be enacted into law.

Thus, if one stopped with the Constitution and its provisions in this area, one would have to conclude that the President could not possibly have the influence he does have on lawmaking. The answer to the riddle is again the growth of extraconstitutional practices (plus congressional legislative reaction to them), and the means of persuasion in the hands of the chief executive. This is, of course, what has happened.

To compensate for his lack of authority to *compel* Congress to act, skillful Presidents have developed a dazzling array of techniques for persuasion and inducement through which Congress can be prevailed upon to act. Examples include patronage, and the promising of jobs of some importance to congressmen's supporters. One of the best ways, however, to influence a congressman, as the lobbyists have discovered, is through his constituents. Presidents since at least Jackson's day have understood and acted upon the congressmen's predilections for the opinion of the home folk upon whom the incumbents depend for re-election. If the man in the White House can stir up demands for action at the grass-roots level, these might well be directly and indirectly felt in the capitol and hopefully action will be forthcoming from the legislature. The development of means for doing this, for the President to reach and activate the public to agitate their representatives to follow him in some matter or other, is one of the most important and far-reaching changes that has taken place in the executive office. By the 1960's and 1970's, it had become possible for a President to be in almost instantaneous contact with the whole nation. By virtue of his office, he receives free time from radio and television networks whenever he deems it in the public interest that he speak to the people. Realizing that some of the most influential press and many of the most influential radio-TV commentators were critical of his policies, Richard Nixon has used this "direct-to-the-people" technique a number of times, in talks about his Vietnam policy, domestic programs, and, once, to explain his reasons for vetoing an appropriations bill passed by the Democratically controlled Ninety-first Congress. Such ready access to his constituency has not always been possible, of course.

Until this century Presidents could do little more than use veto messages as political manifestos, as Jackson did, make speeches or inspire editorials in the press, or travel round the country spreading their message—the oft-cited "swing around the circle." Then, with the technological changes in the nation's communications system (the same kind of developments that began to tie the congressman and senator closer to his district and state), the President was able to "educate" the people more efficiently and directly. The mass circulation newspaper, in the last quarter of the nineteenth century made possible by the introduction of power presses, automatic typesetting, and the like, gave the President unsurpassed means of reaching the public mind (or at least those who read the papers).

The development of the presidential press conference, tentatively with Theodore Roosevelt, on a formal basis with Wilson and Coolidge, became the method for exploiting the press. Then came radio. Silent Cal, suprisingly enough, was the first President to put this to effective White House use. It was, of course, the old master at public relations, FDR, in his famous "fireside chats," who really employed radio to the full as a means of reaching the whole nation simultaneously, and without the distorting intermediary role of the journalistic fraternity, though FDR made good use of the press in his informal press conferences in getting it to publicize his views too. Most recently came television, which has changed not only the image of the President in the mind of the people but the entire technique of campaigning for public office. No one has yet really done with television what FDR did with radio. (The Republican party is thankful that television was not available to FDR.) But television has enormous potential as the televised debates in the 1960 presidential campaign graphically demonstrated.

The spotlight of publicity, press, radio, and television points at the President. The Congress simply does not have this national podium on such a continual basis. Individual senators and congressmen may indeed have the attention of the communications media for short intervals, but only the President has the nation's reporters and national networks at his beck and call. To be effective, nevertheless, the President must still reach out to the people and travel to all parts of the country, to bring the Presidency to the people, despite the advantages of the communications media. Nixon, as other Presidents, has traveled extensively to show himself directly to the people in an attempt to get across his message. If the President has been elected by a close margin, as was the case of Kennedy in 1960 and Nixon in 1968, it is particularly important for him to expand his image in the public mind as the people's President, not only to build up his constituency for the next election but, just as important, to create the national sense of legitimacy for his policies while in office. The kind of attention the President must pay to the public in an age of instantaneous communication has its drawbacks too. The President must always be careful of what he says in an unguarded moment lest a *faux pas* be blown up out of proportion to the context by those who hear and communicate his words to the public. And he must take care not to oversell himself and thus cause the public to tire of him. To lose the support of the people, *or to appear to,* is to weaken his hand in dealing with the Congress and, indeed, other nations.

Changing developments in the national community have also brought pressure to bear on the office of the President. Crises, ranging from depressions and national strikes to wars. have necessitated both a centralization of attention and concerted executive action. The growth of business, which has had its concomitant, bigness in government, has forced the nation to center its need for political direction in the Presidency. The Congress, too, has recognized this, and has, as a result, fallen victim to it by legislating the further development of the presidential office, and thus handing over piecemeal the legislative initiative to the President.

A glance at the growth in the Executive Office of the President in the past two or three decades provides impressive evidence. The Reorganization Act of 1939 established the Executive Office of the President to meet the incessantly increasing demands on the executive branch for an organizational structure to cope effectively with the problems of the day. The early EXOP consisted of the White House Office with a few assistants who reported directly to Roosevelt; the Bureau of the Budget (about which we shall have more to say) that had been created by Congress in 1921, and until 1939 was part of the Treasury Department; a National Resources Planning Board; an Office of Government Reports; and a Liaison Office for Personnel Management. The 1940 *Congressional Directory* was able to list all the personnel of EXOP on just two pages. In 1970 EXOP consisted of 576 employees, was composed of fourteen different sections, further subdivided into their components, and took up twenty pages of the 1970–1971 *U.S. Government Organizational Manual.*

Since the end of World War II, the Cabinet-level Departments of Health, Education and Welfare, Housing and Urban Development, and Transportation have also been added to the immediate executive family. The Departments of War and the Navy were combined into a single Department of Defense, and the rapid expansion of that department since 1947 alone is very well known. In 1970 the Post Office De-

TABLE 4 Executive Office of the President (EXOP)

1942 (FDR)	1966 (LBJ)	1970 (RMN)
White House Office	White House Office	White House Office
Bureau of the Budget	Bureau of the Budget	Office of Management and Budget
National Resources Planning Board	Council of Economic Advisors	Council of Economic Advisors
Executive Mansion and Grounds	National Security Council	National Aeronautics and Space Council
	National Aeronautics and Space Council	National Security Council
	Office of Economic Opportunity	Office of Economic Opportunity
	Office of Emergency Planning	Office of Emergency Preparedness
	Office of Science and Technology	Office of Science and Technology
	Office of the Special Representative for Trade Negotiations	Office of the Special Representative for Trade Negotiations
		National Council on Marine Resources and Engineering Development
		Office of Intergovernmental Relations
		Council on Environmental Quality
		Domestic Council
		Office of Telecommunications Policy

partment ceased to be of Cabinet-level and became an independent government agency, run by a Board of Governors (similar to the organization of the Federal Reserve Board). As of 1971, the eleven departments of the executive branch were

1. Department of State
2. Department of the Treasury
3. Department of Defense
4. Department of Justice
5. Department of the Interior
6. Department of Agriculture
7. Department of Commerce
8. Department of Labor
9. Department of Health, Education and Welfare
10. Department of Housing and Urban Development
11. Department of Transportation

The Congress permits the President to reorganize his executive branch within certain limitations. Sometimes these are written right into the law. But, for the most part, the President can reorganize any part of his executive branch provided one or the other house does not veto the proposal within sixty days. This unicameral veto has been used by either the Senate or the House eighteen times between 1949 and 1965. However, a total of fifty different plans for executive reorganization have been approved in that same period of time.[1]

By far the most significant aspect of presidential leadership vis-à-vis the Congress has been the assumption of the legislative initiative by the executive branch, as already noted. The institutional development of means for presenting to the Congress an anuual comprehensive legislative program began to take shape in the Truman years. During the Administrations of Franklin D. Roosevelt the State of the Union message was more often the statement of a general theme, in philosophical and warm tones, but with the definite proposals and specific guidelines left for later. As a legislative leader FDR operated along very personal lines, just as he did in other

---

[1] *Congressional Record*, 17 February, 1965, p. 2795

matters of governing. When Truman became President at Roosevelt's death in 1945, during the last year of World War II, he began to use the State of the Union message as a kind of bill of particulars. Whereas FDR eventually sent to Congress an *almost* prepared bill on some matter or other, Truman gave to the Congress several specific, outlined proposals and left it to them to come up with the actual program. As Wilfred Binkley has pointed out, Truman "dumped mere proposals in batches."[2]

When the off-year elections in 1946 returned a Republican majority to the Congress for the first time since before the New Deal days, Truman's State of the Union message in 1947 was an appeal for study of legislative measures and a set of warnings to the newly elected Congress. By 1948, Truman was looking forward to that election and fully intended to use the record of the Eightieth Congress as an issue. At the same time, the foreign policy was then centered on the Truman Doctrine in Greece and Turkey, and the Marshall Plan. These two instruments of foreign policy were carefully tied to domestic policy in legislative matters and in 1948 Truman's three important messages (State of the Union, budget message, and economic report) were specific recommendations, sharply defined by the President.

He then began the practice of sending special messages to Congress almost every week with an approved draft of a bill following. True enough, Truman was using this technique to embarrass Republican leadership but there were clear lines of legislative initiative in the executive branch. As Richard Neustadt has said, "specificity" became the order of the day.[3] Eisenhower adopted and further developed this pattern. His administration was almost completely dominated by the theme of institutionalization and organization of a planned chain of command in legislative as well as other matters. The Kennedy, Johnson, and Nixon Administrations have expanded

[2] Wilfred E. Binkley, *President and Congress* (New York: Random House, 1962), 342.

[3] See Richard Neustadt, "Presidency and Legislation: Planning the President's Program," *American Political Science Review*, Vol. 49 (December, 1955), 980–1021. See also his "Presidency and Legislation: The Growth of Central Clearance," *Ibid.*, Vol. 48 (September, 1954), 641–671.

the idea of presidential initiative and today it is thoroughly accepted, and at times welcomed, by both party leaderships in Congress.

The key to the process of presidential leadership in legislation is the Office of Management and Budget. Eighteen months before the beginning of the fiscal year the OMB starts to gather up requests for expenditures from all the departments and agencies of the government. Naturally, new administrative programs in any department or agency are tied to the need for funds to carry out those programs. It becomes the duty of the OMB to synthesize these needs and requests into a workable budget which then becomes closely linked with the Administration's proposals for action in all fields. A department or agency can do little that does not require funds. The cost estimates then are debated back and forth between agency and the Office of Management and Budget. Consultations take place with the Council of Economic Advisors, the National Security Council, the Domestic Council (which formulates policy positions on broad domestic questions for the President), and any other part of the executive that must consider the effects of spending on national security, the economy, and foreign affairs.

In final form, the budget is really the President's budget and his legislative program at one and the same time. It is the key to the President's entire program, because everything he wants to do with his administration to satisfy public and interest demands, party pressures, national security, and his own conception of what should be done must be considered within the context of spending money.

The rough working-up of a presidential program to be placed before the Congress for its authorization and appropriation is a collective job, in which OMB also plays the key staff role, but which, like the budget, of course emerges bearing the stamp of the President. Every legislative proposal the President might want to endorse, from setting a new minimum wage, to school lunches, or a new weapons system, must go through the hands of the OMB. It is the funnel for preparing the President's legislative program. From the proposals accumulated and analyzed by the OMB, the White House staff and speech writers prepare the State of the Union message drafts the President receives and ultimately the special messages which will later outline proposals in more detail. Implementing legislation, also prepared in the White House, will usually follow.

It may seem strange to have legislative matters considered in a chapter on the Presidency, but that is the political reality of today's congressional life. Indeed, even if some Democrat in a Democratic Congress with a Democratic President comes up with a good idea for a legislative program, one can surmise that if it's good enough to bear consideration it will become part of the President's program in due time. Actually, without the approval of the White House, it stands much less chance of getting through. Of course, a member of the President's opposition party in Congress can always offer alternatives and even original bills, but the cards are stacked against such bills being successfully passed by the Congress. Only when a party is in a majority (or if a minority also has control of the White House), can it hope for legislative success. And then, the originator of what might be a major bit of legislation has first to sell it to the executive branch, whose approval, however, need not ensure passage. Even if the congressional majority is of a different party from that of the President, it still waits for the President's legislative program. He remains the legislative initiator.

A glance at the use of the presidential veto and congressional reaction to it will attest to the development in recent years of the President as the leader of legislative proposals. The use of the veto has declined in recent years. Because the President does not have an "item" veto power, but must approve or reject the whole bill which comes to his desk after passage in Congress, there is a tendency for the President to settle for a share of what he asked for and what he can obtain from the Congress. Although the Congress may well have altered what he proposed, the bill the Congress sends him is still basically his own proposal in different dress. If he vetoes that, he is setting aside, to some degree, his own desires, and thereby denigrating his own legislative leadership and taking the chance that two thirds of both houses might override his veto and thus further his embarrassment. President Nixon used the veto in the Ninety-first Congress (1969–1970) with some degree of success. But a fair measurement of the effectiveness of Nixon's use of the veto must await the final count at the end of his term as President.

One more development in this century needs elaboration as to its effect on the Presidency. Since the days of Harry Truman, all Presidents have had the awesome responsibility of directing a nuclear potential and an extensive military machine. Even though the Congress has set up committees for nuclear and space problems as counterparts to the expansion of these areas in the executive branch, they serve more as watchdog committees on policy making after the fact. The truth is that presidential decisions in matters of foreign policy and military affairs have become all-important in contemporary society. That the President has the sole responsibility for the control of nuclear weapons and the direction of the armed forces, whether through a Secretary of Defense or not, means that the entire nation, if not the world, looks to him for the right decisions at the right time. No other element in the American governmental system has this great power at its command. It has never existed before in such magnitude.

The President has indeed become a political leader who must educate, persuade, and lead an entire nation. The parties and Congress are preoccupied with local interests and problems, and unable, or unwilling, to subordinate these in order to tackle truly national problems and issues. These must often be solved at the expense of local and parochial interests. What better example today than that of civil rights? Without the presidential leadership of Eisenhower, Kennedy, and Johnson in this area, none of the recent civil rights acts would be on the books, regardless of the Court's ruling in 1954.

Historically, and especially since the beginning of the twentieth century, the nation has had to look to the Presidency to develop and sell solutions to these national problems, and preside over the total development of the pattern of national policy. The strictly constitutional powers of the President for doing this are rather inadequate from a strict reading of the Constitution. But a combination of the vigor

TABLE 5 Presidential Vetoes (1933–1970)

Years	President	Congressional Party	Regular Vetoes	Pocket Vetoes	Total Vetoes	Vetoes Overridden
1933–1945	F. D. Roosevelt Democrat	Democratic 13 years	371	260	631	9
1945–1952	Truman Democrat	Republican 2 yrs Democratic 6 yrs	180	70	250	12
1953–1960	Eisenhower Republican	Republican 2 yrs Democratic 6 yrs	83	118	201	3
1961–1963	Kennedy Democrat	Democratic	14	11	25	0
1963–1968	Johnson Democrat	Democratic	17	14	31	0
1969–1970	Nixon Republican	Democratic	7	4	11	2

of a one man office with its singleness of purpose, the fixed presidential term that keeps the President in office for at least four years and prevents disenchanted groups from replacing him over some single issue, and the broadening base of popular support in an expanding electorate with a truly national constituency establishes for him the indispensable platform from which to operate as a national leader.

Then, the tools of persuasion which the mass media especially put into his hands, when skillfully used by a true leader and adroit politician, can be made to do the rest.[4] With these resources the President can *usually* counteract the centrifugal forces that play on the Congress, parties, and interest groups in their approach to policy problems. We say *usually* because this enormous reliance on the Presidency to make the system work has its dangers in the last analysis. Because the President must act through skill, persuasive ability, craft, and certainly knowledge and wisdom, the whole thing rests on the fragile base represented by the abilities and judgment of the one man out of 204 million chosen for the office. If he is not equal to the task, the nation is in serious trouble. A congressional district can suffer the ineptitude of a poor congressman, and a state can put up with the caprices of a whimsical senator, but the nation cannot put its trust in an unwise and unskillful President.

A growing number of observers of the American system and of the role of the President in it have recently been citing a different, and opposite danger: that the office concentrates *too much* arbitrary power. Uppermost in their minds has been American involvement in Southeast Asia, and foreign policy generally. If it is true that the powers of the President may be barely adequate to solve the contemporary perplexities of domestic policy, a case can and has been made that his power to pursue a course of foreign policy that is acutely unpopular with a major segment of the national population is much too great. Judgments of this sort may be transient, provoked by

4 See Richard Neustadt, *Presidential Power: The Politics of Leadership* (New York: John Wiley and Sons, 1962); Elmer E. Cornwell Jr., *Presidential Leadership of Public Opinion* (Bloomington: University of Indiana Press, 1965).

some current frustration. However, the frequency with which the office is damned for being either too weak or too strong, for pulling its punches or overstepping its constitutional boundaries, underscores again both the crucial importance of the President in the system, and the lingering ambiguities surrounding his precise role.

Six

The Congress

N REPUBLICAN GOVERNMENT, said James Madison in the fifty-first *Federalist Paper,* "the legislative authority necessarily predominates." As a group the framers obviously shared this view. Matters dealing with the Congress are in the *first* article, occupying as much space as the remainder of the Constitution. When one says that the national government is one of enumerated powers, the reference is to that article which lists in a rather straightforward manner the powers and authority vested in the Congress. The conferees in Philadelphia in 1787 had a good theoretical basis for this preoccupation. If sovereignty rests with the people in a republican form of popular government, the legislature, more than any other branch, is directly and immediately the people's representative, being, in theory, a microcosm of all.

In any discussion of legislative bodies and functions one is bound to raise two key aspects of the legislative system: the representative role and the law-making role. The representative role is basic, and should claim first attention. How can the membership of a representative assembly, in practice, be the true agent of the citizenry? How should the representatives be chosen? How, once chosen, should the members behave in order to carry out their function as agent?

Edmund Burke, the great eighteenth-century English statesman and classical, conservative political thinker, told his constituents in Bristol, who had chosen him their Member of Parliament:

> Your representative owes you, not his industry only, but his judgment; and he betrays, instead of serving you, if he sacrifices it to your opinion.[1]

This is still a widely held belief. Once chosen, the representative should act on the basis of, as Burke said, "his unbiased opinion, his mature judgment, his enlightened conscience" and not be a mere errand boy for his constituents.[2] In this view, the basis on which he is chosen becomes relatively unimportant so long as he is somehow elected popularly. The only trouble with this approach is that if the representative presses it too far, he probably would be defeated at the next election because most people are concerned with their *representatives* looking out for *their* interests and protecting their individual and collective enclaves. The hard facts of the matter are that there are articulate and watchful interests in any constituency, which are going to demand representation on *their* terms, or they will attempt retaliation at the polls.

Perhaps Burke was wrong altogether. Why not frankly recognize the existence of these interests and groups within the electorate, and represent them directly? Why not work out a scheme whereby each interest group of consequence would have the right to elect one or more members of the national legislature, thus providing for functional rather than geographic representation? Not only would all interests and points of view be directly and clearly represented in the councils of the nation, and thus provide a legislature that was truly a microcosm of the "pattern of interests" of the electorate, but it might solve the Burkean problem as well. Each representative, inasmuch as he was chosen from a homogeneous group with a common overriding interest, would himself *share* that interest and objective. He would indeed be "one of them." Hence the need to compromise his judgment and conscience,

---

[1] Election speech, November 3, 1774, quoted in Ross J. S. Hoffman and Paul Levack, eds., *Burke's Politics* (New York: Alfred A. Knopf, 1949), 115. See also William T. Bluhm, *Theories of the Political System* (Englewood Cliffs: Prentice-Hall, 1965), 405–407.

[2] Ibid.

based on differing views of his "constituency," would be minimized.

This is not so farfetched as it sounds. Both the German Weimar Republic and the Fourth Republic of France provided for such a body as an advisory group to the national legislature. Yet logical and sensible as this approach to representation sounds, it undoubtedly would be quite unworkable. This kind of scheme for interest group representation might very well formalize the whole business of interest articulation, but it would by the same token make aggregation of interests in the legislature virtually impossible. Because each member would be there to represent one and only one interest, and his whole position would depend on safeguarding that single purpose, he would have little or no incentive to compromise with other interests, and virtually no sense of responsibility for the over-all conduct of government. Complete deadlock would almost certainly result, because no one would have a vested interest in arranging accommodation. Clearly it would seem that the pendulum has swung too far to the other extreme from Burke's view.

Suppose, instead, that a disciplined two-party system exists, one capable of fielding a group of candidates pledged to a well-integrated and comprehensive set of policy proposals. A legislature elected on this basis will comprise two disciplined groups: a minority whose program lost, and a majority whose party proposals won the public confidence. By the time the legislature meets, the job of negotiation and accommodating among the various interests will already have been done. The members will then be representing two large segments of the total pattern of interests, or two alliances cemented by prior party activity, and will not really be presenting individual interest at all. The members' roles are then reduced to a simple (*pro forma*) job of voting on strict party lines to place the official stamp of approval on the majority party platform. Maybe a scheme like this is the answer. It seems both neat and workable. It poses, however, its own problems.

First and foremost, such a scheme is wholly dependent on some extralegislative entities, such as political parties, for its success. At the same time, it might very well cause such a close tie of the parties to the legislative system that the net effect would be abdication of the legislative function to the parties, or other extraconstitutional bodies. The extreme form of this is in the one-party system where the party and legislature are effectively one and the same. Second, it reduces the role of both the individual member and the legislature itself to the performance of a largely meaningless ritual. Indeed, it might easily lead to one-party domination over such an extended period that a complete loss of the representative function of the legislator would follow.

Where does the United States Congress fit into the picture? What is its role in the articulation and aggregation of interests? The simple and quick answer is that the Congress partakes to some degree of all these possibilities. The membership of the Congress is elected on the basis of geographic rather than interest or functional constituencies. Senators and a few congressmen have whole states as their electoral district. Most members of the House, however, are elected from single-member districts with roughly 1/435 of the population (ignoring the malapportionment that was so prevalent for many years, but which now is slowly disappearing under Supreme Court interpretation of the Constitution in *Wesberry v. Sanders* in 1964).

This system has several important manifestations in terms of the foregoing discussion. First, it means that members of the Congress do not represent homogeneous groups of people with only one major interest in life. Even House members from single-crop farming districts represent a more varied constituency than would be the case in a pure interest group representative arrangement. Senators from the largest states represent widespread arrays of interests and groups that cover the whole spectrum of industry, agriculture, socioeconomic and ethnic groups, religions, and so on. This geographic basis of representation has significant consequences. Each member of the Congress must be a little aggregator in his own right. Each must somehow come to terms with the array of interests in his home area and go to Washington as a kind of living embodiment of compromise. Because the interest groups must superimpose their organizational structures and systems upon the federal and bicameral nature of the American government, it is only natural that part of the job of accommodating those interests is done at the very outset by the individual congressman and senator. Each member of the Congress must weigh and balance out the various stresses and strains impressed upon him by the kind of constituency he has, state or district. It is almost impossible for a member of the Congress to make a legislative decision without having in the back of his mind the effect of his decision on his own people at home. When this is added to the pressures placed upon him as a member of an organization, the Congress itself, as we shall see, it is little wonder that the national legislators are a kind of hybrid. Every member of the Congress has to contend with this problem, and all because he represents a specific geographic area which itself is different in degree, and at times in kind, from every other district or state.

Second, the federal structure of government and our staggered national electoral system also play their part in mitigating party cohesion and discipline in the congressional party. The President is elected by a national constituency once every four years and is limited to two terms of office. The House, on the other hand, is elected from its smaller geographic constituencies every two years, without any limitation on the number of terms, and one third of the Senate is elected every two years by state constituencies also without limitation of terms. Elections that are staggered in this manner do not make for party cohesion on a continuous basis. Nor do they force presidential, congressional, and senatorial candidates to link their respective campaigns together through the political party. Our federal system thus results in varying majorities in the Congress and, at times, in congressional majorities that are different from the party holding the Presidency. Table 6 depicting the party line-up of the Congress and Presidency from 1947 to 1972 shows this lack of party cohesion and uniformity of political strength in the Congress.

Third, given the nature of the American party system, there is only a partial tendency for congressmen and senators to

TABLE 6　Party Makeup of Congress and the Presidency, 1947–72

Congress	President	President's Per Cent of Two-Party Vote	Per Cent of Majority Party Control of Senate	Per Cent of Majority Party Control of House
80 (1947–48)	Truman		Rep.-53.2%	Rep.-56.6%
81 (1949–50)	Truman-Dem.	52.3%	Dem.-56.3	Dem.-60.6
82 (1951–52)			Dem.-51.0	Dem.-54.0
83 (1953–54)	Eisenhower-Rep.	55.8	Rep.-50.6	Rep.-51.2*
84 (1955–56)			Dem.-50.6	Dem.-53.3
85 (1957–58)	Eisenhower-Rep.	57.8	Dem.-51.0	Dem.-53.8†
86 (1959–60)			Dem.-66.0	Dem.-64.8
87 (1961–62)	Kennedy-Dem.	50.1	Dem.-64.0	Dem.-60.0‡
88 (1963–64			Dem.-67.0	Dem.-59.3
89 (1965–66)	Johnson-Dem.	61.3	Dem.-68.0	Dem.-67.8**
90 (1967–68)			Dem.-64.0	Dem.-57.0
91 (1969–70)	Nixon-Rep.	50.4	Dem.-57.0	Dem.-56.5***
92 (1971–72)			Dem.-54.0	Dem.-58.6

Adapted from George Goodwin, Jr., *The Little Legislatures: Committees of Congress* (Amherst: University of Massachusetts Press, 1970), 16.

* Eisenhower's election in 1952 brought in a Republican majority in the Congress, although a very slight one.

† Despite Eisenhower's increased percentage of the popular vote in 1956, the Democrats continued to gain ground in the Congress, beginning with their taking back control in the election of 1954.

‡ Although Democrat Kennedy won the election in 1960, his party lost ground in its total majority in the Congress from the previous Congress.

** The Johnson sweep in 1964 also saw a heavily Democratic Congress elected with him.

*** The Democrats steadily lost ground in Congress after 1964, although they kept control of Congress despite the election of Nixon in 1968. It is also signicant to note that Nixon's percentage of the *total* vote in 1968 was only 43.4%, with the Democrats winning 42.7% under the candidacy of Hubert Humphrey, and George Wallace capturing 13.5%. The Democrats lost a little strength in the Senate in the 1970 election but gained slightly in the House. It should also be noted that since 1947, the President has been of a different party from the majority in the Congress six out of thirteen times. Indeed, since the Civil War, the House has been in the control of the opposition party to the President six times (the 44th, 45th, 48th, 52nd, 62nd, and 72nd Congresses); the Senate has been in the control of the opposition party to the President twice (the 49th and 50th Congresses); and both the House and the Senate have been in the control of the opposition party to the President eleven times (the 39th, 40th, 46th, 54th, 66th, 80th, 84th, 85th, 91st, and 92nd Congresses).

represent parties or party-integrated bodies of interests. Political parties are only one factor in the over-all operations of the Congress. A glance at the Tables 7–10 will show that party identification in voting is at best spasmodic. It is particularly significant that in the Ninetieth Congress (1967–68), when the Democrats were in control of both the Congress and the Presidency, their Party Unity Scores were the same as in 1969, when they controlled the Congress but not the White House. Republican solidarity, on the other hand, dropped six percentage points (from 68 per cent to 62 per cent) with Nixon as President in 1969. Sectional differences of party voting are also apparent from the following tables.

Party Unity and Opposition to Party scores in Tables 9 and 10 are composites of individual scores, and show the percent-

TABLE 7   Party Unity Scoreboard

	Total Roll Calls	Party Unity Roll Calls	Per Cent of Total
		1970	
Both Chambers	684	219	32%
Senate	418	147	35
House	266	72	27
		1969	
Both Chambers	422	144	34%
Senate	245	89	36%
House	177	55	31
		1968	
Both Chambers	514	172	33%
Senate	281	90	32
House	233	82	35
		1967	
Both Chambers	560	198	35%
Senate	315	109	35
House	245	89	36

Reprinted from *Congressional Quarterly,* 29 January 1971, p. 238.

TABLE 8   91st Congress (1969–1970) Victories, Defeats on Party Unity Votes

	Senate		House		Total	
	1969	1970	1969	1970	1969	1970
Democrats Won, Republicans Lost	60	88	31	44	91	132
Republicans Won, Democrats Lost	29	59	24	28	53	87
Democrats Voted Unanimously	7	4	1	1	8	5
Republicans Voted Unanimously	5	2	2	0	7	2

Reprinted from *Congressional Quarterly*, 29 January 1971, p. 238.

age of time the average Democrat and Republican voted with his party majority in disagreement with the other party's majority. Failures to vote lower both Party Unity and Opposition to Party scores.

Fourth, because many congressmen come from safe districts where their re-election is rarely in doubt, or there are relatively few interests they need concern themselves with, and, because party discipline *is* loose and thus congressmen are often free to ignore party leadership demands without serious risk to themselves, at least *some* of the independence of judgment and conscience Burke argued for is also exercised by the American legislator. He is often sufficiently free of both party and constituency ties to vote his own view, at least on some kinds of issues. (In so doing he may, in reality, represent broad

TABLE 9   Party Unity and Opposition to Party Scores

	1970		91st Congress (1969–1970)	
	Dem.	Rep.	Dem.	Rep.
Party Unity	57%	59%	59%	60%
Senate	55	56	58	59
House	58	60	59	61
Opposition to Party	23%	23%	24%	24%
Senate	22	23	22	24
House	24	23	24	24

Reprinted from *Congressional Quarterly*, 29 January 1971, p. 238

TABLE 10   1969 and 1970 Sectional Support, Opposition

	Support		Opposition	
	1969	1970	1969	1970
SENATE				
Northern Democrats	71%	64%	14%	13%
Southern Democrats	46	38	40	40
Northern Republicans	62	54	26	25
Southern Republicans	70	67	18	15
HOUSE				
Northern Democrats	73%	66%	13%	15%
Southern Democrats	40	43	45	40
Northern Republicans	59	59	26	23
Southern Republicans	74	63	16	20

Reprinted from *Congressional Quarterly*, 29 January 1971, p. 238.

currents of thought in the country only vaguely related to his own district: "conservatism" or "liberalism," pro- or anti-big government, and so on.)

Given the way its members are chosen, and the nature of the American party system, the individual members do part of the job of accommodating interests (in their districts) and the parties do another, which is reflected in the modest but important amount of party voting. The previous charts do not depict the whole story. Party unity can be measured accurately only in roll call votes and in some of these such prior agreement has occurred. Many roll-call votes where the parties in the Congress show a substantial amount of unity also display a substantial amount of bipartisanship. By the same token, party unity may well be more the rule than the exception in voice votes, where each individual is counted but his name not recorded.

To put the matter a bit differently, the local point of view and local interest compromises are quite well represented in Congress, and the few major issues upon which the parties have succeeded in getting some kind of national agreement can be acted upon beyond the scope of parochialism. But this leaves a wide range of policy areas that do not come under either of these headings. Most congressmen can and do reflect fairly clear local views from their home areas. But how does national accommodation of interests in the areas of agriculture, labor policy, foreign aid, among others, get done? The answer would have to be found, if found anywhere, in the organizational structure of the Congress, and the system itself.

A legislature is a body of men with different interests to represent and different partisan loyalties. Any such large body can act with effectiveness and dispatch only if there are means to force confrontation of the issues and to extract decisions based on those issues, and if there are leaders who have a vested interest on having decisions made (or not made!), plus the means of bringing them about. In the American Congress, party cohesion is not enough in itself to assure results or non-results, and though the individual members must do a good bit of compromising, they have few incentives beyond those rooted in their home districts or states to cause them much worry. Individually, much depends on one's own particular position in the power hierarchy of the congressional structure. Collectively the Congress itself becomes a constituency to protect against the executive branch and even the Court. The bicameral nature of the Congress, too, makes each house a constituency unto itself, versus the other house. This is not only a further extension of the check and balance concept, but it can also lead to a complicated, confusing, and slow-acting body. Mechanisms must be provided to impel action and compromise.

This opens the whole question of the internal functioning of Congress as a legislative body. Basically, the committee system and leadership roles within Congress are designed to facilitate the job of legislating and of compromising interest demands which must precede legislating itself. To begin with, one must first recognize the role of party in "organizing" the Congress.

Party is the vehicle for the organization of Congress. It should be realized, however, at the very outset, that the word *party* as used here means the congressional party only. Both parties in the Congress bitterly resent outside forces attempting to dictate to them who should be in charge of what, and who should do what. Each house, as judge of its own rules, is led by its *own* party leadership, clothed with that leadership only by the members of the respective parties within each house. At the beginning of each new Congress, in the odd-numbered years, the Republicans and Democrats in each house separately gather to choose their leaders. The leader selected by the majority party in the House of Representatives is then elected speaker by the vote of the House itself, which divides along party lines as a rule, the minority casting its votes for the person they have chosen minority floor leader. The rest of the party leaders (the majority floor leader, the chief whips or assistant floor leaders) are designated by the party membership of each house.

Despite the fact that the entire House of Representatives is elected every two years, the leadership maintains a great deal of continuity because roughly three fourths of the House are in little danger of losing their seats from election to election. Congressional district lines are so carefully drawn that by and large one-party control claims a little more than 300 congressional seats, and most of the House is returned from Congress to Congress. Thus seniority patterns, and general acceptance of the leadership status quo, are fairly well established. Even the 1964 Democratic landslide, which resulted in the capture of several ordinarily Republican seats by the Democrats, caused the defeat for re-election of few leaders in Congress.

True enough, seniority, the system whereby a person climbs the ladder in rank according to the number of years he has served in the Congress and/or on a committee, does not always have the final word in the selection of party leadership. The House Republicans have voted their floor leader out of office twice in recent years (Joseph Martin of Massachusetts in 1959 and Charles Halleck of Indiana, who had led the coup against Martin, in 1965). But in general the choice of leadership is quite stable, particularly in the Senate, where only one third of its membership is elected every two years. Senators are elevated to floor leadership positions only after considerable service and experience in Congress. Mike Mansfield became the Senate majority leader of the Democrats in 1961 when Lyndon B. Johnson, the incumbent, was inaugurated Vice-President. Russell Long, of Louisiana, was elected as Mansfield's assistant only when Hubert Humphrey became Vice-president in 1965. John McCormack, of Massachusetts, became the number one Democrat in the House after the death of Sam Rayburn of Texas, who had served as Speaker and majority leader for many years. McCormack's place as Speaker was taken by Carl Albert of Oklahoma after the former's retirement at the end of the Ninety-first Congress in 1970. Everett McKinley Dirksen of Illinois assumed leadership of the Senate Republicans in 1959 and served until his death ten years later, when he was replaced by Hugh Scott of Pennsylvania.

Both parties in the Senate and the Republicans in the House hold party conferences infrequently. The House Democrats, however, do not maintain a party caucus in form for party cohesion purposes. When party conferences do occasionally take place, no decision is binding on the members. Party cohesion on policy, although not on selection of party leaders in Congress, is relatively ineffective among the Democrats because of the significant split between the Southern Democrats and their colleagues who tend not only to have different accents but also different views on most national issues. This is true both in the Senate and the House. Attempting to bring together such a severely divided party would only exacerbate the division within the party. Indeed, Democratic party leadership tends to be continually preoccupied with affecting compromises.

A vast majority of senators and congressmen from the Southern states of Alabama, Arkansas, Florida, Georgia, Kentucky, Louisiana, Mississippi, North Carolina, Oklahoma, South Carolina, Tennessee, Texas, and Virginia are Democrats. Generally they can be considered quite conservative in their political, social, and economic views. Most of the other Democrats in the Congress, although by no means all, tend to be more liberal in their views than their Southern counterparts. Thus a Democratic majority on paper does not necessarily imply that the Democrats will remain a voting bloc on even the most important issues they face. If the Southern Democrats, or most of them, ally themselves on specific issues with the Republicans, the so-called Democratic majority falls apart. Even though there are a few Southern Republicans in the Congress, they, too, to all intents and purposes, vote generally along the same lines as Southern Democrats anyway. There is then a potential bipartisan "conservative coalition" on any controversial matter before the Congress. The strength of this coalition can be measured to some degree by examining roll-call votes on significant issues through the years. Of course this is only a partial measurement because the "coalition," purposeful or not, can always operate in the committee system as well. Table 11 shows the relative success of this "coalition" in recent years.

TABLE 11

	Coalition Appearance Percentage of Roll-call Votes, 1961–1970	Coalition Victories		
		TOTAL	SENATE	HOUSE
1961	28%	55%	48%	74%
1962	14	62	71	44
1963	17	50	44	67
1964	15	51	47	67
1965	24	33	39	25
1966	25	45	51	32
1967	20	63	54	73
1968	24	73	80	63
1969	27	68	67	71
1970	22	66	64	70

Reprinted from *Congressional Quarterly*, 29 January 1971, p. 243.

The low point of the "coalition's" success was in 1965 when the Democrats enjoyed a very powerful majority following the election of 1964. In this session of Congress the Southern Democrats were relatively weak in influence because so many Republican districts outside the South had gone Democratic in 1964; hence a good deal of "liberal" legislation was passed in that session. The "coalition" began to gather strength after that, however, and in Johnson's last year in the Presidency it had reached a high point of 73 per cent victories on 24 per cent of the total roll-call votes taken. In 1969 and 1970, with a Republican in the White House, the "coalition" lost some of its power in the Senate but improved its position in the House. Indeed, with a relatively conservative Republican as President, the "coalition" found an ally in Nixon and could now cast itself as a defender of presidential leadership rather than as an obstructionist group. All this goes to prove that on many issues and problems, even beyond those represented by roll-call votes on the floor of both houses of the Congress, it is necessary for Southern and Northern Democrats to compromise with each other in the over-all decision-making process in the Congress. The skill of leadership of both parties comes into play, not only in floor leadership but also in the many pockets of leadership in the committees themselves. If the "liberals" want a victory, they have to give a little (or a good deal) to ensure a voting majority. Either that, or they have to ally themselves with the relatively few "liberal" non-Southern Republicans on specific issues. It can be readily seen that party cohesion and unity in the Congress is flimsy at best.

Another important reason for the lack of more party cohesion on policy matters is that most members of both parties regard the congressional party as the medium for getting elected and not for putting forth a specific legislative program, as is the case in Great Britain. The Republicans in both houses do tend to be more united than the Democrats, but two reasons probably account for this. First, they have been a minority in the Congress (except for the years 1947–1948 and 1953–1954) since before the days of the New Deal. Thus they have been more or less forced to adhere to one another within the Congress to present a united front against the majority (the bigger the majority, the greater the problems of its leadership to keep the pack together). Second, the United States is an urban society, and for a number of socioeconomic reasons, the Democratic party is the urban party. As a result, the Republican party in the Congress seems to be more homogeneous because of its representation of the nonurban portion of the national community—increasingly the suburban areas. The congressional Democrats are simply more heterogeneous. Add to this the homogeneous group of Southern Democrats as a super-imposition on all the Democrats, and the result is a Democratic party in the Congress that can more easily go off in different directions. Again, one can discern in the Congress the effect of the geographic system of representation.

Both congressional parties in each house maintain their own campaign committees, quite independent of the national committees, for the purpose of helping "their own" get re-elected and, sometimes, to raise financial aid for their own party candidates seeking to oust members of the opposition. They exist as fund-raising committees, separate and distinct from other party organizations, which, of course, helps to maintain the separate identities of the congressional party from the national party, or, as noted before, the presidential party organized to capture control of the White House.

The congressional committee system is by far the most important element of the internal organization of the Congress. There are 17 Senate and 21 Permanent (or Standing) House Committees to which flow the vast mass of bills. (In the Nineteenth Congress (1967–68), 20,587 bills were introduced in both houses and only 1,002 bills actually were enacted into law.) The party division of the committees is roughly equivalent to the relative party strength in each house. In addition, the committees are subdivided into over 140 subcommittees in the House and over 100 subcommittees in the Senate. Add to this several Select (or Special) temporary committees and joint committees and one can see the complexity and pervasiveness of the congressional committee system.

Table 12 lists the Standing Committees in the Senate and House in the Ninety-second Congress (1971–72) and their party ratio.

The bill-passing process follows an often slow and usually tortuous path, although the Congress is capable of speeding a bill through the congressional maze if it so wills. A bill may be formally introduced in the Congress only by a member of that particular house, although companion bills are sometimes introduced in the other house at the same time in order to hasten the process. In that way both houses may well be

TABLE 12

Senate	Party Ratio Dem.–Rep.	House	Party Ratio Dem.–Rep.
1. Aeronautical and Space Sciences	6–5	1. Agriculture	22–14
2. Agriculture and Forestry	8–6	2. Appropriations	33–22
3. Appropriations	13–11	3. Armed Services	25–16
4. Armed Services	9–7	4. Banking and Currency	22–15
5. Banking, Housing and Urban Affairs*	8–7	5. District of Columbia	15–10
6. Commerce	10–8	6. Education and Labor	22–16
7. District of Columbia	4–3	7. Foreign Affairs	21–17
8. Finance	9–7	8. Government Operations	23–16
9. Foreign Relations	9–7	9. House Administration	15–10
10. Government Operations	10–8	10. Interior and Insular Affairs	23–15
11. Interior and Insular Affairs	9–7	11. Internal Security‡	5–4
12. Judiciary	9–7	12. Interstate and Foreign Commerce	25–18
13. Labor and Public Welfare	10–7	13. Judiciary	22–16
14. Post Office and Civil Service	5–4	14. Merchant Marine and Fisheries	22–15
15. Public Works	9–7	15. Post Office and Civil Service	15–11
16. Rules and Administration	5–4	16. Public Works	23–14
17. Veterans' Affairs†	5–4	17. Rules	10–5
		18. Science and Astronautics	18–12
		19. Standards of Official Conduct	6–6
		20. Veterans' Affairs	16–10
		21. Ways and Means	15–10

* Prior to 1971 known as Banking and Currency.
† Added as a new committee in 1971.
‡ Prior to 1968, known as Un-American Activities Committee.

considering similar legislation at approximately the same time. If one house finishes the process first, the other may indeed "substitute" the finished bill for its own and in that way avoid, if it wishes, the lengthy investigatory process in its own chamber. Revenue bills, however, constitutionally must be considered by the House of Representatives first. It has become traditional for the Senate to await House action on appropriation bills as well. Figure 6 represents the usual way a bill is passed.

The primary reason for the existence of the committees is to act as a screening mechanism for the flood of measures presented to the Congress. The House or Senate would be hopelessly inundated if it attempted to do any significant proportion of this screening as a body. The party plays a role here too, for each committee and subcommittee is always in the hands of the same majority as that of its house.

Because of the safe district system (a constituency that is usually dominated by one party) and the stable return of the same members to Congress, the seniority system becomes all important. The concept of seniority is well established and so firmly imbedded in the congressional system that it will endure for a long time. It means that members of each party on each committee advance in rank according to the length of continuous service on the committee. Gradually, then, a member edges himself toward leadership of his committee, majority or minority. If he stays there long enough, he may even get to be the chairman, or the ranking member of the minority party. And, by that time, he has become one of the elders of his party who for the most part control the whole system. It is no wonder, then, that an individual congressman or senator does not really mind if his party suffers defeat nationally in the Congress as long as *he* does not. In the event of a party setback, he is rid of a few of his own party who might rank above him on his committee. And, that's one quick way of advancing one's own seniority! It also means a wider choice of office space, for seniority rules here too!

The seniority system has come under increasing attack in recent years. Not only does the longest continuous service of the majority members of a committee determine the committee's

BILL - PASSING PROCESS

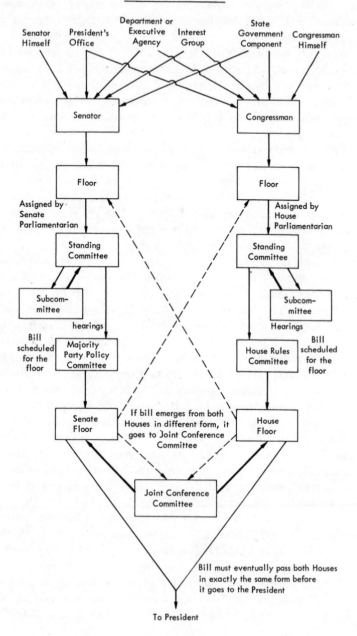

chairmanship, but seniority is also a factor in the chairman's appointment of chairmen of his committee's subcommittees and of key appointments to joint conference committees temporarily established to iron out differences between House and Senate versions of the same bills. Seniority results in relatively older men being chairmen of committees. In 1970, 6 chairmen of Senate committees and 9 chairmen of House committees were over 70 years of age, and 3 of the latter were at least 80. The average age of chairmen in the Senate (Democrats) was about 65 in 1970 and the same held true for the ranking Republicans on their respective committees. Seniority also leads to less efficient use of highly competent members of the Congress who must bide their time before rising to senior rank on their committees. This often leads to frustration and alienation on the part of many in the Congress. They not only cannot "lead" as early as they would like, but they must also at times cater to the whims of chairmen in order to obtain favorable subcommittee assignments. Their respective constituencies, in effect, often have to wait until their representatives in the Congress rise in seniority before they have enough influence and power to "do things" for the constituencies. If a congressman stays in office long enough, he is then able to use the seniority that accrues to him to prove to his constituents that he is indeed influential in Congress on their behalf.

Furthermore, the seniority system, when coupled with the great number of "safe" districts in the nation, results in an imbalance of sectional representation at the top levels of the committee system and a narrow congressional bias, not the broad party view that is associated with the national presidential party. Seniority creates a further obstacle to party cohesion and unity, for the chairman is firmly ensconced in his position and can disregard with impunity his party's or his President's policy.[3] In the Ninety-first Congress (1969–70), with a Democratic majority, committee leadership was pretty much the same as in the past Congress. The winds of change blow gently

[3] The House Democrats in the Ninetieth Congress, 1967, performed the rare feat of removing a chairman from his number one position (Powell, Dem. of New York) for his flagrant violations of House standards of conduct, giving the South another chairman (Perkins, Dem. of Kentucky).

and intermittently in the hierarchy of leadership. In the Senate, 12 of the 16 chairmen were from Southern and border states, with Louisiana and Arkansas each having both their senators chairing important committees. Of the remaining 4 chairmen, 2 were from the State of Washington and 1 each from Wyoming and New Mexico. The Eastern, Midwest, and North Central States were not even represented in the upper reaches of the Senate committees. In the House, 14 of the 21 committees were chaired by representatives of Southern or border states, with Texas having 4 chairmen, Maryland 3, and South Carolina 2. Of the remaining 7 chairmen, 2 were from New York, 2 from Illinois, and 1 each from Pennsylvania, Colorado, and California. There, too, the sectional controls of the Southern Democrats are very much in evidence.

The Republican side is similar, except the ranking members of the committees represent states and districts that for the most part are nonurban oriented, although the Northeast is more fully represented in Republican leadership than Democratic in the Senate. In the upper house, Vermont had 3 ranking Republicans, Maine 2, New Hampshire and New York 1. The Midwest and Farwest had the bulk of the others. In the House, although Pennsylvania had 3 ranking Republicans and New Jersey 2, most of the remaining Republican senior members of House committees were from the Midwest and Farwest; Ohio having 5, Illinois 3, and California 4. From these brief statistics it can be seen that seniority and safe districts to a considerable extent mitigate rapid change in legislative leadership and make for pockets of resistance as well as power in the legislative process. It is no wonder that the urban society and its representatives have been trying, albeit unsuccessfully, to do away with the seniority system. Although there have been serious attempts to do this, most of the Congress are comfortable with the system, and despite some procedural reorganization that took place in 1970, the seniority system has been left intact.

The process of assigning members to a committee is fairly selective. The Senate Democrats have a steering committee (composed of its own leadership and key old hands) and the Republicans a Committee on Committees (consisting of ba-

sically the same type as the Democrats), which make committee assignments of new senators and those desiring to switch
committees. This is done in a rather informal manner in
consultation with the chairman of the committee being considered (in the case of the majority party) or the ranking
member of the minority on the committee and the preferences
of senators. When John F. Kennedy was United States Senator
from Massachusetts, he actively sought an open position on the
Foreign Relations Committee in 1956, after the elections. He
contacted Senator Theodore Francis Green of Rhode Island,
who, by seniority, was slated to be the next chairman of the
committee. Green, who had been on the Democratic Senate
Policy Committee for several years, arranged it with Lyndon
B. Johnson, then the Democratic Majority Leader, who directed the assignments of Democratic senators almost single-
handedly. The process is similar in the House.

The leadership of both parties, in both houses, act as the
funnels for assignments and changes in committees through
their respective key people on the Steering Committees. The
Democrats in the House use the Democratic membership of
the Ways and Means Committee as the handlers of assignments. This does not imply the necessity for party cohesion,
but rather for playing the game with party leaders or the
"establishment" according to their fancies, desires, and political predilections. Political mavericks and "loners" do not find
it easy to obtain choice assignments. As the late Speaker
Sam Rayburn used to say, "If you want to get along, go
along."

Leadership of the committees rests on a parochial base.
The bulk of the membership of the Congress must work with
and through its established committee leadership. The power
of the committee chairmen is great. They establish the agenda
of the committee, practically control the committee calendar,
appoint the subcommittees and their chairmen (paradoxically
the committee chairman of the Democratic majority is often
much the same breed as his opposite number, the ranking
Republican, and between the two of them they pretty well
manage the work of the committee); assign members of the
committee to act as floor managers for bills reported out of

committee; usually veto or accept new members of their committees; and so on. Most like this system, because almost everyone in Congress wants eventually to be in a position of power (that's why they are there in the first place) and because the system does need guidance and direction.

The party leaders of the Congress, over-all and within the committees, are a loosely organized group themselves, who work closely together when they want to, or feel compelled to. The leadership of the President's party, if the majority, often takes its cues from the executive branch on matters of legislation, whereas the minority leadership acts as a fluid opposition, contributing something in the course of law-making, at times forcing changes in form and substance, but rarely originating successful legislation, unless it happens to have control of the Presidency.

Far from acting as generals commanding the troops, the party leaders really act as brokers; the majority leader attempts to negotiate a pattern of majority support, draws largely on his own followers, but curries the votes of favorably disposed members of the opposite party as well. Accordingly, his successes are limited in scope and number, and depend far less on party discipline than on the gradual emergence of a nonpartisan consensus, which he may help crystallize but cannot create. Even the party leaders, then, although they do contribute a further increment to the total process of interest aggregation and policy-making, still cannot have the broad national responsibility for policy leadership. It remains for the President to take this upon himself on behalf of his party in Congress, whether it is of the majority or not. The other party, even though it might be a majority in Congress, has little choice but to flounder in a sea of rhetoric, hopefully waiting for a chance to win the White House and *thus* seize control of the legislative initiative.

It must be remembered, at the same time, that the congressional system is a friendly one. The members of Congress may be of different parties and views, but they are cut from the same representative type bolt of cloth. The pressures on all may vary in kind and degree, depending on the type of district or state that is represented, but pressures there are and they are on all.

Any senator or congressman is concerned with the relationships he must maintain with (1) his party leaders in the Congress itself, for they control his legislative destiny in great measure; (2) his fellow committeemen, with whom he must come into contact more than any other group and whose respect he must earn and keep; (3) the chairman of his own as well as other committees, particularly if he wants to move ahead and obtain choice assignments; (4) his friends or the "class" with which he entered the Congress, for mutual support and commiseration; (5) his personal staff and that of the committee of which he is a member, for their expertise and knowledge of the political and legislative process as well as the substance of the material covered by his committee; (6) the federal agencies and executive departments with which his office and committee must deal as well as their professional staffs on whom he must depend for information, facts, and figures to supply his constituency and whom he must contact on behalf of his constituents at any time; (7) the White House Staff, particularly if the President is of his party, for cues, and contacts; (8) the President himself, for his image (to imitate or to ridicule), for the coattail effect (in fact, Republican Congressman Martin used to say that when he was floor leader of the House he was able to get more out of Democratic Presidents than Eisenhower); (9) the regional interests of his state, for example, oil, silver, coastal development, conservation, and so on; (10) his state and local party organizations, to keep his political fences at home mended and his ties close to ensure his renomination; (11) the pressure groups important to him and his constituency, for he is their political outlet, as they are his; (12) his party principles, as he sees them and as he has campaigned on them, be they "conservative" or "liberal," for high or low taxes, "big" government or "little" government; and (13) how he sees his own personal role. Is he a creator of public opinion at home, or does he follow it? Does he educate the folks back home, or is he taught by them? Or is it some magical combination of both? The student of congressional behavior can at least see that when a member of the Congress casts a vote, conscience (Edmund Burke notwithstanding) is not his only source of thought or motivation.

The over-all role of Congress is extensive. Because so much originating of legislation is now done by the executive branch, Congress appears to have a secondary role in legislative matters, the theory being "The President proposes, the Congress disposes." But Congress constantly reasserts its own legislative function. Proposed presidential legislation is exposed to long and minute examination in committee. More often than not, what comes out of Congress bears little resemblance to the original proposal. Lately, the Congress has added new weapons to keep its position vis-à-vis the President viable. Often the Congress, in giving the President authority to do something, adds the proviso that a concurrent resolution may take it back. A concurrent resolution does not have the force of law nor does it require a President's signature and thus is not subject to a presidential veto. But, if incorporated within an act or statute passed by Congress and signed by the President, it then has the force of law, as part of that statute, and thus acts as a potential brake on presidential exercise of power. The Congress is careful to include the unicameral veto mentioned previously in its legislation supporting executive reorganization. The Congress can wipe out executive action in this field by the vote of only one house.

Corresponding to the decline of legislative initiative in Congress (because of wars, depression, the growth of administrative centralization, and the proliferation of agencies) has been the increase in the use of the investigatory power by Congress. Congress can investigate anything, as long as it is tied to a legislative purpose, no matter how trivial or remote. Congress must stay within constitutional bounds, but the investigatory function is broad. Although congressional committees hold open and closed hearings on pending legislation, they also can and do hold hearings to determine whether or not legislation is necessary in some area. Often the legislation that does come to the Hill from the White House is based upon leg work done originally by the congressional committee and its staff. Add to this the overseeing aspect of investigation, that is, to keep watchdog vigil on the executive branch and its policies, and one has a fair idea of how powerful a force in the political process the Congress really is.

Congress holds hearings on a host of matters; drug addiction, auto safety requirements, the Ku Klux Klan, the electoral college, crime, student unrest, etc. In its capacity to oversee the executive branch, the Congress investigates the foreign aid program, foreign commitments in China and Vietnam, the cost of finding the hydrogen bomb lost off Spain (about $5 million), the management techniques of conducting the war in Vietnam, the American role in NATO, and other areas. Congress keeps Defense and State officials on steady call to appear as witnesses before various committees. Congressional hearings serve an important educational function for the public by calling attention to problems, issues, and mistakes. In this way, Congress does very much affect both domestic and foreign policy. Congressional hearings compel the executive to defend its policies and practices, reassess them, and, indeed, at times, to change them. In 1967 and 1968, the Ninetieth Congress carried out about 500 investigations at a cost of $22 million. The Eighty-ninth Congress spent $18 million and the Eighty-eighth $15 million. Congress had obviously extended its energy in the direction of legislative oversight as well as investigation for very broad legislative purposes. In the Ninetieth Congress the Senate Judiciary and Government Operations Committees and the House Appropriations, Government Operations, and Education and Labor Committees spent the most money.[4]

The appropriation power of the Congress is mighty. The presidential budget may begin in the executive branch but it goes through—in no uncertain terms—the Congress. The President can say what he wants to do, but most things cost money and thus require congressional authority to raise and spend it. In the final analysis, a President can do little without money. The power to appropriate money gives the Congress a forceful lever in affecting the policy of the military establishment, departments, and agencies. Because Congress

[4] *Congressional Quarterly*, 4 July 1969, p. 1197.

holds the purse strings, others must come, if not cater, to it. Congress plays on this theme, collectively and individually in committees. For example, when one agency sends its emissaries to Congress to seek more money than is allotted it in the presidential budget or to defend the amount that is, Congress is just as liable to play that agency off against another, or the President himself, to prove a point: that of congressional power. When a President wants to create a new department, agency, or bureau; or he wants one already established to be empowered with more authority; or seeks more money to do more things, he must come to Congress.

Congress is a living organism, just as much as the Presidency. Congress is a vitally important factor that helps make democracy work. The executive, by its very nature, tends to be secretive and enmeshed in the entanglements of its own bureaucracy. Only the Congress, which can focus the spotlight of the investigatory principle of its branch, can compel the executive to speak out on policy, make it gather together its loose ends, and supply a public arena for opposing interest groups to use as a platform to articulate their desires and needs.

The Congress, however, not only lacks internal party discipline that might, if present, oil the legislative wheels that grind slowly and crunchingly indeed, but it is also so structured internally that leadership is fragmented among a host of feudal barons in the form of committee chairmen. Congress, as a focus of the aggregating function (done only partially and poorly by our parties), is able to do only bits and pieces of the job of accommodating interests and making policy. Yet, the Congress is in a sense the first branch of government, and it has also held its own in a world of executive leadership.

One of the characteristics of a governmental system of separated powers is that attitudes toward the branches, and as a result their relative positions in the scheme, can and do change. The waning hours of the 1970 session of the Ninety-first Congress in late December saw a monumental legislative log jam, for which the laggard pace of the Senate was largely to blame. Behind this lay lengthy, time-consuming struggles by groups of senators to block or alter presidential policies—

on Cambodia, the supersonic transport, welfare reform, and other matters. The same interests that currently deplore overextended presidential power have sought out the Congress as a counterweight. And the Senate responded in 1970 with a more massive effort to reassert legislative power than the Capitol has seen for a long time. Eventually, other groups, impressed by congressional obstructionism or recalcitrance to act on a new range of issues, will again call upon presidential leadership to "save the republic." Thus, the pendulum has swung back and forth since earliest days.

Seven

The Role of the Bureaucracy

UBLIC POLICY in theory is supposed to be the result of the bargaining that goes on among the chief actors in the political process. So far we have viewed in the perspective of the over-all system the functions of pressure groups, political parties, the President, and Congress. Another group of people remains who, because of their own vested interests, very often act just as politically in their own way as the components already described. For lack of a better descriptive term, we can call them the bureaucracy, the group that does the job of carrying out the intentions of the executive and legislative branches.

Some bureaucrats, like those employed in the Executive Office of the President, are so closely linked to the President and his entourage that, to all intents and purposes, they are "the President's" people. Others, like such regulatory commissions as the Federal Communications Commission (FCC), Interstate Commerce Commission (ICC), Federal Trade Commission (FTC), Federal Power Commission (FPC), Federal Maritime Commission (FMC), and so on, are almost as close to the Congress as to the President. True enough, the President is the Chief Administrator in the United States and generally held accountable for the whole executive establishment. But it must be realized that he has little direct control over much of the bureaucracy, for they are in practice "independent" of him in many ways. Several of them—such as the National Labor Relations Board (NLRB), Civil Aeronautics

Board (CAB), National Mediation Board (NMB)—are multi-headed organizations that owe special status to legislative action. The Congress defines the jurisdictional boundaries and limits the authority of all agencies as it sees fit. Furthermore, Congress is the body that supplies the money for continued operations, and the resulting congressional presence in the mind of the bureaucracy is evident. The heads of many agencies are appointed by the President for a set term.

Because the heads of agencies come for the most part from the "political" ranks (as opposed to the career people) and their terms are staggered, a President often finds it difficult to direct them to follow his personal policy until the second or third year of his administration. President Kennedy certainly found this a great problem when he took over the White House after eight years of Republican patronage in the Eisenhower Administration. A President clearly has less difficulty with the heads of the eleven departments composing the Cabinet, because they serve at his pleasure, even though they need Senate confirmation for their original appointment. The members of the White House Office in EXOP do not need even that.

The people govern, and in the United States almost 3 million are necessary to do the job in the national government alone, not taking into consideration the millions working for state and local government. Broadly speaking the bureaucracy consists of the personnel in the executive departments, the independent agencies, and the federal regulatory commissions. Table 13, based on a report by the Joint Committee on Reduction of Federal Expenditures in 1970, tells a revealing story. Obviously the civilian employees in the military agencies (Department of Defense, Army, Navy, and Air Force) represent the greatest single number. The Postal Service is next, followed by the Veterans Administration, the Departments of Agriculture, Treasury, Health, Education and Welfare, Interior, and Commerce. Then come the Federal Aviation Agency, the Department of State, General Services Administration, NASA, and the Department of Justice. The agencies with the fewest number of employees are the regulatory commissions, such as the AEC, CSC, ICC, FCC, FPC, FTC, and SEC.

TABLE 13   Average civilian employment and payroll costs for each of the fiscal years in the 10-year period 1960–1970 broken to show the civilian agencies, the military agencies, and totals, follow:

	Average Employment			Payroll (In millions)		
FISCAL YEAR	CIVILIAN AGENCIES	DEFENSE DEPT. (CIVILIAN EMPLOY- MENT)	TOTAL	CIVILIAN AGENCIES	DEFENSE DEPT. (CIVILIAN EMPLOY- MENT)	TOTAL
1960	1,320,032	1,054,740	2,374,772	$ 6,804	$ 5,760	$12,564
1961	1,323,567	1,037,356	2,360,923	7,546	6,026	13,572
1962	1,373,485	1,058,676	2,432,161	7,898	6,318	14,216
1963	1,417,937	1,063,720	2,481,657	8,659	6,603	15,262
1964	1,434,104	1,042,552	2,476,656	9,297	6,818	16,115
1965	1,443,376	1,024,482	2,467,858	10,403	7,102	17,145
1966	1,500,349	1,074,080	2,574,429	10,875	7,732	18,607
1967	1,605,919	1,234,474	2,840,393	11,727	8,668	20,395
1968	1,654,973	1,280,853	2,935,826	12,919	9,395	22,314
1969	1,655,976	1,305,664	2,961,640	13,840	10,298	24,138
1970	1,694,157	1,264,207	2,958,364	15,621	11,213	26,834

Reprinted from *Congressional Record*, 8 September 1970, S14933.

The total number of employees has increased in the past ten years, and the size of the federal payroll for these employees has increased some 50 per cent since 1960. If allowances are made for inflation in those ten years, the payroll cost of the bureaucracy has remained relatively steady.

The bulk of federal employees are under civil service and their jobs are protected as a "right." They cannot be removed or, theoretically, appointed for political purposes. Congress or the President by Executive Order can erase the jobs themselves, but not the jobholders. These people are directly responsible, through a definite chain of command, to their superiors. The top echelon of the civil service group sometimes, but not usually, supplies people whom the President appoints as the "political executives"—the Secretaries of the Departments, the heads of agencies, and the top administrators. It cannot be denied, either, that political favoritism plays a great part in choice of job assignments, speed or delay in promotions, and the like, even though civil service in theory rules out politics. But political relationships among people will always exist and the rules in the civil service are broad enough to permit some leeway in the career service itself.

However, we are not concerned with the everyday role of most of the government workers, but rather with the top levels of the bureaucracy who, for the most part, administer what both the President and the Congress have created, oftentimes at the initiation of the bureaucracy itself. Congress says to the President, "Here is what you asked for, an agency to do something you have successfully argued needs doing. Here are the ground rules under which it shall operate and here is a down payment for a year to pay the expenses. Next year, we'll take another look." Thus, the tools the President needs to execute policy in a society that is rapidly changing, expanding, and becoming more complicated come from Congress.

The President can then exhort this and other agencies to do the job his way, he can use the politically appointed heads of the departments and agencies as his agents, and he can call into use various key members of the Executive Office, particularly from the Office of Management and Budget and the Domestic Council, to bypass those who seem to block his policy by having them "twist" arms, threaten budgetary reprisals, or promise a bigger slice of the annual budget. Much depends on how skillful the President is in handling his subordinates and in persuading people to do what President Truman once said "they should be doing anyway." A President can create and develop a conflict system whereby he plays one group off against another, as Agriculture against Commerce (over foreign aid), Treasury against the Federal Reserve Board (over monetary policy), or even the Army against the Navy (over weapons systems). Such was the technique of Franklin D. Roosevelt. Or he can establish his own personal chain of command, a formal set of institutional levels, where decisions of varying importance are made along the ladder, leaving the most important ones for himself. Such was the method of President Eisenhower. Or he can do what the late John F. Kennedy tried to do, make the system more fluid and "cooperative," and less competitive. President Nixon has tried to keep his finger on the pulse of the bureaucracy through EXOP. By creating the Domestic Council in 1970, making the old Budget Bureau into the Office of Management and Budget, and placing trusted political confidants in key positions in the new executive offices, Nixon hoped to keep more presidential control of the bureaucracy. He also reshuffled duties and responsibilities of the bureaucracy in order to make it more closely attuned to his own ideas of institutionalized control.

The President and his office are the focal points for administrative direction. The executive branch attempts, with different degrees of success, to bring together under one roof a presidential policy in all areas. The theory is that the President is responsible for the execution of the laws of the land, the rules and regulations by which all are governed. But in practice the system is so vast and complicated, areas of jurisdiction overlap and compete so much with one another, that it is a formidable task and one which few Presidents have been able to master. The Office of Management and Budget, as of late, has come to play a major role in the shaping of policy on behalf of the President. The Director (who handles management) and the Deputy Director (who handles the Budget) have become key figures in the presidential family in giving guidance to new programs and to the continuing expansion or curtailing of old ones. They convey the President's wishes as to what should be cut, what added, and what trimmed to fit into the broad picture of presidential policy— be it in the field of agriculture, foreign aid, labor regulations, drug control, or what not.

A politically appointed head or commissioner is not usually as expert in the field as the permanent, civil service, career employee. The top career people easily take a hand in shaping the policy wants and needs of the agency or commission and the political head often finds himself leaning on the career people for guidance in financial matters. A close relationship exists between the professional careerist and his counterpart on Capitol Hill, the professional staff personnel of the congressional committee handling the legislative aspect of the agency's field. The careerist needs the political head to represent him in the jostling and haggling that goes on among the top agency executives and with the White House. In short, there is a whole additional political process that goes on within the administrative and bureaucratic network that is so important a part of government.

It would be useful at this point to describe the types of bureaucratic entities that exist and demonstrate how they fit into the over-all pattern of administering the nation's laws.

We can first consider the upper level departments, the eleven that comprise the Cabinet. The heads of the eleven departments, although subject to Senate confirmation, are almost invariably approved by the Senate under the theory that the President should have those whom he wants occupying such positions. Because they serve at his pleasure, in effect, they have functions that relate chiefly with the President and his policy. Usually, the department heads will be chosen for political reasons, either because they are "representatives" of the sort of group with which the department must deal or because they have shown that they can do the job the President expects. Thus the Secretary of Commerce will be someone on good terms with business, the Secretary of Agriculture will have close and strong ties to the agricultural community, the Secretary of Defense will have had broad experience in matters of management, directing a large corporation, and/or banking, although Nixon's Secretary of Defense, Melvin Laird, came directly from Congress. Ordinarily the Secretary of State will have had long experience in the field of international relations. John Foster Dulles, Christian Herter, and Dean Rusk, Secretaries of State under Eisenhower, Kennedy, and Johnson, were active in international politics prior to their service. William Rogers, on the other hand. Nixon's choice for Secretary of State, was not. Nor was Nixon's second Secretary of the Treasury, John Connally of Texas, active in banking circles, although previous Secretaries indeed had been. It is expected that Secretaries of the Department of Health, Education and Welfare, the Department of Housing and Urban Development, and the

Department of Transportation will have some knowledge, or at least a "feel," for the problems with which these departments deal.

Nixon was not beyond shifting some of his top political heads in the first two years of his administration. When Secretary of the Interior Walter Hickel, former Governor of Alaska, earned the wrath of the President for having openly challenged the direction of the Nixon Administration's policies in 1970, he was let go. Believing that Robert Finch, the first Secretary of HEW, could not cope with the problems of that Department and was unable to redirect the aims of the Department, Nixon placed a high State Department official, Elliot Richardson, at its helm and moved Finch into EXOP. The President has considerable direct control of policy in the eleven departments of Cabinet level by virtue of his power of appointment, but even this may not be enough to ensure that his policies are observed throughout the vast departments, for their bureaucracies are staffed with many officials protected by civil service rules and regulations. Bureaucrats of this sort are often difficult to redirect once they are entrenched in their positions, and a major portion of the time spent by their political superiors is in trying to push through the policies of the President.

The heads of the Cabinet departments have a particularly difficult task: supervising and running their staffs and departments, managing the internal workings of their administrative machinery, and overseeing the administration of the policy as laid down by the President (and by themselves) to make certain that the department is indeed carrying out these policies. This means they have to ride herd on the vast numbers of personnel in key positions who must implement that policy in hundreds of ways. Now, if a President also uses these heads of departments as an advisory board, that is, as a full-fledged Cabinet, they must also know something about the rest of the important high level departments. Furthermore, today's business of government being what it is, it is not unlikely that the affairs of one department and another will overlap. No better example exists today than that of the

Departments of State and Defense. At times it becomes quite difficult to delineate between the two.

Then again, the department heads must also concern themselves with what the agencies in allied fields may be doing that might be counter to the policy direction of the departments. A directive of the Department of Commerce might be interpreted quite differently by the Interstate Commerce Commission and/or the Department of Justice. Then, the department heads must prepare (and defend) their budgetary requests, first for the Office of Management and Budget and then before the Congress in its examination of the entire presidential budget. This alone occupies much time of the top level executives. In general, however, it can be safely said that the functions of these top people draw them toward the President, rather than the Congress. The departments are the old-line executive appendages. In fact, when a new agency reaches Cabinet status (such as Housing and Urban Development), the Congress has definitely petrified another area in the presidential forest. It is a formal congressional approval of the need for upgrading the work of that executive entity, and in the words of Charles E. Jacob, "They enjoy a high degree of autonomy in their spheres of competence."[1]

A second category of politically appointed officials, and one of great importance, comprises the regulatory commissions—"quasi-judicial" or "quasi-legislative" groups (or both), which have been given extremely broad authority by the Congress to act within certain spheres. They perform judicial and legislative functions in that they make decisions that have the binding effect of law or adjudicate conflicts that exist in an industry or between economic groups. During the past several years, the regulatory commissions have had more to do with everyday life as their influence has become greater and greater. The Interstate Commerce Commission, for example, regulates railroads, the bus service, and the trucking industry. These industries alone, branches of transportation in general, are often in conflict with one another over rates, rules, and

[1] Charles E. Jacob, *Policy and Bureaucracy* (Princeton: D. Van Nostrand Company, 1966), 78.

conditions. Add to the list the Civil Aeronautics Board, which is responsible for the regulation of the nation's airlines and their rates, routes, and mergers, and one has the makings of a difficult web to unravel. The airlines want higher rates, less supervision, and government subsidies to speed up the process of developing and obtaining faster planes. The railroads want mergers and shutdowns, and less favoritism to the airlines, whereas the trucking industry casts a plague on both houses. Imagine a President trying to formulate a transportation policy, given the opposing nature of the different modes of transportation. Add to the already difficult situation such pressure groups as the Airline Pilots Association (who argue that the Federal Aviation Agency, charged with regulating air safety, should be telling the airlines to establish newer and better safety precautions in their aircraft), the mechanics unions (who argue they should be better paid because they are as important to flying as the pilots—as one said, "Where're you going to go at 20,000 feet if something goes wrong?"), and noise abatement civic groups who rebel at having planes fly over their homes in the first place, and an even more sticky morass of problems materializes. The foregoing example can serve as just one of many to depict the complexities of administering the nation's laws. Actually, a specialized regulatory agency must do the job.

Take another example. The Federal Communications Commission, instituted in 1934 to regulate wire and radio communications, has jurisdiction over radio, telephone, telegraph, submarine or underwater cables, and television. Among other things, the FCC oversees safety regulations and has the important job of distributing licenses for radio and television stations. The FCC is a seven-man commission, appointed by the President with approval by the Senate. The FCC conducts hearings, makes rules, can acquire or deny extension of services of radio and television stations, allocates air channels, assigns frequencies, and also can issue cease and desist orders on advertising over the air. (Advertising practices are also regulated by the Federal Trade Commission.)

During the Eisenhower Administration one of the commissioners, the Congress found in an investigation of the FCC, had apparently been in collusion with an individual who sought a license to operate a television station in Florida. Allegedly the commissioner had been lent money and been given interests in an insurance company by the same person. The insurance company did business with an airline which owned the company applying for the television license! A veritable conflict of interest, one might say. The commissioner resigned under fire.

When Kennedy became President, he appointed one of his early backers, Newton Minow, to the vacant chairmanship of the FCC. In May, 1961, Minow generally assailed the broadcasters in his famous "TV is a vast wasteland" speech before the National Association of Broadcasters (this is the same as telling the AMA it is doing a disservice opposing Medicare, at their invitation!), making it clear that they should improve the quality of television programs and eliminate excessive violence. He told them that when the individual licenses came up for renewal their performances would be compared with their promises. Needless to say, the applause that greeted Minow's speech was somewhat less than deafening.

The power of the chairman of the FCC was severely limited in that he could not delegate tasks to individual members. Most of the commissioners did not share Minow's iconoclastic views on broadcasting and when the Kennedy Administration attempted to put more authority into the chairman's hands, the House vetoed Kennedy's reorganization plan. Minow was too strong a head for the broadcasters, and they had too much power in their access to the Congress. The administrative requests were watered down to the point where the chairman could delegate certain tasks to other members of the commission, but only with the formal approval of three of them. Three and one make four, the majority of seven. That, the Congress accepted. The FCC can always be viewed as an agency in conflict with other agencies, with Congress, or with pressure groups which are their "clienteles." In November, 1961, Senator Russell Long, Democrat of Louisiana, had all seven commissioners before his Senate Small Business Subcommittee and blasted all of them for the way the FCC had been handling the space satellite communications project.

The battle was then shaping up over the establishment of COMSAT. Life is not easy for administrators, particularly political heads. Mr. Minow never did fill out his full term, but resigned some time later.

In a complex society, someone has to set the terms of group relationships. It apparently cannot be left to automatic adjustments within the community and thus agencies like the FCC are established, proliferate, and expand their authority. Lately the FCC has ordered an investigation of the entire costs, rates, and earnings of the American Telephone and Telegraph Company, cracked down on several stations for having excessive commercials by renewing their licenses for one year instead of three, ordered a Mississippi broadcaster on probation for racial segregation editorials, issued a proposal to curb economic domination of the television industry by the big networks, and refused to allow a community antenna service to compete fully with the Texas television station owned by Mrs. Lyndon B. Johnson.

In the summer of 1970, on a complaint from several groups, the FCC ruled that President Nixon had made such extensive use of TV in the election campaigns to defend his administration's policies on Vietnam that the networks had to give free, prime time to the President's opposition. Of the 5 voting in the majority, 3 were Republicans (including 2 who had been appointed by Nixon in 1969) and the 2 dissenters were Democrats. (By law no more than 4 on the FCC may be of the same political party at one time.) A "significant imbalance" had been created by the President's free use of TV to explain his position, and thus the networks, who are regulated by the FCC, were forced to give free time to several United States senators in opposition to President Nixon; all in the name of the public interest and despite the fact that the FCC, in a certain sense, is part of the presidential branch of government.

The Federal Trade Commission, established in 1914, and headed by five commissioners appointed for seven-year terms with a limitation of no more than three members of the same political party, issues cease and desist orders for advertising abuses (it ordered Carter's Little Liver Pills to drop the word *Liver* from its advertising), and administers the Clayton Act of 1914 to limit restraints of trade. It was the FTC that helped investigate, along with the Attorney-General of the United States, the cases which sent several top General Electric executives to jail for short terms for collusion on price-fixing on electrical products. The FTC ordered a drug company to stop making false claims of germ-killing and pain-relieving properties for its throat lozenges, and under the commission's own authority, attempted to force the cigarette companies to label cigarettes as a health hazard. The reaction to this regulation was so strong that Congress entered the fracas and wrote its own law for such regulation, a less stringent one at that. (Southern Senators are not to be trifled with.) Taking on the drug makers, the FTC in 1963 ruled that six of them had rigged antibiotic prices. Between 1959 and 1969 a running battle between the FTC and the makers of a product called Geritol centered on whether or not the majority of tired people felt that way because of "iron-poor" blood, a central claim of Geritol's advertising. In 1970 the FTC extracted a promise from the Campbell Soup Company to remove the marbles from its soup advertisements. Clear glass marbles had been placed in the bottom of the bowls of soup shown on TV and in newspaper advertising to give the public the impression that the solid ingredients in the soup looked greater than they actually were. Deception in advertising is one of the primary areas for FTC investigation, and the regulatory commission is constantly involved in issuing cease and desist orders to industry. Of course, all orders of the FTC, as of any regulatory agency, are subject to court appeal, usually a federal circuit court, and many of the orders sent out by the agencies are delayed while the issue makes its tortuous way through the court system. Several anti-trust suits resting on FTC charges are now pending in the courts.

Little need be said about the role the Food and Drug Administration has come to play in the execution of federal law regarding drugs, narcotics, and patent medicines. A strong head can generate considerable respect and attention among those within the agency's field of regulation. The Securities and Exchange Commission has tightened its regulatory hold on the stock exchanges and indeed has asked for even more regulatory authority from Congress, and obtained it. Some regulatory agencies, such as the National Labor Relations Board, have their major problem in adjudicating conflicts. When this five-man board decides, let us say 3–2, that a union has been guilty of an unfair labor practice under the law, the unions claim the government is pro-management. When the ruling goes the other way, management says that labor rules the roost. The life of the administrator is not easy.

Other types of federal agencies include the government corporation, such as the Federal Deposit Insurance Corporation (FDIC), which insures bank deposits; a government business such as the Tennessee Valley Authority, which makes and sells power to a vast region in the Tennessee Valley and operates in much the same manner as any large business corporation serving millions of people; government agencies that run institutions, such as the prisons and Veterans Hospitals; and others such as the Bureau of Standards, Internal Revenue Service (which exerts great power over taxpayers merely by its own interpretation of the rules), the Postal Service, the General Services Administration, the Fish and Wildlife Service, and so on.

Administrative agencies and the bureaucracy that runs them really do the day-to-day business of government, and affect public policy if only by the way in which the laws are interpreted. These too are engaged in a continuous task of adjustment of conflicting interests. Leadership exerts itself, within that process, from different places. But a President, despite the advice given in countless books, cannot be many men at the same time, but only one man at a time. Therefore, continuous leadership does not always stem from the executive. A lax chief executive may well give the reins of power in some area to a few administrators by appointing a weak political executive to head an agency or department. The "pros" may then end up with the authority that rightfully belongs to the commissioner or chief administrator. And in their hands the carrying out of what the President wants may be quite different from what the latter had in mind. Then, too, such independence might never even be discovered. Much, therefore, depends on whom the President appoints and what his budgetary policy is. One can never escape from the latter. The final weapon in the President's hands, as well as Congress', is the power of allocation of funds.

As Paul Appleby has said, in *Policy and Administration,* public administration "is not autonomous, exclusive, or isolated policy making. It is policy making on a field where mighty forces contend, forces engendered in and by the society. It is policy making subject to still other and various policy makers. Public administration [for that is what this is all about] is one of a number of basic political processes by which this people achieves and controls governance,"[2] hopefully, one might add. In theory, the administrator does governmentally what the politician does politically. He acts as a balancer of the interests that compose society, some more important than others, and others more representative of the public than some.

Administrative agencies undoubtedly play an important role in American society. Naturally, individual agencies have different degrees of significance. The regulatory commission acts more directly than other types on the people. Quasi-judicial bodies deal with specific segments of the society and the government corporation with others. These segments may be physical, class, geographic, economic, or even social. Certainly the new agencies being established to deal with health and poverty programs, education and welfare areas, are examples of the proliferation of government activity in today's society.

Although administration can easily be broken down into types, functions, sizes, and so on, one thing can be said about all administrators and administrations. They do things, they manage other people, and events. Anthony Downs has pointed out that expansion of bureaucracies is closely linked "with the tendencies of modern societies to grow larger in total population, more complex in specialization, more sophisticated in technology, more urbanized, and wealthier per capita as time passes."[3] Government bureaucracy at federal, state, and local

[2] Paul Appleby, *Policy and Administration* (University: University of Alabama, 1949), 170.
[3] Anthony Downs, *Inside Bureaucracy* (Boston: Little, Brown and Company, 1967), 255.

levels easily becomes inflated as more demands for services, regulation, pump-priming, and funds are made by people and newly formed groups. Government becomes a negotiator, mediator, and even an arbitrator among interest groups as well as a supplier of laws and funds. The question can then be asked: Are the people in danger of being totally managed by government? Certainly there are indications of this possibility. On the other hand, it can be argued that the growth of administration in government as well as in private business is merely the evolution of another human technology in man's adaptation to his environment. In other words, the development of clearer lines of authority, more efficient decision-making (someone has to decide who gets which slice of which pie), as well as greater and more specific use of administrators, is the same thing in human terms that the development of machinery is in the scientific and technological development of society. More machines appear, but people are still needed to decide what the machines shall be fed, and for which purpose. Just as the scientist, the business leader, and the labor union head must be flexible as different problems and crises occur, so must the administrator of government.

It bears repeating that the society of 1972 is not that of 1787. Trends toward bigness and impersonality are common to large organizations be they in business, labor, or any kind of social or educational institution—or the government. The country has to learn to live with organization and develop an art of administration that can get a job done, when a job needs doing. Bigness is here, isolationism in the daily life has disappeared even more completely than in international relations. All the bemoaning of the facts, all the claims that the bureaucrat is nothing but a fat cat without a care in the world for the people he directs, will not improve the situation. The problem is how to make the bureaucrat act more efficiently to get his job done. In a democracy, the problem exists of keeping the administrative staff and the organization of government from acting in nondemocratic ways. How does a democracy handle the growth of as large a scale public service system as the bureaucracy of the federal government?

One of the major problems of a large administration is to functionalize or distribute the work load into smaller units without sacrificing the advantages of large-scale operations, central coordination, and unified planning. (The paradox is that big business has this problem just as big government has, and yet big business has never seemed to realize that government must also learn to cope with the problem; it will not go away.) How do a people coordinate the activities of government to have an efficient system—one without waste of money, time, or people—and at the same time, keep things small enough to accomplish what must be done at the state and local level? Experience has shown that without federal government controls, an inordinate amount of federal grant money is lost in the states through political ineptitude, favoritism, or just plain graft. But, without a definite line of responsibility within the agencies and departments, the bigness of the federal government does indeed lead to impersonal government, slowdowns, and inefficiency. Someone must answer to someone else, clearly and specifically, or that person ends up answering only to himself. The result is the complete loss of the purpose for which government was contrived in the first place, "to establish justice, ensure domestic tranquillity, provide for the common defense, promote the general welfare, and secure the blessings of liberty to ourselves and our posterity."

The bureaucracy must also be kept within the bounds of governmental responsibility. The public suffers if a top career man in some agency hampers presidential policy by unwittingly or deliberately obstructing the authority of the agency head. The same is true when the professional bureaucrat feeds information to the opposition in the Congress solely for personal gain without regard to his own executive responsibility. The career man who in reality is the captive of the pressure group his agency is supposed to regulate can do the same damage to the commonweal that a conspirator might contrive. Inasmuch as bureaucracy tends to be concomitant with modern government, it must be kept from encroaching on private lives. It must be directed and controlled so that it will not use its great power for evil. Misuse of power, the giving out of false and misleading information, and the failure to use initiative are all possibilities in a bureaucracy.

The only preventive weapons that seem to be available belong to the President and the Congress. The checks and balance system must be constantly called into play. Presidents must give direction and then see to it that the bureaucracy follows that guide. They must persuade those who are so firmly rooted in the system that not even Presidents can order. The Congress, itself, must be ever watchful of the bureaucracy, too. Through its power of appropriation and investigation, the Congress has to check possible abuses by the bureaucracy of the authority granted by the Congress. For the bureaucracy is its *own* constituency and *itself* acts as any other pressure group, prodding and probing, expanding and then consolidating its own position, and yet always aware of the power that belongs to the legislature. After all, it is the Congress that giveth, and Congress can taketh away when provoked.

Eight

Policy and Administration: The Military

TO UNDERSTAND fully the politics of administration and the complex web of relationships, formal and informal, that tie the *administration* of policy with the *making* of policy, one must examine a specific area of governmental activity. The area of military policy is the logical example to choose. As we noted in the previous chapter, nearly half the federal civilian employees work in the military establishment. We all know what a vast amount of the federal budget is devoted to financing the armed forces. Finally, there are many perplexing moral and philosophical questions involved regarding the role of the military in national life and in shaping national policy, the pattern of linkages between the defense establishment and the national economy—the "military-industrial complex"—and the use of America's armed might abroad in ways that many Americans profoundly disapprove.

THE DEFENSE DEPARTMENT

The Department of Defense is of course the focal point for the contemporary military establishment. Up to and including World War II this department as we know it today did not exist. The military was represented directly to the President via his Cabinet through the Secretaries of War and the Navy. The Marine Corps, a unit of the Navy, as it still is, and the Army Air Force, a unit of the Army, communicated

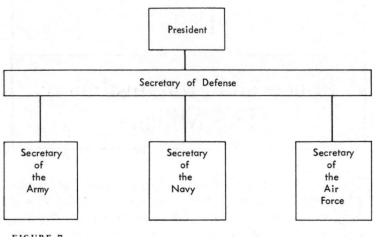

FIGURE 7

through and were under the jurisdiction of these same Secretaries. Following World War II, the National Security Act of 1947 was passed. This provided for the establishment of a Department of Defense combining as three coequal subdivisions the renamed Department of the Army, the Department of the Navy, and a new Department of the Air Force under the over-all supervision of a Secretary of Defense.

The Secretary of Defense was made the "principal assistant to the President in all matters relating to the Department of Defense." By law and intent, then, a civilian authority was created to be immediately subordinate to the President, superior to the other civilian Secretaries of the various military departments, and superior to the military branches themselves. Whereas the individual service Secretaries could go directly to the President before passage of the 1947 Act, they now have an intervening authority placed between them and the President. If they want to "go directly" to the President under the 1947 Act, they can do so only after first informing the Secretary of Defense of their intention. The three new service Secretaries of Army, Navy, and Air Force also have a dual function. First, they head their individual military departments and, in effect, represent departmental opinions to the Secretary of Defense; and second, they represent the Secretary of Defense (whole policy guidelines in the final analysis depend upon the President) to their own individual military departments. Thus they are advisers as well as administrators. And this has proven to be a heavy burden indeed.

The Secretary of Defense has the duty of making what Samuel P. Huntington calls force-level recommendations.[1] His function is to advise the President along the specific lines of (1) the strength of the armed services, the number of bomber wings, ships, and divisions, etc., (2) the size of the armed services, the number of personnel and strength of divisions etc., (3) the readiness of the various armed services, and (4) their deployment. The Secretary is a *civilian* spokesman for the military and superior to its hierarchy. As such, the military chiefs must come to him, advise him, and consult with him. They can disagree with his decisions and try to circumvent him by going directly to the President (if they dare and the President gives them access), by appealing to the key members of the Congress on specific committees which deal with the military services, and by leaking information to the press, thus embarrassing the Secretary. The Secretary of Defense, however, is the final military decision-maker, subject only to the dictates of the President himself and/or the pressures inherent in a relatively open political system such as our own.

The Secretary must of necessity be a business manager of tremendous ability. It is he who decides what should be presented to the President, the office of Management and Budget, and the Congress in the way of systems analysis, recommendations about weapons and delivery systems, and estimates of the capability of potential adversaries. Throughout the short history of the Defense Department, the years have been marked by running battles with and among the military branches over the allocation of money and resources. It is rare indeed when the Air Force fully agrees with the amount

[1] Samuel P. Huntington, *The Soldier and the State* (New York: Vintage Books, 1964), p. 440.

of money the Secretary finally decides should be allocated for research, supplies, and construction. The Army is never really satisfied with the size of the regular army or the standby reserve. Navy Admirals want more ships, more men to man them, and greater control over their assigned missions. The Marines look with disdain on the other branches of the service, and the Naval Air Arm cannot understand why it does not hold a separate identity from the Navy Department. Somehow or other, the Secretary of Defense must juggle these discordant elements and come up with a workable and efficient defense system. When the exigencies of war are added to his problems, it is no wonder that his office is one of the most precarious and burdensome in all the national government.

Some critics of the military ethic may well point to the danger of military dictation emanating from the Joint Chiefs of Staff and the hard line of military chiefs. On the other hand, the military chiefs, collectively and individually, can often be found crying "civilian dictatorship" as they point to the Office of the Secretary of Defense and bemoan its failure to understand the needs of sound military strategy and tactics. And the Secretary can be caught in the crossfire emanating from Capitol Hill as the hard-line approach is intensified by key committee chairmen seeking to cement their relationships with the military branches which they supervise. When that occurs, a Secretary of Defense finds himself fighting a holding action with his own military chiefs while he wards off attacks from the Congress. Because the President must carefully choose his moments to battle with the Congress over many other matters, the Secretary can be left on his own to sink or swim in the congressional labyrinth. Each Secretary brings with him his own concept of administration to a vast, complicated network. He may well view his position differently from the man he replaces, although his views must naturally coincide with those of the President. If the President leans on him for military advice and policy strategy, the Secretary's role is one thing. If, on the other hand, the President looks more to the Joint Chiefs of Staff, as is his privilege, for policy strategy, the Defense Secretary's function must necessarily shift toward management and administration rather than policy-making.

Policies related to the conduct of war are in the domain of the President and his immediate advisers, the *entire* military establishment, and the policy-planners of the State Department. The Secretary of Defense can well be a policy strategist *before* major American engagement in escalated military operations, but once the nation commits itself (or is committed by specific actions on the part of the President, the Congress, or both—as in the case of Vietnam), a sense of uneasiness about the role of the Defense Secretary begins to creep into the thinking of the Congress and the people. The names of generals at times supersede the Secretary in headlines. To those in the Congress who think that the Secretary of Defense is too omnipotent over the military authorities, he is an unqualified civilian, unable to comprehend the broad strategic and tactical necessities required. To those in the Congress who think that he is too quiescent in controlling the "hawkish" tendencies of the military authorities, he is acquiescing to the militaristic notions of a group of people (the military) who do not appreciate the democratic tradition of civilian control. To the "dovish," as to Clemenceau, war *is* too important to be left to the generals, and it is all the more encumbent upon the Secretary to reassert civilian authority.

When the chips of military action are down, however, it becomes obvious that both of these extreme positions are over-simplified rationalizations. In reality, both the Secretary and the military authorities are under the command of the President himself. It is he who must make the final determination as to which course to take in matters of military action—to cease bombing or increase it, to commit more troops or to stabilize the numbers of men committed to combat. How important a share of the partnership in the decision-making process is permitted to the military is in the domain of the President. During a nonwar condition, the military finds itself having to go through a thick layer of civilian domination as personified by the Secretary of Defense and exemplified by his huge civilian organization. Eventually, however, in time of war or military operations, the advice of the military is more sought out not only by the President but by the Congress as well, and here may lie danger to American democracy. For if the civilians in the government, the President and the members of the Congress, lean too heavily on the militaristic portions of the government for military advice, it is all too easy for them to begin to lean on the professional military chiefs for policy advice as well. This problem is compounded if there happen to be in key positions in the civilian branches people who *themselves* are militaristic and seek military solutions for political problems. The partnership changes to one of the military authorities and the "hawks" in the executive branch and the Congress. "Political policies" then become secondary to "military necessity." It is all too true that civilian Secretaries (and Presidents) come and go, but the military outlook remains constant through the inherited influence of the military.

In the final analysis, then, it all depends on the President. He is recognized as *the* "civilian" head of the Armed Forces, and he is indeed, constitutionally, the commander in chief. It is he, no one else, who must bear the burden of maintaining civilian authority in keeping with the democratic tradition. If he falls victim to militaristic thinking, the nation follows that path unless the Congress, in its legislative wisdom, denies him the funds and authority to act. Congress, however, has a tendency to appropriate the funds requested for military purposes, almost without question. To deny appropriations of such nature for our young men fighting and manning far-flung posts in the Pacific, Europe, and Southeast Asia would appear to be irresponsible and traitorous. The only other recourse is for the people to put the brakes on a President's taking the militaristic path. But they can do this only at election time, and then it is very, very difficult to deny those same young men the people's support. The President can therefore play on his role as commander in chief in his campaign for re-election. When all is said and done, the civilian-military partnership of the Defense Department, the Joint Chiefs of Staff, and the military branches can only be likened to a Board of Directors. The President is Chairman of the Board. The Secretary of Defense and chairman of the Joint Chiefs of Staff are *his* vice-chairmen of the Board. Hopefully, *his* leanings will be in the democratic tradition.

THE MILITARY BRANCHES

As previously pointed out, the Defense Department was born *after* the conclusion of World War II, as part of the National Security Act of 1947. The concept of organized civilian control through the person of one Secretary of Defense came about as an aftermath of that war. But the "union" of the various military chiefs came about in 1942, *during,* not after, the war because of the exigencies of military necessity. There was need for a unified command within the nation for military purposes in order to join that command with the Allies through the Combined Chiefs, a wartime name for the partnership of Allied military chiefs.[2] Beginning in 1942 the Joint Chiefs of Staff (JCS) operated immediately under the supervision of President Franklin D. Roosevelt as his military advisers.

Roosevelt fancied himself a military strategist and maintained a rather close relationship with the military though this arrangement was originally based only on an exchange of letters between General George C. Marshall and Admiral Ernest King, American Army and Navy chiefs. In addition, Admiral William Leahy was very close to Roosevelt and acted as his principal liaison with the military commanders during the war. Leahy in fact was the first real head of the Joint Chiefs. During the rest of Roosevelt's Administration a distinct dichotomy existed between the civilian Secretaries of War and Navy and the JCS. For the most part, the military adhered to its principal function of dealing with military problems. Most of the time, although not always, Roosevelt took the advice of the JCS on military matters.

Toward the end of the war it became clear that the JCS, and the military in general, wanted to remain free of civilian control in peacetime. As Admiral Leahy said in 1945 to the Congress, the JCS wanted to be responsible solely to the President, not to civilian Secretaries, and wanted to advise the President directly on the national defense budget, thus cutting

[2] See Demetrios Caraley, *The Politics of Military Unification* (New York: Columbia University Press, 1966), 14–20.

out such an intermediary as the (then) Bureau of the Budget, which was beginning to grow in over-all influence in legislative matters. But the Congress decided otherwise in 1947 and the Joint Chiefs of Staff remained purely military. Only military, not political, responsibilities were put on the JCS, who were placed under the authority and direction of the President *and* the Secretary of Defense and therefore subordinate to civilian authority. But no coordinated system at the top was spelled out in detail. The JCS was established as a *committee,* with a chairman selected by the President. There

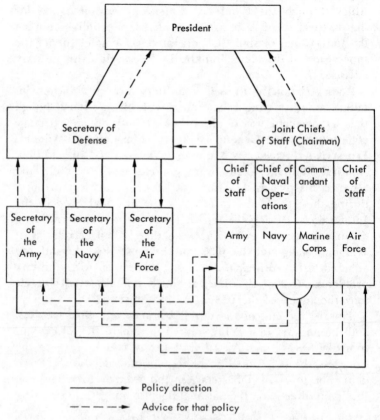

FIGURE 8　The Civilian-Military Relationship.

is *no* one military man at the head of *all* the military services.

The functions of the JCS are to (1) prepare strategic plans and provide for strategic direction of the armed forces, (2) prepare joint logistic responsibilities to the armed forces, (3) establish unified commands in strategic areas, (4) review major material and personnel requirements of the armed forces, (5) formulate policies for joint training of the armed forces, (6) formulate policies for coordinating education of members of the armed forces, (7) provide for representation of the United States on the Military Staff Committees of the United Nations in accordance with the UN Charter, and (8) perform such other duties as the President or the Secretary of Defense may prescribe.[3]

Many functions of the wartime JCS were changed by the National Security Act of 1947 and later amendments. (1) Overall national security policy formulation was taken from the JCS and transferred to the National Security Council, thus limiting the role of the JCS to a purely military one. (2) Military research and development was placed under the Secretary of Defense (and became the basis for future controversies over weapons systems). (3) Central Intelligence Agency was given the job of coordinating *all* intelligence efforts of all agencies, including the military. (4) The Atomic Energy Commission was established by the McMahon Act of 1946, thus placing the development of atomic energy in civilian, not military, hands. (5) The development of our space programs, at a later time, was also located in a civilian agency (NASA). (6) All emergency planning was placed in the Executive Office of the President, a separate body from the JCS.

But these arrangements did not prevent the JCS from engaging in non-military areas, under the guise of giving the "military viewpoint." The chairman of the JCS emerged as the bridge between the JCS and the White House and in so doing he was able to represent the political views of the Administration to the military chiefs of the separate services. Conversely, their military views were represented by the chairman to the Administration. The first two chairmen, Admiral Leahy and General Bradley, were very strong personalities

[3] See *Congressional Record*, 17 June 1970, pp. S9173–S9174.

who spoke their minds about what kind of military posture the nation ought to take against our potential adversary, the Soviet Union. Admiral Leahy was noted for having great faith in the concept of sea-air power and was oriented toward Asian problems, whereas General Bradley was European-minded, an expert on land warfare, and a strong believer in the policy of containment. Between 1947 and 1953 these two highly respected officers made the position of chairman of the JCS meaningful in high administrative affairs and established the JCS on a sound footing.

But it was during the Eisenhower Administration that the JCS began to take a more active part in nonmilitary policy decision-making. Secretary of Defense Charles E. Wilson instructed the JCS, in the spirit of the Eisenhower "team" approach, to include in their thinking every point of view, not solely the military. This helped ease the JCS and their chairman into a politico-military advisory position to the civilian authority. Once decisions were made, however, it was expected by Eisenhower that the JCS would adhere to the established position and not speak out in opposition to Administration policy. But the military chiefs were not very happy with the Eisenhower Administration as far as budgetary limitations were concerned. Testifying before Henry M. Jackson's Senate Subcommittee on National Policy Machinery on June 14, 1960, General Maxwell Taylor, former Chief of Staff of the Army (and later to become Chairman of the JCS in the Kennedy Administration), argued that the services had each year received "rigid budget guidelines which control the growth, direction, and evolution of the Armed Forces. These guidelines [were] often set with little knowledge of their strategic implications."[4] Taylor, who was an ardent spokesman for complete unification of the armed services,[5] claimed that we lacked "a system of politico-military bookkeeping to assure that commitments and capabilities are kept in balance."[6] The following year, Robert S. McNamara

[4] *Hearings,* Subcommittee on National Policy Machinery, Senate Committee on Government Operations, 87th Cong., 1st Sess., 1961, Vol. 1, p. 769.

[5] See Maxwell D. Taylor, *The Uncertain Trumpet* (New York: Harper & Row, 1959).

[6] *Hearings,* Subcommittee on National Policy Machinery, *op. cit.,* p. 769.

brought that very concept with him to the Office of the Defense Department.

Secretary of Defense McNamara increased the influence and prestige of the Defense Department. Not only was he aided by the legal authority given his office, but, as Colonel Robert N. Ginsburgh has pointed out, the Joint Chiefs of Staff held widely divergent views in the years of the Kennedy Administration. As a result, the JCS did not often present a united "military" front to the Secretary of Defense. McNamara was therefore free to choose alternatives he thought more feasible without depending very heavily on the JCS. Unanimity, difficult to achieve at best, was the exception rather than the rule, and the Defense Department (and McNamara) gained relatively more authority and power than the military chiefs.[7]

But this is not to say that the JCS was not a powerful body. Because McNamara established such a centralized Defense Department from the civilian angle, it seemed that the JCS fell in importance. In reality, however, the JCS has held its own in defending its military mission, that of supporting a strong military posture and presence wherever it would do the most good. When the military felt that it was being pushed around by the Defense Department, it played to the Congress and the press. This continued under Secretary Melvin Laird. The Joint Chiefs of Staff is pretty much controlled by the Secretary of Defense. But the military chiefs can strengthen themselves by playing on the tension inherent in the executive-legislative struggle, which is a continual one in our system of government. An Air Force Chief of Staff who feels his Secretary of the Air Force and/or the Secretary of Defense is limiting his budget too much or is cutting down what he believes to be a necessary Air Force weapons system can always run to the Chairman of the Senate Armed Services Committee who himself is quite willing to carry the ball for the military. At times, the Congress can help the military in opposition to the Secretary of Defense and/or the President.

A great deal will depend on who is President and in which direction he leans for advice and comfort, the Defense De-

[7] Robert N. Ginsburgh, *U.S. Military Strategy in the Sixties* (New York: W.W. Norton and Company, 1965), 33–44.

partment and its civilian staff or the military on the JCS. When Eisenhower was President this problem was not as pronounced because of his military reputation and experience. When John F. Kennedy became President in 1961, the military became a bit uneasy. Not only did the military services begin to feel the effects of the McNamara "way of life," they were also skeptical about Kennedy. It did not help their disposition either when Kennedy showed a predilection for leaning on General Maxwell Taylor as his personal representative early in his administration. This was deeply resented by the military as Taylor had already retired from active duty, and when Kennedy chose him to become Chairman of the Joint Chiefs, it was looked upon as one more slap in the face of the military. Kennedy had bypassed other high-ranking officers on the JCS and the leading military figures in the Armed Forces and instead had selected a retired officer in whom he had much trust. Pentagon personnel apparently hastened to read Taylor's *The Uncertain Trumpet* to see what might be in store for them. In June, 1961, a number of high military commands were changed, prompted by what McNamara thought was some rather serious undermining of his position by various officers in their dealings with Congress and the press. The JCS was also stripped of some of its nonmilitary advisory jobs and by the end of 1961, the military was chagrined, to say the least.

THE NATIONAL SECURITY COUNCIL

The experience of World War II had left in its wake at least three major problems relating to America's machinery and procedures for making military (and coordinated military-foreign) policy. One had to do with the coordination of the branches of the armed services themselves. The creation of the Department of Defense was aimed at providing such coordination, and though, as we shall see shortly, it by no means represented a complete or fully accepted solution to the problem, it was a major step forward. Second, there was the problem of coordinating the military command structure under the President. As we have seen, this problem emerged early in the war itself and was solved provisionally by the creation of the Joint Chiefs of Staff, later formalized in the same legislation that established the Defense Department. The third problem was the formulation of over-all military policy at the level of the President *and* the meshing of that policy with the foreign policy of the nation.

Organized cooperation between the State Department and military authorities is only a recent phenomenon. During the First World War, politico-military coordination was usually on an *ad hoc* basis, for specific matters of a temporary nature. In the early part of World War II, the Secretaries of War, Navy, and State had more or less informal Cabinet-type consultations among themselves, placing military matters within the context of our over-all political commitments to our Allies. But this too was of a temporary nature; there was no formal agenda, lines of responsibility were confused, and formal authority was lacking. To meet the clearly demonstrated need for cooperation for the purpose of carrying out the war, a standing interdepartmental committee known as SWNCC (State-War-Navy-Coordinating Committee) was formed in December, 1944. SWNCC, however, was used only as a clearing-house for information passing between the military and State Department and had little to do with actual policy-making.

As the war neared an end, it became apparent that a new type of politico-military cooperation would have to come about in order to provide for the future security of the nation. The reorganization of the civilian side of defense policy (the Department of Defense) and the military components (the Joint Chiefs of Staff) was one thing. But there had to be some sort of "institutionalized manner of consciously integrating military policy with all aspects of high-level foreign policy."[8] This was the conclusion reached by the special group established by Secretary of the Navy James Forrestal in 1945 and headed by Ferdinand Eberstadt, a former high official of the government involved with coordinating war production and the manufacture of munitions. When the National Security Act of 1947 was finally passed, a number of things suggested by

[8] Caraley, *op. cit.*, p. 41.

the Eberstadt Report were incorporated in it. The National Security Council was one of these.

The NSC was both an advisory group and evaluations "board" consisting of the President, Vice-President, Secretaries of Defense and State, and Director of the Office of Civil and Defense Mobilization (now defunct with its function transferred to the Office of Emergency Preparedness). The Chairman of the Joint Chiefs of Staff and the Director of the Central Intelligence Agency were made *advisers* to the NSC, but *not actually members of* it. The NSC itself was soon placed in the Executive Office of the President and the Special Assistant for National Security assigned as the President's close adviser. During the early years, between 1947 and 1950, the NSC was principally an advisory body to President Truman, giving him the benefit of its unanimous as well as divided opinions. It was also taken for granted that despite the broadness of the act establishing it, the NSC would be primarily concerned with matters of foreign, not domestic, policy.

Prior to the outbreak of the Korean War, the greater number of policies considered by the NSC dealt with particular foreign countries, or larger areas which presented some sort of critical significance at the time. Long-range problems were brought into focus as papers covering countries and geographic areas were prepared by the professional staff of the NSC. The policy paper was usually brief, giving an analysis of the problem and drawing some conclusions. The NSC then debated the matter and the Executive Secretary passed the problem on to the President. He would then place the NSC position in context with other papers and reports he might have from the Joint Chiefs or other parts of the government and then approve or disapprove the conclusions of the NSC. If he approved, the NSC position became national security policy on that particular subject. Technically, the decisions were to be implemented by all the affected agencies of the government (for example, individual military services, specific desks in the Secretary of State's domain, etc.). For the most part, however, in the early days of the NSC this overseeing role fell on the Secretary of State. During the initial phase of the NSC, therefore, it operated as an advisory body, organizing itself and feeling its way into a comfortable niche in the President's official family.

By the time of the Korean War in 1950, the NSC was a well-established, functioning organization within the Executive Office of the President and under his personal control, through his Secretaries on the NSC and his Executive Secretary in charge of the NSC Staff. As a direct result of our military involvement in Korea, the President usually presided at NSC meetings. The size of the NSC was enlarged by adding representatives of the Bureau of the Budget and the Economic Cooperation Administration (foreign aid agency). The overseeing of NSC decisions was also made more exact by creating within the NSC a small unit to work with responsible departments and agencies to ensure that reports on the status of programs approved by the NSC and the President were made available to them. The Korean War also brought the NSC more into line as an inner war council.

With the election of Dwight D. Eisenhower in 1952, the NSC underwent further metamorphosis. In his campaign Eisenhower had pledged a revitalization of the NSC, and after his inauguration he appointed Robert Cutler as his Special Assistant for National Security Affairs. Cutler immediately began to upgrade the NSC as an advisory body. Under Truman, the NSC tended to be a group of debaters, but under Eisenhower, in keeping with his own ideas of institutionalization and placing greater emphasis on staff work, the NSC became a more corporate group of advisers. The NSC was enlarged to include the Secretary of the Treasury, George M. Humphrey, in whom Eisenhower had tremendous confidence, the Director of the Budget, and the Chairman of the Atomic Energy Commission. Sherman Adams, who held the post of Assistant to the President and who was probably the most influential staff chief of all of Eisenhower's assistants, played a most important role in bringing the NSC to a position of prominence. The professional staff was enlarged and other agencies, such as the United States Information Agency, were represented on the NSC every so often. Precise staff work, previously distributed agendas, the cutting off of some members and the adding of others pointed up the importance that Eisenhower placed in the new look of the NSC.

An important aspect of the use Eisenhower made of the NSC was the establishment of an Operations Coordinating Board for the "integrated implementation of national security policies." In Truman's day, a few staff people did the job of overseeing the process of following through with NSC decisions. Truman could then put his finger on the process through his contacts with the staff people or his Executive Secretary on the NSC. But Eisenhower, again in keeping with his concept of staff work and institutionalization, went a step further with the OCB, which was organized not to force compliance with decisions as much as to provide the details and plans that could be used to put those decisions into operation. The OCB was a kind of trouble-shooting group which could take upon itself the implementation of policy decisions. Policies agreed upon by the NSC and the President were usually very general. The OCB was supposed to furnish the wherewithall, much like the way an executive officer or chief of staff performs this function in a military sense. The OCB assisted the agencies and departments to carry out their planning responsibilities to national security policy. As Cutler pointed out, the OCB had no power to intervene, order, or come between the President and his own responsibilities as President. For the most part the OCB was composed of Under Secretaries and Assistant Secretaries who were responsible for the carrying out of the decisions made by the NSC. It was only an arm of the NSC, nothing more.

When he became President in 1961, John F. Kennedy placed his reliance on personal contacts with people with whom he had been relatively close. The White House Office, within the Executive Office of the President, was revamped and deinstitutionalized. His Special Assistants for various policy areas were *his,* not the Executive Office's, agents probing and prodding departments and agencies. Wanting to make certain that he had *his* finger on the pulse of government, and was not dependent on any one Special Assistant, Kennedy began his Administration with the idea of superimposing the personal method of governing that had been Roosevelt's on the enlarged Presidency that had developed since New Deal days. To do this he needed trusted lieutenants, not an expanded committee system, who would do his bidding.

A month after his inauguration as President of the United States, John F. Kennedy made sweeping changes in the National Security Council system. In an Executive Order on February 19, 1961, he abolished the Operations Coordinating Board, centering responsibility for much of the Board's work in the Secretary of State, Dean Rusk. Kennedy had decided to have the work of the Board coordinated in his own office, the State Department, and, whenever necessary, in the United States Information Agency.

Kennedy transferred the function of making certain that national security policy decisions were executed properly from an interdepartmental committee that was hard for the President to supervise and control to McGeorge Bundy, his National Security Special Assistant, and Bundy's deputy, Walt W. Rostow. The Bundy team now had the job of monitoring the President's decisions, particularly on security policy, throughout the executive department, to make certain they were carried out, and to coordinate all the Government's foreign policy activities as monitors, under the State Department.[9]

Kennedy's approach to the purpose of the NSC and the OCB was in line with his attempt to make *his own* direction of policy a more personal one than the way things had been under Eisenhower. Just as bringing in General Maxwell D. Taylor as his personal representative and then Chairman of the Joint Chiefs of Staff showed the professional military people that Kennedy would be no "pushover," so too the abolishment of the OCB reflected a new personal touch in policy responsibility that Kennedy believed was lacking in the institutionalized staff system of Eisenhower.

The Kennedy Administration "deliberately rubbed out the distinction between planning and operation which governed the administrative structure of the NSC staff" in the Eisenhower Administration. This latter point was stressed in

[9] Arthur Krock, "The President's New Way to Get Policy Compliance," *New York Times*, February 21, 1961.

remarks made by William D. Carey, Executive Assistant Director of the Bureau of the Budget in 1962, at a conference for Federal Executives in Virginia. Carey pointed out that President Kennedy had espoused the theory that "responsibility belonged with individuals instead of institutions." McGeorge Bundy and his "group" worked informally, with a minimum of paperwork, to expedite the flow of information to the President and orders from him. In his own office as Special Assistant for National Security Affairs, Bundy was doing what the old OCB had tried to do before, but with more informality. Bundy, said Carey, was a convener and catalyst, "alert to spotting gaps in the fabric of national security planning" and moving in to close them. The Kennedy Administration upgraded the immediate presidential family in the decision-making process throughout the government. In the area of national security, the President tied foreign policy matters more closely to it and made the Secretary of State more of a coordinator than policy-maker. He kept for himself the shaping of foreign policy, military planning, and national security. Kennedy's changes in the NSC and the abolishing of the OCB were part of the more general redirection of the office of the President, from the institutionalized format to the informal communications network with which he was more at ease.

When the Cuba missile crisis occurred in the fall of 1962, Kennedy created the Executive Committee of the NSC, consisting of Secretary of State Rusk, Secretary of Defense McNamara, and Bundy. "ExComm," as it became known, began to function along the lines of a War Council. Robert F. Kennedy, the Attorney-General, was also a close associate of his brother and had much to do informally with the deliberations and decisions of ExComm. The elaborate structure of the NSC had been largely obliterated and the "inner Cabinet" of Rusk, McNamara, and the President's brother, aided by National Security Affairs Special Assistant McGeorge Bundy, was the principal adviser to the President on national security from then on.

From 1962 on, this group dealt with the important security issues of the day and left the less important, where presidential decisions were not absolutely and immediately necessary, to the staff of the downgraded NSC. There were no more series of elaborate studies and position papers by the NSC staff itself. Rather the NSC existed as a kind of "backstop" for McGeorge Bundy and Rusk. Kennedy preferred to deal directly with McNamara and/or the Joint Chiefs of Staff chairman on military matters and, therefore, there was no necessity for the JCS to spend valuable time as *advisers* to the NSC. As Stanley L. Falk has pointed out. "The NSC under President Kennedy, it is clear, was thus a flexible organization within the overall national security structure."[10]

Kennedy had respect for the military but in his own conception of the Presidency no military chief was going to be in a superior position to the President. Kennedy, too, asked questions of his military, demanded answers and the reasons for those answers. After the Bay of Pigs disaster in April, 1961, in which the JCS had fared badly in his eyes, for not giving him proper advice, Kennedy distrusted the military even more.

But Lyndon B. Johnson's approach to the military side was quite different. Johnson rarely considered the substance of foreign policy in his senatorial years. More concerned with the "hows" rather than the "whys" of policy-making, Johnson was also relatively ignorant of the role of the military in American life, despite his legislative experience, and he brought this deficiency to the White House. He treated the NSC structure with even less concern. "ExComm" continued as the working structure but the term NSC, as applied to Rusk, McNamara, Bundy (and later Walt Rostow, who took the latter's place), and the other civilian and military leaders on whom Johnson leaned, was used more out of habit than anything else. At times, for example, the NSC was used to study past performances and future capabilities of the government of South Vietnam. But Johnson basically depended more on individuals—Rusk, McNamara, Bundy, and the Joint Chiefs —than had even Kennedy.

There is one specific factor in the Johnson Administration

---

[10] Stanley L. Falk, "The NSC Under Truman, Eisenhower, and Kennedy," *Political Science Quarterly*, Vol. 79. No. 3 (September, 1964), 433.

that points up the necessity to have such bodies as the NSC in operation. Presidents Roosevelt, Truman, Eisenhower, and Kennedy were all, in one fashion or another, personally aware of military strategy, policy, and potentiality. Roosevelt, whose experience went back to his role as Assistant Secretary of the Navy in World War I, was considered to be a fair military strategist. He enjoyed playing off his military leaders against one another, as he did with his political leaders and administrators, and never permitted the "military establishment" to get into the position where it began to think "it" knew more than he did. Truman distrusted the generals and the admirals even more. The MacArthur firing epitomized Truman's belief that no military man should be so powerful that he was on par with the President, let alone superior to him. Eisenhower's military expertise caused him to look to his military chiefs for advice and answers to *his* questions. The institutionalization of his Administration, in particular the NSC, created layers of insulation between the JCS and his own office. Although the Chairman of the JCS certainly enjoyed access to Eisenhower, there were all sorts of chains of command with which the JCS Chairman had constantly to associate: the weekly meetings of the NSC, the importance of the full Cabinet in Eisenhower's concept of staff, the growing centralization of civilian authority in the Department of Defense, and the power of Sherman Adams. In short, the military was only a section, important though it might well be, of the over-all national security and foreign-policy decision-making process.

The downgrading of the NSC, as a sifter of national security and foreign policy problems, was begun by Kennedy and completed by Johnson. Now with very little insulation between it and the President (what with the NSC practically done away with and the personnel of the White House Office almost completely changed), the military establishment, in particular the JCS, was in ascendancy. Rusk, Bundy, and Rostow, had been "hard-liners" in the Kennedy Administration, but their collective impact had been attenuated by others close to Kennedy (his brother Robert, Theodore Sorensen, Richard Goodwin, Arthur Schlesinger, Jr., etc.). McNamara, too, intent on civilian control of the military for his own reasons of defense management was apparently an indirect sobering influence on the military. But as we became more deeply committed to military action in Vietnam, the influence of the military chiefs and "hard-liners" Rusk and Rostow on Lyndon Johnson began to increase.

Richard Nixon brought to the Presidency in 1969 his previous experience as Vice-President during the Eisenhower Administration. Nixon's legalistic approach to decision-making resulted in his affinity for employing the NSC as a common meeting ground for his chief civilian and military advisers. In a special announcement on February 7, 1969, he restored the NSC as a "principal forum for the consideration of policy issues" and established a group of supporting NSC subcommittees "to prepare forward planning for the Council as well as to facilitate the handling of more immediate operational problems within the context of the NSC system."[11] It was the President's intention to bring together the State and Defense Departments and the Joint Chiefs in one body in order to help him make national security and foreign policy decisions. The NSC was thus revitalized, and the military chiefs given a more coordinated role *with* the civilian components of the government. Interdepartmental groups, *ad hoc* groups (such as the Vietnam Special Studies Group and the Washington Special Actions Group), review groups, and an Undersecretaries Committee were soon established as a new institutional arrangement in the Nixon Administration. Significantly, the JCS was also now fully represented in fact and practice on the NSC.

Melvin Laird, Nixon's Secretary of Defense, was the first such Secretary ever to have come to the position directly from the Congress, where he had been thoroughly involved in military matters. In his House career, Laird had been a critic of McNamara's proclivity for civilian "dominance" of the military and had been considered by the military indeed as a friendly congressman. Nixon, however, also put great stress on

11 "The National Security Council: New Role and Structure," Senate Subcommittee on National Security and International Operations, 91st Cong., 1st Sess., Committee print, 7 February, 1969, p. 1.

the role that his Special Assistant for National Security, Henry Kissinger, would play, and by 1970 the latter's institutional role (as well as the personal, confidential role as adviser to the President on foreign policy) clearly recreated an insulating layer between the President and the JCS in the day-to-day, normal decision-making process. This is not to say that the President could not go directly to the JCS or any one of them if he so chose. But the staff system, in which Nixon believed, did not make it easy for the military chiefs to have the President's ear at *their* request. The NSC structure, in the first two years of the Nixon Administration, became an ongoing forum and decision-making structure on matters of national security and military policy-planning. Once again, the military was brought into partnership with, not domination of, the process. Naturally, the President could shift his emphasis one way or the other according to circumstances and issues. His

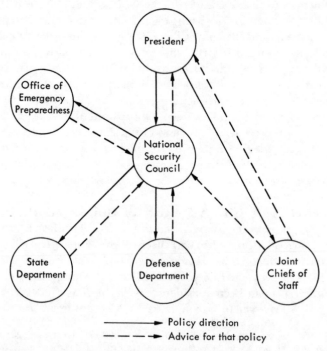

FIGURE 9 Administering National Security Policy.

powers as commander in chief permit him to pick and choose, as he sees fit. But it would still be incorrect to view the role of the military establishment as superior to the civilian in the American governmental system.

INTER-SERVICE RIVALRY

Well below the rarified heights of the President as commander in chief and foreign-policy-maker, the level of the national security, and even the level of top military policy-making in the office of the Secretary of Defense, administrative life in the defense establishment looks much like administration elsewhere in the executive branch. In fact, perhaps nowhere is the pluralism and the intense competition of bureaucratic life in Washington more evident than in the defense area—even in the post-World War II era of elaborate industrial "coordination."

When the Second World War ended, it was natural for each of the military branches to attempt to obtain as great a share of the annual federal defense budget as possible. The awesome power of the atomic bomb which had been so graphically displayed at Hiroshima and Nagasaki in 1945, bringing about the fall of Japan, was also demonstrated in a series of tests in the South Pacific in 1946. American possession of a nuclear deterrent, in the form of a bomb dropped from an aircraft, brought about a new faith in air power. The Air Force now considered itself a full-blown partner of the Army and Navy, and the separation of the Air Force from the Army and establishment of another branch of the military services emphasized the coming of age of air power. Each of the military services continued to press for the uniqueness of its own mission (the Navy never forgot that the atomic bomb tests in the South Pacific, after the end of the war, had taken place with Navy ships as stationary targets, as if to stress the obsoleteness of surface vessels). Although there was some positive direction in a few quarters for armed forces unification at the top level of command, for the most part each military branch fought for its own autonomy in the post-World War II military reorganization. The Army, Navy, and

Air Force, for example, competed with one another in setting forth reasons for or against Universal Military Training, the size of the new Air Force, the role of Navy aviation, and the future function of the fleet.[12]

The battle over Truman's Secretary of Defense Louis Johnson's cancellation of construction of a large new aircraft carrier in 1949 can serve as a case in point. The Air Force, pressing strongly for more emphasis on air power and less on naval vessels, greeted Johnson's order with great pleasure. Navy brass was very agitated at this downgrading of their service. Aircraft carriers had played a major role in World War II, and the Navy felt certain that the carrier would continue to be the backbone of the fleet. The great potential of the nuclear-powered submarine as an offensive weapon had not yet been realized by most of the high-ranking naval officers. They sincerely believed that a carrier, with a complement of relatively short-range planes, was a more effective weapon of war than a large group of long-range, land-based heavy bombers. The Navy took its case to the Congress (in what has become known as "the revolt of the Admirals"), and in a series of congressional hearings high-ranking naval officers castigated the Defense Department's undue reliance on the United States Air Force. During the controversy, Captain Arleigh A. Burke (USN) and a compatriot passed on important and confidential data supporting the Navy's case to the press. After the ensuing uproar died down, the Navy finally obtained congressional sanction for its carrier, but the acrimonious battle between the Air Force and the Navy left many scars.[13]

Inter-service rivalry became rather commonplace. The military services, despite the use of the nomenclature "Joint

[12] Samuel P. Huntington, *The Common Defense* (New York: Columbia University Press, 1961), and his "Inter-Service Competition and the Political Roles of the Armed Services," *American Political Science Review*, Vol. LV, No. 1 (March, 1961). See also Demetrios Caraley, *The Politics of Military Unification* (New York: Columbia University Press, 1966), and Paul Y. Hammond, *Organizing for Defense*. Princeton University Press, 1961).

[13] Jack Raymond, *Power at the Pentagon* (New York: Harper and Row, 1964), 198–201.

Chiefs," were not united in an understanding of their combined military mission, the roles of the various weapons delivery systems, or the size of their respective services. Was there sense in having both the Army and the Navy, not to mention the Air Force, develop missile systems? True enough, the missile was a high-powered substitute for the shell, and each of the military services used a different type of shell for its mission—the Army used the artillery shell for land bombardment and an anti-aircraft shell for defense against planes; the Navy used large shells for bombardment of shore installations from the sea; and the Air Force used small shells for air-to-air purposes. Although missiles appeared to be essential as a new offensive and defensive armament, and the military branches were rooted in the past as regards developing their own fire-power systems, the propulsion of the missile was for all intents and purposes basically the same. Why could not the services unite in order to perfect a common missile system and thus lower the tremendous costs of research and development in this highly complex armament field?

The individual services argued that such competition, even though there was a good deal of repetition and duplication, refined research and development to such an extent that each service would obtain a better weapon in the long run. Each service could thus take advantage of the other's mistakes and successes. Place research and development together under one command and mistakes would be compounded or go undetected for too long a time. Competition, not collusion, was the rule of thumb for the services. Although there is some truth to this argument, it was, however, basically imbedded in inter-service jealousies. Each of the services carefully guarded its own prerogatives under the guise of a unique military mission in the event of war. The services disagreed on troop strength of our European commitment, the issue of "massive retaliation" against a potential foe versus the degree of limited-warfare capabilities, and, of course, in the size of budget reductions. As Samuel P. Huntington has written of the 1950's, "At no point in the history of military policy after World War II were the President and the Budget Bureau confronted with a truly joint, integrated military program, publicly announced and supported by all military men as the indispensable minimum for national security."[14]

Civilian agencies often found themselves in the position of acting as mediators in inter-service quarrels, with the result that the military services were forced to become "politicized," adopt a less professional bearing in their military attitudes, and develop a political sophistication in dealing with one another.[15] The respective services turned to the public in order to create more favorable images of themselves as guardians of democracy. They also developed their own individual, outside "think tanks" to help them present the best possible case for their points of view. Thus the RAND Corporation of California was employed by the United States Air Force in order to take advantage of its physical, applied, and social science techniques; the Research Analysis Corporation worked closely with the Army (spending a good deal of time showing the Army how to combat the widening influence of the Air Force on policy decisions at high levels of government); the Massachusetts Institute of Technology's Operations Evaluation Group was hired by the Navy to help develop and refine the Navy's role in the political-military world; and the Institute for Defense Analysis became the outside research company for the Joint Chiefs of Staff *and* the Department of Defense.[16] The military services, moreover, used their own pressure groups, whose activity was expanded in the post-World War II period, to "backstop" their public image. All the military-related associations—the Navy League, Air Force Association, Reserve Officers' Corps, Marine Corps League, National Guard Association, among others—were in the fore-front protecting their "clienteles." In addition, the military professional groups with their journals played their part in sustaining the integrity and vital importance of their respective services. Organized in the post-Civil War era, they continued to be formidable organs of the military services'

---

[14] Huntington, *The Common Defense, op. cit.*, p. 379.

[15] Ibid., p. 380.

[16] Colonel Robert N. Ginsburgh, "The Challenge to Military Professionalism," in David B. Bobrow, ed., *Components of Defense Policy, op.cit.*, p. 133.

propaganda. The most influential ones were (and are) the U.S. Naval Institute, established in 1873 and which began publication of its *Proceedings* in 1874; the Military Service Institute (1879); the Cavalry Association (1885), with its journal begun in 1888 and now interested in armor and mechanization; the *Journal of United States Artillery* (1892); and the *Infantry Society Journal* (1893).[17] The military services were also aided by the industries that served their needs. The Air Force, for example, could always count on the aircraft manufacturing industry (which also got into the missile construction business) for advice and comfort.

Each of the services could also intensify its liaison activity with the Congress and appropriate key congressional committees. Army, Navy, and Air Force Reservists in the Congress particularly are catered to because of their built-in biases on behalf of "their" military branches. Thus in indirect ways the military services could continue to bypass their civilian secretaries and pressure senators and congressmen on the basis of constituency interests, and whenever necessary they still do. One result of the military-congressional liaison has been the exacerbation of inter-service rivalry. If money is appropriated for two destroyers, it may have to be taken from aircraft research and development, thus incurring the wrath of the Air Force. When the nation becomes deeply engaged in an armed conflict, the Congress usually pulls out all stops on military appropriations. All the services then seem to be a bit happier with their slices of the budget pie. But in a relative peacetime situation, when economy becomes of greater concern to the Administration and the Congress, the services compete more sharply for funds and authorization of strength. Congress can be the center of the military's attention in their individual battles with the Secretary of Defense over military policy, organization, and development. A President who exerts a strong leadership in matters of foreign policy, with which military strategy and policy as well as national security are closely related, can have relative success in limiting the military services' dealings with the Congress.

The intensity of our military involvement in Vietnam did

17 Huntington, *The Soldier and the State*, p. 243.

not bring about a unified "military outlook" on needs, strategies, and tactics. Indeed, command problems in the field seemed to aggravate and contribute to the continuation of inter-service rivalry.

THE CIVILIAN-MILITARY PARTNERSHIP

As the preceding sections of this chapter make very clear, one can see in the area of military policy illustration of all the standard problems of administration and policy coordination. In reality, however, and especially since 1945, the stakes for American democracy have become much higher than just the solving of problems of military rivalry and coordination, however monumental these may be. With the acceptance by the United States of the role of "leader of the free world" came a new series of challenges and responsibilities. For the first time in our national history, we were forced to develop and continually maintain a world-wide foreign policy posture. In support of this posture, we were also compelled to maintain an unprecedented huge and powerful military capability. Furthermore, the nation has been drawn into a whole series of situations, stretching around the world, in which her foreign policy has involved military threats or actual operations. Korea and Vietnam come to mind most quickly, but Quemoy and Matsu, Lebanon, Greece and Turkey, Cuba, the Dominican Republic, Berlin, and a host of other points on the globe have been involved.

Our foreign commitments, sanctified by treaties and accentuated by our widening national interest, brought about a marked increase of the military share of the total national budget. There were, of course, fluctuations in the military percentage of the budget until the outbreak of the Korean War in 1950, and although this development was gradual, it was relatively steady. The military percentage of the total national budget has grown to a point where the defense establishment, including all the components responsible for our national security, accounts for roughly half of all national government expenditures. In fiscal 1949, the Army, Navy, and Air Force spent approximately $14 billion, or 35 per cent, of the $40 billion total spent by the United States government. The Air Force's share of the $14 billion was a scant $1.69 billion. Fifteen years later, in fiscal 1964, the three major branches of the military spent $48.7 billion, about 50 per cent in its total outlay as compared with fiscal 1949.[18] Since 1964 the military portion of the total national budget has increased even more, with the exceedingly high cost of the Vietnam War being put at roughly $2 billion per month Nor do these figures take into account the militarily related expenditures of our space programs under the National Aeronautics and Space Administration (NASA). The extent of American military spending staggers the imagination. The economic impact of military spending on the nation's general economy alone is enough to make us take stock of the military establishment's influence at the top levels of decision-making in the United States government.

The issue, however, is even broader than that, for the development of our international position has been so vast and our military alliances are so widespread that almost every major political decision is made in the context and climate of a military environment. The rapidly advancing technology of weapons and delivery systems has also brought into the political-military picture the industrial complex, which has become a business partner with the military establishment. The military man is no longer an isolated and insulated individual concerned solely with developing his own military expertise. In the last twenty years many generals and admirals have come to occupy sensitive diplomatic posts, and a great number, after retirement, have become lobbyists and executives for important industrial concerns doing business with the defense establishment. One thing is certain, in the contemporary United States the generals and the admirals now have more to do with *political* decisions made at high levels of the national government than ever before.

There has been a growing fear, since the advent of the Vietnam War, that the military establishment has come to command a greater importance in the over-all executive

[18] See Clark R. Mollenhoff, *The Pentagon* (New York: G. P. Putnam's Sons, 1967), 416–417.

branch than should rightfully be the case. The degree of military involvement in political decisions (to escalate or not, negotiate or stall, use the offices of the United Nations or engage in unilateral diplomatic activity) is far more complicated than the oversimplification that the civilian authorities are dominated by the military. In truth, "historically, the character of civil-military relations in the United States has been dominated by the concept of civilian control of the military."[19] As Colonel Robert N. Ginsburgh has pointed out, "although the American military have not always been submissive to the civilian controllers, they have never seriously challenged the right or the tradition of civil control."[20] On the other hand, civilians and the military have a *new set* of relationships, intertwined, mutually dependent on each other for advice and support. There exists today a political-military fusion which, although deplored by some analysts, will continue to muddy the waters of civilian-military relationships. Just as American government is in reality based on a fusion or sharing of executive and legislative power (although we use the terminology of separation of powers), so too within the executive branch itself there is a commingling, or fusion, of people and minds about policy decisions in the field of national security and foreign policy. The simple concept that the civilian authority is up here and the military down there, subordinate to and led by the civilian, is indeed tenuous. The complexities of the civilian-military relationship are further aggravated by the role that the Congress plays in shaping and approving national security, and thereby military, policy.

Until the Cold War, which set the stage for world-wide rearmament, was ushered in at the end of World War II, the American democratic tradition placed the military establishment (Departments of War and Navy under the pre-1947 arrangement) in a position clearly subordinate to civilian

---

[19] Gene Lyons, "The New Civil Military Relations," *American Political Science Review*, Vol. LV, No. 1 (March, 1961), 61.

[20] Robert N. Ginsburgh, "The Challenge to Military Professionalism," Davis B. Bobrow, ed., *Components of Defense Policy* (Chicago: Rand McNally, 1965), 132.

authority. The President is constitutionally the commander in chief of all the armed services, although interestingly enough there is no constitutional provision that he must be a civilian. We have elected several military men to the Presidency; they conveniently doffed their uniforms and donned mufti while occupying the White House. Yet traditionally, most Americans so often consider the President the *civilian* head of the government that they automatically assume that civilian authority is superior to the military. Civilian control of the military, however, is basically extra-constitutional,[21] and most Americans agree that the superiority of the civilian over the military is a foregone conclusion and a necessary prerequisite to maintaining a democracy. Throughout most of our history, in fact, the prestige of the soldier has been relatively low, and only since the end of World War II has the military increased its stature in the eyes of most Americans.

That the professional military man is now considered an integral part of the executive branch of government, rather than a poor country cousin called upon only when the nation is at war, is no better exemplified than in the late President John F. Kennedy's speech to the graduating class at West Point in June, 1962. President Kennedy told the newly commissioned 2nd Lieutenants in the regular army that America depended upon them as never before.

> Your strictly military responsibilities, therefore, will require a versatility and an adaptability never before required in either war or in peace. They may involve the command and control of modern nuclear weapons and modern delivery systems, so complex that only a few scientists can understand their operation, so devastating that their inadvertent use would be of world-wide concern. But so new that their employment and their effects have never been tested in combat conditions.
>
> On the other hand, your responsibilties may involve the command of more traditional forces, but in less traditional roles. Men risking their lives, not as combatants, but as instructors or advisors, or as symbols of our Nation's commitments. The fact that the United States is not directly at war in these areas in no way

21 Samuel P. Huntington, *The Soldier and the State*, p. 190.

diminishes the skill and the courage that will be required, the service to our country which is rendered or the pain of the casualties which are suffered.[22]

The non-military role of the military in the decision-making process was further elaborated upon by the President:

> The nonmilitary problems which you will face will also be most demanding, diplomatic, political, and economic. In the years ahead, some of you will serve as advisors to foreign aid missions or even to foreign governments. Some will negotiate terms of a cease-fire with broad political as well as military ramifications. Some of you will go to the far corners of the earth, and to the far reaches of space. Some of you will sit in the highest councils of the Pentagon. Others will hold delicate command posts which are international in character. Still others will advise on plans to abolish arms instead of using them to abolish others. Whatever your position, the scope of your decisions will not be confined to the traditional tenets of military competence and training. You will need to know and understand not only the foreign policy of the United States, but the foreign policy of all countries scattered around the world who 20 years ago were the most distant names to us.
>
> Above all, you will have a responsibility to deter war as well as to fight it. For the basic problems facing the world today are not susceptible of a final military solution. While we will long require the services and admire the dedication and commitment of the fighting men of this country, neither our strategy nor our psychology as a Nation, and certainly not our economy, must become permanently dependent upon an ever-increasing Military Establishment.
>
> Our forces, therefore, must fulfill a broader role as a complement to our diplomacy, as an arm of our diplomacy, as a deterrent to our adversaries, and as a symbol to our Allies of our determination to support them.[23]

Thus the military has come of political and diplomatic age. Without doubt our social values and institutions are now

[22] *Selected Papers on Administration of National Security.* Senate Subcommittee on National Security Staffing and Operations. Committee Print, 87th Cong., 2nd Sess., 1962, p. 17.

[23] Ibid., pp. 18–19.

subordinate "to considerations of military potential," and the military is now in an advantageous position in the decision-making process as an equal and formidable partner with their civilian counterparts.[24]

[24] Harold D. Lasswell, "The Garrison-State Hypothesis Today," Samuel P. Huntington, ed., *Changing Patterns of Military Politics* (Glencoe: Free Press, 1962), 62–63.

Nine

The Judicial Branch

HE JUDICIAL BRANCH in the United States, unlike most national judicial systems, wields great political power and must be counted as part of the American political system. Its methods may not be those of the politician actively seeking support from groups for his policies or election, but instead are more passive. It must wait for cases to come before it and then decide on the facts, as interpreted by the judges and applicable to the law and Constitution. Someone or some group must go to the court first; the court does not take the initiative.

Federalism involves complicated governmental relationships between the component parts of the political system—especially the national and state governments. All kinds of constitutional questions inevitably arise in such a governmental scheme. Do certain acts of the federal government infringe on the powers reserved to the states, and, on the contrary, do actions taken by a state violate provisions and guarantees of the United States Constitution, which is by definition legally superior to state acts in conflict with it? Do presidential directives impinge on the legislative authority of Congress and thus offend the principle of separation of powers? It is only natural to look to the courts to decide these and other such similar questions. For the American tradition is thoroughly imbued with the concept of the rule of law, and the acceptance of this concept implies the community's willingness to view the courts as the final arbiter.

The American conception of the sanctity of law is indeed deeply imbedded in the nation's history, and derives from the higher law background the United States inherited from Europe and England. English law, in particular, was the normal heritage of Americans of the late eighteenth and early nineteenth centuries. In the break with England, the colonists constantly appealed to a higher law, a natural law, they claimed to be superior to the mere acts of the British government. The declaration of Independence and the Constitution are colored with this notion of the rule of law. When the colonists declared their independence, it was natural for them either to rework their colonial charters or adopt new constitutions for their new state governments, and later the Constitution of 1787 for the entire nation. The fact that they felt compelled to have constitutions, and *written* ones, strongly implied belief in law superior to legislative acts and executive decrees.

Although some scholars dispute the idea, it can be cogently argued that the courts are seen as the institutions that safeguard the supremacy of higher law, a substantive set of truths that are superior to the procedural rules. Indeed, the late Professor Edward S. Corwin, a noted expert on constitutional law, stated that judicial review was "an attempt by the American democracy to cover its bet."[1] The Constitution, moreover, is a higher law in itself, superior to all other written laws and the courts are the logical enforcers and interpreters of it as well. Government acts take the form of legislation passed by Congress and state legislatures; presidential executive orders, proclamations, executive agreements, and presidential use of the elastic clause (Article II, Section 3); and interpretations, rulings, and decisions of the departments, regulatory commissions and boards, and agencies (or the bureaucracy in general) of the government. They can all, in time and under specific circumstances, be judged by the courts for conformity with the Constitution and higher law. In so doing the judiciary branch functions as a normal feature of the American political system and is accepted by most of the people as such.

[1] Quoted in Alpheus T. Mason, *The Supreme Court: Palladium of Freedom* (Ann Arbor: University of Michigan Press, 1962), 164.

Strangely enough, however, despite the sanctified position Americans tend to accord the courts in the system, the very process of selection of those who sit on the federal bench (not to mention the state bench) is out and out political. That these political considerations *have* often coincided with legal ability is a happy coincidence for all. Table 14 will establish the simple fact that Presidents, at least recent ones, tend to appoint to the federal bench people of their own political persuasion.

Furthermore, the judges throughout the federal system are usually men who have had active political careers in their own states. In most states, judges are elected to the state courts, and they must by the nature of the case get into the political wars. Because federal judges are appointed by the President, with Senate confirmation, those who do come from the state bench, often come from the field of politics, albeit in an indirect fashion. Whether they do or do not, appointments to the federal bench invariably require access to the President or his close advisers. Political considerations simply *do* play a part in the process of selection. Many federal judges have had state legislative experience too, and have used their state political connections to move into the judicial service, usually through the patronage system.

Prior judicial service is not an absolute prerequisite for appointment even to the United States Supreme Court. Of all the Justices and Chief Justices appointed since 1789, a shade under 40 per cent of them never had any kind of judicial experience in either federal or state courts. Indeed, of the 23 members of the Supreme Court appointed from the time Franklin D. Roosevelt took office in 1933 until the Nixon Administration began in 1969, 12 (or 52 per cent) had none at all (including two Chief Justices, Harlan Stone and Earl Warren). Nixon's two appointees in 1969 and 1970, however, were from the federal bench.

Table 15 shows the composition of the Supreme Court as of January 1, 1971.

No better example of the political importance and nature of the Supreme Court exists than the circumstances of President Nixon's appointments of Chief Justice Warren Earl

TABLE 14 Court Appointments—Party Affiliation: 1933-63

Courts[a]	Roosevelt (D) (3/4/33 to 4/12/45)		Truman (D) (4/13/45 to 1/20/53)		Eisenhower (R) (1/20/53 to 1/20/61)		Kennedy (R) (1/20/61 to 11/22/63)	
	Total	Republicans	Total	Republicans	Total	Democrats	Total	Republicans
Supreme Court*	9	1	4	1	5	1	2	—
Circuit Courts*	54	4	27	3	45	3	20[d]	—
District Courts*	140	2	98	6	129	6	102	11
Territorial Courts†[b]	29	—	18	—	8	2	2	—
Hawaii Circuit Courts‡	28	7	15	4	11	—[e]	—	—
Hawaii Supreme Court‡	9	3	7	1	2	—[c]	—	—
Court of Claims*	4	—	2	1	2	—	1[e]	—
Court of Claims and Patent Appeals*	3	—	3	1	5	1	1	—
Customs Court*	7	2	4	1	3	—	—	—
Total	283	19	178	18	210	13	128	11

Reprinted from *Congress and the Nation* (Washington, 1965), 1444. Administrative Office of the U.S. Courts.

Note: Party affiliations are as of date of appointment.

* Life appointments.   ‡ Term appointments.

[a] Do not include: District of Columbia Municipal, Juvenile and Police Courts; U.S. Courts; Supreme Court of Puerto Rico.

[b] Includes the District Courts of Canal Zone, Guam, Puerto Rico, and Virgin Islands. Also included was the Territorial Court for the District of Alaska until changed to a U.S. District Court upon admission of Alaska as the 49th State Jan. 3, 1959, and the Territorial Court for the District of Hawaii until changed to a U.S. District Court upon admission of Hawaii as the 50th State Aug. 21, 1959.

[c] Jurisdiction of the Hawaii Circuit Courts and Supreme Court was transferred to the State of Hawaii Aug. 21, 1959.

[d] Includes one Liberal party member.

[e] No party affiliation.

TABLE 15 The Supreme Court as of November 1, 1971

Name	Appointed by	Year	Party Affiliation	Prior Experience	General Political Views	General Economic Views
Warren Earl Burger Chief Justice	Nixon	1969	Republican	Circuit Court of Appeals	Conservative	Conservative
Hugo L. Black (retired September 1971)	Roosevelt	1937	Democrat	U.S. Senator (Alabama), former police court judge	Liberal	Liberal
William O. Douglas	Roosevelt	1939	Democrat	Law Professor Member of SEC	Liberal	Liberal
John Marshall Harlan (retired September 1971)	Eisenhower	1955	Republican	Circuit Court of Appeals	Conservative	Conservative
William J. Brennan, Jr.	Eisenhower	1956	Democrat	Judge of N.J. State Supreme Court	Liberal	Liberal
Potter Stewart	Eisenhower	1958	Republican	Circuit Court of Appeals	Moderate	Conservative
Byron R. White	Kennedy	1962	Democrat	Deputy Att.-Gen.	Conservative	Moderate
Thurgood Marshall	Johnson	1967	Democrat	Circuit Court of Appeals-Sol.-Gen.	Liberal	Liberal
Harry Blackmun	Nixon	1970	Republican	Circuit Court of Appeals	Conservative	Conservative

Burger in 1969 and Associate Justice Harry Blackmun in 1970.

Except for the Senate's rejection in 1930 of President Herbert Hoover's nominee John J. Parker to the United States Supreme Court, no other presidential appointment to the highest court of the land had been defeated by the Senate in the twentieth century until 1969. President Lyndon Johnson's nominations of Associate Justice Abe Fortas as Chief Justice and Federal Judge Homer Thornberry of Texas as his replacement on the Supreme Court had both been withdrawn by Johnson in 1968 when Fortas came under fire from Senate critics. The Fortas case is politically linked to Nixon's appointments in the first two years of his administration and must first be recounted here.

Abe Fortas was a successful Washington lawyer and lobbyist, as well as close friend of Lyndon B. Johnson, for whom he had acted as legal counsel in Johnson's disputed election from Texas to the Senate in 1948. A native of Tennessee and a political liberal, Fortas' fine legal mind, and constitutional and political skills were recognized by many liberal advocates of civil liberties and rights. In 1965 there was little difficulty in having the Senate confirm him as an Associate Justice of the Supreme Court, by voice vote, to replace Justice Arthur J. Goldberg, a John F. Kennedy appointee in 1962, whom Johnson had convinced to leave the Court in order to become Ambassador to the United Nations, thus permitting Johnson to place his old friend on the nation's highest bench. The Senate debate was remarkably short in 1965 with only half-hearted opposition stemming from a few senators.

Three years later Chief Justice Earl Warren wrote to President Johnson on June 13, 1968, that he *would* (italics added) retire effective at the pleasure of the President. In his reply to the Chief Justice, the President said he would accept the resignation "effective at such time as a successor is qualified." Warren's retirement would have given Johnson, who was leaving office in 6 months, a chance to fill only one vacancy except for the President's decision to appoint Fortas as Chief Justice of the United States. Raising Fortas to the number one position on the Court would then permit Johnson to place another old Texas friend on the Court as an Associate Justice,

Homer Thornberry, a federal judge on the 5th Circuit Court of Appeals and a former member of the House. When Johnson announced his nominations, he said that he had discussed them with several senatorial leaders and he saw no trouble ahead in obtaining confirmation. But the President was in error. It did not take long for opposition to Fortas to begin to develop among Republicans and Southern Democrats. Nineteen Republicans in particular made it public that they would oppose Fortas. Believing that Johnson should not appoint a Chief Justice as a "lame-duck" President, they stated that the newly elected President (hopefully, a Republican) should have the opportunity to fill Warren's position. There is little doubt that Warren was announcing at this time his impending retirement to make certain that there would be no possibility that Richard M. Nixon, in the event of his election in November, 1968, would have the opportunity of replacing him with someone having more conservative views. Because of their aversion to such a "lame-duck" appointment, the 19 Republican senators announced they would "vote against confirming any Supreme Court nomination of the incumbent President."

With this as background Senate Judiciary Committee Chairman James O. Eastland (Dem. of Mississippi) opened hearings in mid-July on the Fortas nomination. Fortas' close ties to Johnson were common knowledge and Senator Robert P. Griffin (Rep. of Michigan), one of the 19 dissident Republican senators, attacked the appointment on the "lame-duck" charge as well as that of "cronyism." There was some indication that Fortas had continued to be part of LBJ's inner advisory council, which a number of the Senate felt showed lack of judicial restraint if not integrity. Although Senate Republican leader Everett Dirksen of Illinois supported the President's choice, there was an obvious mood of irritation among many of his cohorts. If most of the Southern Democrats linked up with enough Republicans, Fortas could well be in trouble. A filibuster on the nomination would certainly not enhance LBJ's last few months in office either.

On July 16, 1968, Fortas himself testified before Eastland's committee. The first nominee as Chief Justice and the first confirmed sitting Associate Justice ever to testify before the Senate Judiciary Committee, he refused to answer several questions on past Court decisions, put to him by Senator Thurmond, on the grounds of judicial impropriety. But he did admit to having once called a prominent businessman and friend to complain about the latter's public criticism of Johnson's Vietnam policy. Fortas saw nothing wrong with that. Rather than having a quick confirmation, Fortas was beginning to have strong opposition. Time was running out on the Johnson Administration and Senator Eastland saw no chance for a Senate vote on confirmation before September.

Senate opposition had indeed begun to harden and President Johnson publicly stated that he was displeased at the recalcitrance of a "small sectional group" of senators. The Dean of the American University Law School, B. J. Tennery, then testified that Fortas had been paid $15,000 for having conducted a series of seminars at the Law School for nine weeks during the summer of 1968. Further investigation showed that the money paid Fortas had been raised by his former law partner, Paul A. Porter. It had come from several people, some of whom were clients of Fortas' former law firm of Arnold and Porter, with which Mrs. Fortas, also an attorney, was still associated. Fortas' opponents immediately smelled conflict of interest, collusion, and judicial impropriety, and began to zero in on the Justice. When Fortas declined to reappear before the Eastland Committee, he was even more suspect. Yet the Committee, by an 11–6 vote, sent his name to the Senate floor on September 27 with the recommendation that he be confirmed as Chief Justice.

Never before had a filibuster been attempted in the Senate over a confirmation to the Supreme Court. Senator Griffin was irate over the matter of the $15,000 fee and the mysterious extrajudicial activities of Fortas with the President. Southerners saw an opportunity to attack the liberal learnings of the Warren Court through Fortas. For five days the Senate debated the Fortas nomination in a mini-filibuster. The Senate did not stay in continuous session (as is the custom in a full-fledged filibuster), and it did transact other business. But, as is their prerogative, several Republican and Southern Democratic senators continued to attack Fortas' judicial integrity and political liberalism. Finally, Majority Leader Mike Mansfield (Montana) asked for a cloture vote on the debate, to shut off further discussions and vote on the confirmation. On October 1, one month before the presidential election, cloture was defeated 45 to 43, 14 votes shy of the necessary two thirds (59) of those present and voting to close off debate. Twenty-four Republicans, 15 of the Southern Democrats, and 4 Northern Democrats voted against cloture. Voting for it were 10 Republicans and 35 other Democrats. Once again the conservative coalition had been victorious.

Faced with a continuation of the struggle, Fortas asked the President to withdraw his name from consideration and Johnson regretfully agreed, stating that the action of the Senate was "historically and constitutionally tragic." Thornberry's name was withdrawn as well because Fortas, for the moment, would continue as an Associate Justice of the Supreme Court.

Although the President was unmistakably angry at the failure of the Senate to have accepted Fortas as Chief Justice, he did not base his contention in any constitutional "right" of his own to have his nominee confirmed. It was clearly the prerogative of the Senate to delay the confirmation vote as long as one third plus one of the Senate desired to continue the mini-filibuster. Being the politically astute man that he was, Johnson realized that if the Senate did balk at Fortas, the short time remaining before he left the presidency would not give him ample opportunity to secure the nomination. Johnson also realized that by this time he had lost much of his political "muscle," and he was indeed taking a calculated risk in attempting to push Fortas through the Senate. There is little doubt that many in the Senate also resented the manner in which the Chief Justice had resigned. Warren's resignation was never clearcut but rested on the supposition that he would retire upon Senate confirmation of his successor. Johnson had gone to the Senate with Fortas and Thornberry's names before Warren had actually left the court. He was also asking the Senate to think about filling Fortas' seat as Associate Justice and Fortas had not resigned that either. It was obvious that Warren was wary of who might be the next

President. The timing of his letter of intent to resign, for that is what it was, smacked more of politics than it should have. Fortas had failed to gain confirmation (although technically his name had been withdrawn from consideration) because of the developing resistance to him by the conservative coalition, the charge of "cronyism" which seemed to stick and about which Fortas could do very little, and the alleged impropriety of Fortas' having accepted a $15,000 fee for leading a few seminars at a law school while a member of the Court.

Seven months after his name had been withdrawn, Fortas again became the center of controversy over his having received a fee. In May, 1969, *Life* magazine broke a story which charged the Associate Justice with having accepted a $20,000 check in January, 1966, from the Wolfson Family Foundation established by Louis Wolfson. Wolfson was a wealthy industrialist and financier who had been indicted in September, 1966, and then imprisoned in April, 1969, for illegal stock manipulations. Fortas had taken no part in the proceedings relevant to Wolfson's appeal to the Supreme Court in 1969 when the Court denied a review of his conviction. Fortas quickly denied any impropriety on his part and issued a statement in which he said that the Foundation had given him a fee for doing research, study, and writing in the field of racial and religious relations in which the Foundation had great interest. Finding he had no time to do this, Fortas said he had returned the fee. The Justice further denied that he had acted in any improper way with Wolfson or the Foundation since becoming a member of the Court.

Several Republicans and some Democrats in the Congress called for Fortas' resignation, a congressional investigation of the entire matter, new laws regulating tax-exempt foundations, legislation requiring disclosure of outside income of Supreme Court Justices, and legislation making it mandatory for all Supreme Court appointees to have had prior judicial experience in either the Federal Court system or on the highest appellate state courts. (Fortas was then one of the 4 justices on the Supreme Court, including Chief Justice Warren, who had had no judicial experience before coming to the Court.) Fortas was clearly under suspicion and attack in Congress and in the press, particularly because he had kept the $20,000 for 11 months before returning it in December, 1966.

The House Judiciary Committee was asked to look into Fortas' relations with Wolfson and the Foundation to determine if there were grounds for impeachment by the House. Article II, Section 1, of the Constitution states that all federal judges "shall hold their offices during good behavior" and the "Canons of Judicial Ethics" of the American Bar Association state that judges should avoid even giving the impression for suspicion that they are using their high office to enhance improperly in any way business interests or charitable enterprises. Congressman H. R. Gross (Rep. of Iowa) was ready to move against Fortas with impeachment proceedings.

On May 14, 1969, Fortas became the forty-first Supreme Court Justice to resign or retire. He wrote letters of resignation to Chief Justice Warren (who had stayed on when Fortas' name had been withdrawn in 1968) and President Nixon. In his letter to the Chief Justice, Fortas again denied any improper behavior but stated that the public controversy over his relationship with the Wolfson Family Foundation would "adversely affect the work and position of the Court." It had therefore become his duty to resign "to enable the Court to proceed with its vital work free from extraneous stress." The President accepted the resignation.

With Chief Justice Warren having announced his retirement at the end of the October, 1968, term (which ended June 23, 1969), President Nixon would now have two positions on the Court which Lyndon B. Johnson had hoped to fill in 1968 before the end of his presidential term.

On May 21, 1969, Nixon announced the nomination of Warren Earl Burger to succeed Earl Warren as Chief Justice of the United States. A judge of the United States Circuit Court of Appeals for the District of Columbia, to which he had been appointed by President Eisenhower in 1956, Burger was a Minnesota Republican. In just two weeks after his nomination by Nixon, Burger was unanimously endorsed by the Senate Judiciary Committee, and on June 9, 1969, approved by the Senate by a 74 to 3 vote.

President Nixon announced the nomination of Clement F.

Haynesworth, Jr., a judge of the 4th Circuit Court of Appeals, to the Fortas position in August, 1969. The 57-year-old South Carolinian had been a Democrat who had supported Eisenhower in 1952 and 1956 and been appointed by him to the Court of Appeals in 1957. In 1964 Haynesworth changed his registration to Republican. His background was of the "old South," and his nomination was not well received by civil rights advocates. It was generally believed that the appointment of Haynesworth was reflective of Nixon's "Southern strategy," designed to develop political strength for the national Republican party in the South. Nixon's choice, too, was to restore balance to constitutional interpretation by placing another judicial conservative, like Chief Justice Warren Burger, on the high bench so often characterized by Nixon as too liberal.

Almost immediately a question of judicial ethics arose with Haynesworth's nomination. Sensitive to the kinds of things which had emerged from the Fortas controversy, Senate critics were quick to examine the financial holdings of Haynesworth. It was soon learned that Haynesworth had owned a one-seventh interest in a North Carolina vending company that had vending contracts with two textile manufacturing firms. In 1963 Haynesworth had sat on a case before his court (*Darlington Manufacturing Company v. NLRB*) involving a subsidiary of the company in which Haynesworth had the financial interest, small though it was. His court's ruling for the company in that case against the NLRB now became the subject of controversy before Senator Eastland's Senate Judiciary Committee, which began hearings on Haynesworth's nomination in mid-September. During the hearings another issue soon arose. In 1967 Haynesworth had purchased 1,000 shares of stock in a corporation a month after he and two other judges of his court had heard arguments in a case involving the company. A short time later, Haynesworth concurred in an opinion, written by one of the other two judges, affirming a lower court decision that had been favorable to the company. The relative impact on the value of the stock by the court decision was of no significance, but the fact that Haynesworth had purchased the stock while the company was awaiting his court's decision did appear meaningful to some Senate critics.

The Fortas case had obviously left its mark. Fortas had a pro-civil rights and pro-union reputation but had gone down to defeat because of his financial involvements as a Justice. Some who had seen misconduct on Fortas' part in his financial affairs now found themselves defending Haynesworth on the grounds that his financial involvement in companies was very minor. Civil rights advocates saw in this issue a chance to build their case against a man they felt not sympathetic to their cause. Pro-union people saw in Haynesworth's affiliations with Southern textile manufacturing firms, most of them extremely hostile to union organizational attempts, both as an attorney and purchaser of stock, an opportunity to stress Haynesworth's alleged anti-union bias.

The President, who did not personally know Haynesworth but who had selected him on the judgment of his Attorney-General John Mitchell on the basis of age, judicial experience, and constitutional conservatism, was not happy at the fight building up. In a press conference devoted almost entirely to the issue on October 20, Nixon defended Haynesworth's integrity and deplored the attacks on his nominee, saying that ". . . if Judge Haynesworth's philosophy leans to the conservative side, in my view that recommends him to me. I think that the Court needs balance, and I think that the Court needs a man who is a conservative—and I use the term not in terms of economics, but conservative, as I said of Judge Burger, conservative in respect of his attitude towards the Constitution . . ." The President then went on,

> It is the judge's responsibility, and the Supreme Court's responsibility, to interpret the Constitution and to interpret the law, and not to go beyond that in putting his own socio-economic philosophy into decisions in a way that goes beyond the law, beyond the Constitution.

Despite the allegations made against Haynesworth in his financial dealing, the President found him to be an honest man, "a lawyer's lawyer and a judge's judge." The President would stand by him until he was confirmed. To stress the impartiality of his own judgment about Haynesworth's qualifications, Nixon stated that his "acquaintance with Judge Haynesworth can only be casual. If he would walk into this room, I am afraid I wouldn't recognize him." Indeed, Nixon had never met Haynesworth.

Nixon insisted that he would not withdraw Haynesworth's name even though a close vote seemed imminent. The debate over Haynesworth centered primarily on the ethics of his judgment in sitting on cases where his financial interests could be said to coincide. Civil rights and pro-labor union leaders continued to press hard for his defeat. Debate in the Senate began on November 13 and lasted for a week.

On November 21, 1969, the vote was taken and Haynesworth was rejected by the Senate 55 to 45. Twenty-six Republicans, 18 Southern Democrats, and Democratic Senator Mike Gravel of Alaska voted for confirmation, but this time the conservative coalition did not have the numerical strength to dominate. Seventeen Republicans, defecting from Nixon's presidential leadership, joined 38 Democrats to compose the 55 Senate majority. For the first time since 1930 the Senate had defeated a presidential nomination to the Supreme Court.

Labor unions had mounted a strong campaign against Haynesworth and much credit was due to the lobbying efforts in the Senate by the AFL-CIO. But it is clear that a majority of the Senate who had voted against Haynesworth did so because of his having tried cases in which he had some, albeit indirect and minor, personal interests. The focus was on the qualifications of the President's nominee, not on the *right* of a President to *have* his nominee confirmed. But Attorney-General John Mitchell took the Senate action as a senatorial breach of presidential authority when he said that the defeat was a "reflection of the failure of some in the Senate to recognize the President's constitutional prerogatives." This charge can be singled out as the beginning of the separation of powers argument which erupted over Nixon's next nominee to the Court, G. Harrold Carswell of Florida.

On January 19, 1970, Nixon nominated Judge Carswell, a Georgia Democrat who had become a Florida Republican, to the Supreme Court. President Eisenhower had appointed Carswell to the federal bench in northern Florida in 1958, and

Nixon had elevated him to the 5th Circuit Court of Appeals in May, 1969. The White House issued a statement that Carswell had been cleared of any possible conflicts of interest, and Carswell stated that he himself owned no stocks or bonds. In 1948 Carswell had made a white supremacist speech while making an unsuccessful try for a seat in the Georgia state legislature, but he now repudiated his position of twenty-two years before. His Court of Appeals, however, had recently and unanimously made two anti-desegregation decisions which had been overruled by the Supreme Court. The NAACP was not at all happy about the appointment, and neither was AFL-CIO President George Meany.

The Senate debated the nomination on March 13, 16, 17, and 18. Proponents based their arguments on Carswell's being "good enough" for the Court and opponents on his alleged mediocrity. Defending Carswell, Republican Senator Roman Hruska of Nebraska said that mediocrity was entitled to "a little representation . . . we can't have all Brandeises and Frankfurters and Cardozos." On March 25, 1970, Senator Bayh of Indiana released a study that showed that Carswell's decisions as a federal district court judge had been overruled on appeal an inordinate amount of times, and by March 26, 31 Senators (26 Democrats and 5 Republicans) had announced their intention of voting against the President's choice. Fifteen Democrats and 24 Republicans announced for Carswell and 30 (16 Democrats and 14 Republicans) were as yet uncommitted. Clearly Carswell's nomination was in trouble.

Why this time? The issue centered on Carswell's behavior before the Senate Judiciary Committee. Mindful of the issues in the Fortas and Haynesworth cases, the Senate was not going to be bulldozed into letting anyone who was not "pure as the driven snow" slip by. Carswell's forthrightness over his personal activities had been called into question. As a United States Attorney in 1955 and 1956, he had helped incorporate a segregated golf club of which he was a director. He had told the Senate Committee that the segregation motive of the other originators of the club was unknown to him. On the evening previous to that statement, on January 26, he had discussed the issue of the club with two attorneys (one from

Florida and the other a Washington attorney who had been on the American Bar Association committee that had found Carswell "qualified"). That evening Carswell had admitted to them that he had been an incorporator of the club, but on the following day in his appearance before the Senate Committee he acted uncertain of it and in fact had denied that he had been an incorporator of an officer of the club. He was reminded of his role as incorporator by Senator Edward Kennedy, who showed Carswell a copy of the corporate charter with Carswell's name on it. Carswell's uncertainty in January changed to a possible lack of candor in March when the story of the evening conversation of January 26 was broken in the *New York Times* on March 25, 1970. What had appeared to have been a relatively safe nomination in January, with the Senate loathe to have a third hassle over the personnel of the Supreme Court, now began to fester.

Democratic Senator Young of Ohio called Carswell a bigot and pointed out a number of "other distinguished Southern jurists" whom Nixon could well have named to the Court. Playing on the theme previously suggested by Senator Bayh, Young mentioned that 58.8 per cent of Carswell's decisions had been reversed on appeal, three times the average for all federal district judges in the country and two and one half times the average for those in Carswell's jurisdiction. Carswell's defenders did their best to offset the charges of racism and mediocrity that had been leveled at the Florida judge.

Republican Senators Edward Brooke of Massachusetts and Robert Dole of Kansas, representing the Republican liberal opposition to and conservative support for Carswell, engaged in debate over Carswell's qualifications, as the controversy became more acrimonious. Carswell's major champion, Republican Senator Edward Gurney of Florida, stood fast by his state's adopted son, arguing that Carswell's appointment would offer "very real and substantive encouragement to many . . . who have been worried about the direction of the Court in recent years."

But on March 31, 1970, the focal point of the argument shifted from solely that of Carswell's qualifications to that of the President's "right" to have him confirmed. Harking back to Attorney-General John Mitchell's charge at Senate recalcitrance on the occasion of its rejection of Haynesworth, President Nixon sent a letter in support of Carswell to Republican Senator William Saxbe of Ohio. After defending Carswell's qualifications, the President went on to say:

> What is centrally at issue in this nomination is the constitutional responsibility of the President to appoint members of the Court—and whether this responsibility can be frustrated by those who wish to substitute their own philosophy or their own subjective judgment for that of the one person entrusted by the Constitution with the power of appointment. The question arises whether I, as President of the United States, shall be accorded the same right of choice in naming Supreme Court Justices which has been accorded to my predecessors of both parties.
>
> I respect the right of any Senator to differ with my selection. It would be extraordinary if the President and 100 Senators were to agree unanimously as to any nominees. The fact remains, under the Constitution it is the duty of the President to appoint and of the Senate to advise and consent. But if the Senate attempts to substitute its judgment as to who should be appointed, the traditional constitutional balance is in jeopardy and the duty of the President under the Constitution is impaired.
>
> For this reason, the current debate transcends the wisdom of this or any other appointment. If the charges against Judge Carswell were supportable, the issue would be wholly different. But if, as I believe, the charges are baseless, what is at stake is the preservation of the traditional constitutional relationships of the President and the Congress.

The President altered the course of the debate by this letter. First, he had indirectly charged those who opposed Carswell with doing so in order to maintain their own political and judicial philosophy. The fact of the matter was that a number of Carswell's opponents were also strict constructionists but yet were extremely wary of Carswell's testimony before the Senate Committee. The fact that he had not proven to be an "outstanding jurist" was not so much the problem as the possibility that he was a good deal less than a "good jurist." Second, the President had acted petulantly in seeking to have his appointees confirmed as had previous Presidents. The truth of the matter was that of the total of 129 nominees named to the Court since the beginning of the Republic, one in five had failed, for various reasons, to gain confirmation. True enough only the nominations of John J. Parker and Clement F. Haynesworth, Jr., had failed to win Senate approval in this century. But statistically, Presidents do not have a 100 per cent rating in Supreme Court nominations. Third, the President had erred in making the statement that it was his duty to appoint and the duty of the Senate to "advise and consent." Read in context of the Carswell nomination, it appeared that the President was saying the Senate had no constitutional right to deny his appointment. If the Senate did so, constitutional balance would be thrown out, when in truth, if the Senate had no right to reject a presidential nominee, that in itself would be a cause of imbalance.

On April 6, 1970, the Senate first voted on Senator Bayh's motion to recommit the nomination of Carswell to the Senate Judiciary Committee. This was a most unusual thing to do with a presidential nomination that had been voted out of committee. Successful motions to recommit legislative bills are usually a parliamentary way of killing off such bills, since they hardly ever emerge once recommitted. If Carswell's nomination were recommitted, the intent of denying him the appointment would have been obvious, but then again the issues would not have been clearly resolved once and for all. With only 4 Senators not voting, Bayh's motion to recommit failed 52 to 44. When the vote on the actual confirmation was taken, Carswell was defeated 51 to 45. The conservative coalition had broken down again, and Nixon had his second bitter defeat at the hands of the Senate. There is little doubt that, although the question of Carswell's alleged racist attitudes and his judicial integrity were important factors, the issue of the President's prerogatives had also come into play. No one can know if the vote might not have been the same had Nixon not written a letter which made him so vulnerable. But it did indeed add another dimension to the issues on the Carswell nomination. The fact that the Republican and Southern Democratic defenders of Nixon's choice for the Court did not attempt to defend the so-called presidential authority in the matter speaks for itself. The constitutional issue of the separation of powers was a very live one and, more than likely, a decisive one.

Shortly after his defeat at the hands of the Senate, the President sent the name of federal judge Harry Blackmun of Minnesota, a long-time friend of Chief Justice Burger, to the Senate as Associate Justice. The Senate quickly confirmed this choice, and the Court turned the corner toward a more conservative view.

When one considers how much of an impact the decisions of the Supreme Court have had since the New Deal, to say nothing of the recital on the preceding pages, it is difficult to conclude that the Court is an isolated, purely legalistic, branch of government. The members of the Court bring to their office their past political experience and biases and do not operate in a legal vacuum. Even the greatest Chief Justices were actively and controversially involved in politics before being appointed to the highest judicial post in the land, including John Marshall, Roger Taney, Morrison Waite, William Howard Taft, Charles Evans Hughes, and, of course, Earl Warren. This kind of political experience was undoubtedly an asset, not a liability, in making the essentially political decisions often demanded of the Court.

The Constitution vests judicial power in "one Supreme Court, and such inferior courts as the Congress may, from time to time, ordain and establish." So reads Article III. The Constitution does not say how large the Court shall be, nor what the limits of its appellate jurisdiction shall be. These things the Constitution leaves to the Congress to decide. The Congress, then, has a good deal to say about the scope of judicial activity, although the judges have tenure (on good behavior and subject to impeachment) and their positions cannot be vacated during their lifetime, nor their salaries reduced during their continuance in office. The Supreme Court has original jurisdiction in "all cases affecting ambassadors, other public ministers and consuls, and those in which a state shall be a party," but in other types of federal jurisdiction, as briefly outlined in Article III, Section 2, "the supreme court shall have appellate jurisdiction, both as to law and fact with such exceptions, and *under such regulations as the Congress shall make."* (Italics added.) Thus, despite the existence of judicial review, which deals with interpretation of state and federal laws in relation to the Constitution, the Congress does indeed have much to say about what the courts can and cannot do. In fact, the entire federal court structure is predicated upon Congress.

The Federal Courts are organized in an hierarchical manner with the Supreme Court at the very top. The Supreme Court has no disciplinary power over the lower court judges, who also hold office for life (on good behavior) and whose salaries likewise cannot be reduced while in office. The Supreme Court can neither demote nor promote a federal judge. This is the function of the executive branch.

Federal Courts are divided into two major categories. First, there are the legislative courts, created by Congress to deal with matters that require a specialized forum. Such are the court of claims, the court of customs and patent appeals, the customs courts, the tax courts, and the court of military appeals. The judges in these courts do not hold tenure positions but are appointed only for set terms and their decisions are reviewable by one of the second category of courts, the constitutional courts.

There are three major constitutional courts, the district court system consisting of 91 district courts, 4 territorial courts (including the District of Columbia, and at least one in each state), the 11 Courts of Appeals (one of which is for the District of Columbia), and the United States Supreme Court. The district courts have original jurisdiction over cases involving the United States Constitution, acts of Congress, or treaties with other nations; suits between residents of different states where the amount of money involved is over $10,000; admiralty or maritime jurisdiction; cases in which the United States government is a party; cases brought by a state against residents of another state; cases between a state, or its residents, and foreign states or citizens; and cases between two or more states. The Courts of Appeals have appellate jurisdiction in cases brought to them from the district courts and also on appeals on rulings made by the federal regulatory commissions. The Supreme Court has appellate jurisdiction over cases in the lower Federal Courts, the decisions of the highest courts in the individual states that raise federal questions of constitutionality, and the legislative courts. It has, furthermore, wide discretion on what it will in fact hear.

District and Courts of Appeal judges can become involved in the politics of the nation just as much as Supreme Court Justices. Judge Medina's deeds and words as the presiding justice several years ago in the trial of the Communist Party leaders in the United States, out of which rose the Dennis case, formed the basis for much political controversy in the nation at that time. Judge Learned Hand's expression "clear and probable danger" became a byword in American politics in his ruling on that same case on appeal from Medina's court. Judges' activities in labor disputes, seizing of industries at government request, and in their handling of cases with international repercussions thrust them into the political process, whether they approve of such movement or not.

That the Congress is very much aware of the political nature of the court system can be seen by the reluctance of the Democratically controlled Congress during the Eisenhower Administration to provide for much-needed judgeships in the

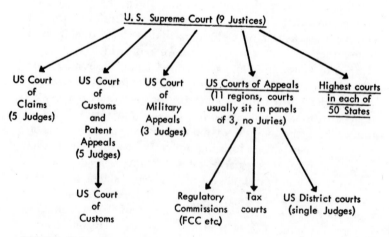

FIGURE 10

federal system. The Congress waited until a Democrat, John F. Kennedy, occupied the White House before creating these new judgeships so that they could be filled by deserving Democrats rather than by Republicans appointed by Eisenhower. Former Congressman Thornberry, a Southern supporter on the Rules Committee of Kennedy's programs, was rewarded with one of these judgeships. In the brief period of the late President's Administration, 117 Democrats went on the federal bench, out of a total 128 Kennedy appointees.

Now that the political nature of the courts has been established, despite the aggravation that such a label might engender in the minds of the members of the bar, it is time to review just what the Supreme Court has done to earn its rightful place as an integral part of the political process in the over-all American political system.

The first Court under Chief Justice John Jay (1789–1795) was uncertain of its role in the new government established by the 1787 Constitution. Yet it was mindful of the fact that what it did would establish the precedent for things to come. Jay refused to supply President Washington with an advisory opinion and ever since then the Court has not been looked to for such opinions. Jay's Court also ruled that the Constitution did not forbid a citizen of one state from suing another state and thus the Chisholm case led to the adoption of the Eleventh Amendment to plug a loophole in the Constitution.

It remained for John Marshall to harden the lines of the Court that had been most fluid prior to his assuming the position of Chief Justice in 1801. He held this role until 1835 and his decisions, for they appeared to be his more than the rest of the Court's whose views he seemed to dominate by the force of his own personality, established the predominance of the national government over the states. Interestingly enough, Marshall had very little formal education and not much more legal training. But his contributions to constitutional law are the foundation for the establishment of national supremacy. His decisions were the work of the judicial politician, who led and demanded from his Supreme Court colleagues utmost loyalty. Almost all the opinions of his court were unanimous, and indeed Marshall's. In the thirty-four years of his reign as Chief Justice, he liberally construed the Constitution so as to uphold national power over states' rights. In several cases (*McCulloch v. Maryland,* 1819; *Cohens v. Virginia,* 1821; *Gibbons v. Ogden,* 1824; not to mention a host of others) Marshall rested his doctrine of national supremacy on the theory that the national government is the superior body to the states and it was the duty of the Court to see to it that the states did not infringe on the sovereignty of the national government.

Marshall left the Court in the era of Jacksonian democracy and Jackson appointed his close associate Roger Brooke Taney. A sixth-generation Marylander, the first Catholic ever to be Chief Justice, and the only Catholic on the Court during the first 100 years of the Republic, Taney was a Jacksonian, which in those days meant a states' rightist. But Taney could not personally control the other members of the court the way Marshall had and there were many divided opinions. The real battle raged between those who leaned toward the national commerce power and those who were inclined toward the broad interpretation of the police power of the states. Immigration and the liquor traffic were beginning to be problems and the states were starting to license the flow of liquor under their police power.

In 1837 the State of New York and the City of New York had a regulation under their police power to have ship masters give information to the city about incoming passengers upheld by the Supreme Court against a challenge that the rule infringed Congress' commerce power. In 1847 Taney ruled that the states could regulate all liquor traffic where they were concerned. But the shift to state power was only in degree and emphasis. In 1852 in the Genesee case, Taney ruled that the power of the national government extended to the Great Lakes. In Taney's time, property rights were still protected and national power still upheld, but with less unanimity and less emphasis on the power of the national government.

The major issue of the pre-Civil War Court was slavery, where emotionalism and sectionalism blurred the legal issues. The Southern states wanted federal legislation supporting their views and the Court in 1842 held that the federal government was indeed responsible for capturing escaped slaves. The *Strader v. Graham* case in 1851 ruled that slaves who had been taken from Kentucky into free territory and then returned to Kentucky were not legally free as far as the federal government was concerned. It was still left to the state having jurisdiction to decide which set of laws of which state applied, slave or free laws. The famous Dred Scott case in 1857 was decided by 5 Southerners and 4 Northerners. According to the Court at that time, a slave sojourning in free territory was not free, the Missouri Compromise of 1820 was unconstitutional (this was the first time a federal law was declared unconstitutional since *Marbury v. Madison*), and that Negroes were not citizens. No one can doubt that the Dred Scott decision had its political effect.

The Court has constantly been involved in political matters even though in theory the Court has tried to stay out of questions of political controversy where one of the two branches of government could decide matters.

The slavery issue was tied with the issue of the nature of the union. The Civil War was fought over this latter question with the North espousing the cause of national power to save the union, although up to the actual beginning of the war the North had been espousing the right of the states to ignore national slave fugitive laws under *their* sovereign rights. After the war the North lined up for states' rights with the growth and industrialization of the national economy.

One reason was the threat to economic interests in the North from the national government, causing the North to espouse states' rights as opposed to national regulation in the field of the economy. As workers began to demand regulation and intervention by government to protect themselves against the power of management, management was thus able to forestall national regulation because the occupants of the White House at the time were reflections of the dominant economic forces in the nation. The first attempt to get the national government into the field of regulation was really made in 1906 and 1907 by Congress with bills to regulate child labor under the national commerce power. No action was taken by Congress, although the Supreme Court did up-hold the right of the Congress to regulate lotteries in 1903, food and drugs in 1911, and to legislate against interstate traffic in prostitution in 1911, all under the commerce power. In 1918 the Supreme Court, under Chief Justice Edward D. White, in a 5–4 decision (*Hammer v. Dagenhart*) ruled that a federal law forbidding child labor in business engaged in interstate commerce was unconstitutional, because *prohibition* was not covered by the term *regulation*. In 1922 the Taft Court ruled in *Bailey v. Drexel Furniture Company* that the taxing power could not be used by the Congress to cut down state power and state jurisdiction because the power to tax was for the purpose of raising revenue rather than regulating some industry in interstate commerce.

The fight over the right of the national government to enter fields previously the domain of the states reached its peak in the New Deal days of Franklin D. Roosevelt. The conservatives of the day looked to the Court to protect property rights and when FDR came into office the Court was made up of nine rather elderly men. Indeed, when Hoover was running for the Presidency in 1928, William Howard Taft had stated that he would stay on as Chief Justice so that Hoover (whom he termed a radical) would not be able to appoint a left-winger. When Taft was convinced that Charles Evans Hughes would replace him, he resigned in 1930. Hughes had good conservative credentials, having represented many large corporations before the Court.

Four Justices, Sutherland, McReynolds, Van Devanter, and Butler, known as the four horsemen, formed a conservative clique to defend property rights and the power of the states as opposed to expansion of national power. The other four, Stone, Roberts, Cardozo, and Brandeis, usually fell on the opposite side. From decisions in the early 1930's it looked as though New Deal laws might have a chance to be declared constitutionally valid under the commerce clause. Either Hughes or Justice Roberts (who had a tendency to swing the other way) could block or accept New Deal legislation.

By 1935, federal legislation along these lines had worked its way through the court system. But the Court began to knock down law after law as violations of the Constitution. In 1935 in *Panama Refining v. Ryan*, the Court by an 8–1 decision struck down a federal law as being a violation of separation of powers. A compulsory railroad retirement pension scheme under the commerce power was declared invalid by a 5–4 decision, and on May 27, 1935 (a date known affectionately as Black Monday), the Court invalidated no less than three acts. Congress was being blocked by a recalcitrant Court. After his sweeping victory in 1936 Roosevelt hit on a scheme that would have added enough justices to the Court to ensure approval of New Deal legislation, provided the new justices were carefully selected for their views.

According to FDR's plan, a new justice was to be appointed for every one over 70 who did not retire at that age, with a maximum number of 15 on the Court. Although the bill would have been perfectly constitutional (remember the Constitution sets no limit on the size of the court and it has varied from 5 to 10 members since its beginning), the furor that was raised in the country is good testimony to the sacrosanct position the Court holds. Granted FDR's position was not very strong (Brandeis was over 70 and he was usually for the legislation that came before the Court), and his political tactics in springing this on his own party leadership so suddenly and without warning were rather imprudent, yet he won the war when the Court began to approve legislation by a 5–4 vote, with Hughes and Roberts abandoning the four horsemen.

There was no "packing of the Court" but the point had been well taken. The Social Security Act, the Wagner Act, and other types of social welfare legislation were upheld. Since that time, no major act of the Congress under the commerce power, on which rests much of this kind of legislation, has ever been declared unconstitutional. The tone of the Court had changed, just as the direction of the United States had. Only because the Court had sanctioned such legislation in the late 1930's has the Congress continued to pass further extensions of the welfare state. In fact, because the Court says it is all right, the Congress looks upon this as blanket approval for other types of action resting on the same reasoning.

This is the political side of the judicial branch. It is, without question, an integral part of the political process. The judges' political role is not a matter of choice but of function. Just as with legislators and Presidents, the judges represent sets of values that they themselves must accommodate. They too must make choices and are subject to the stresses and strains in society just as anyone else. Or, as someone once said, "They read the election returns too." Any attempt by the judicial branch to separate itself from the political arena would be doomed to failure. In fact, when the Court has ruled that something was a political question and not subject to its scrutiny, that in itself was a political act. Deciding that something was political is political in and of itself. And then, sometime later, a Court could well change its mind. As noted in an earlier chapter, this happened with regard to legislative apportionment.

In a series of cases the Warren Court stood firm for the separation of church and state by forbidding in 1962 the recital of a New York State Regents prayer in public schools (*Engel v. Vitale*), and in 1963 forbidding the recitation of the Lord's Prayer and any Bible reading in a public school (*Abington School District v. Schempp* and *Murray v. Curlett*). Both of these areas, the question of malapportionment and separation of church and state, have been the cause of great concern to the Congress. Amendments to the Constitution that would in effect negate the actions of the Court have been introduced. Time will tell whether such amendments will get very far. The one-man, one-vote principle has been widely incorporated into new state laws and the effects of the decisions have reached into all types of legislative bodies. Except for a few hearty stalwarts, the validity of the Court's prayer ruling has been generally accepted too. (Anyway, the last ruling can be virtually ignored in any community that tacitly decides to ignore it. Unless there is overt action on the part of anyone protesting the recitation of a prayer, it can go on as usual.)

In the areas of racial controversy, no one can deny that the Court has been an extremely vital cog in the political machinery. In 1896 the Supreme Court in *Plessy v. Ferguson* ruled that separate but equal facilities were perfectly constitutional in the various states. Transportation facilities in this instance, and therefore any other type of public facility by implication, could also be segregated according to race. The Fourteenth Amendment did not guarantee social equality, said the Court. But in 1954, with the wording of the Fourteenth Amendment unchanged, but with a different American society, with different views, different forces at play, and different tactics being employed by those whose rights were denied to them, the Supreme Court stated that such separation of the races was inherently unequal to begin with and thus a violation of the Fourteenth Amendment. The case of *Brown v. the Board of Education of Topeka* was a landmark decision in American history. A unanimous Court overruled the 1896 decision. The political repercussions are still being heard and will be for years and generations to come.

Many areas of the Bill of Rights could be examined for the effects of the Court's decisions but this is not a text on constitutional law. The simple truth is that the Court and the entire judicial system play a role in the never-ending group conflicts in the United States, and the judicial branch is one phase, sometimes an unheralded one, in the political process. In the current battle for civil rights and the continuing one for civil liberties, the present Supreme Court has taken a rather consistent position in defense of the rights of individuals as opposed to governmental action against them for unpopular views or unpopular acts. It has consistently held to its position on integration, knocking down scores of state laws designed to circumvent the basic ruling in 1954.

The Court has also made several important decisions aimed at protecting the civil liberties of those accused of crime. Indeed, many law enforcement officers have claimed that such rulings have had the effect of shackling police departments in their interrogation of witnesses and searching for evidence. Be that as it may, it is apparent in today's American society that the Supreme Court is the nation's exemplar and disseminator of democratic values (as it interprets them) and has had this role thrust on it. The country has become accustomed to look to the courts for guidelines, standards, and ideals—goals toward which communal action ought to strive. In fact, probably more than the Presidency, the Supreme Court since 1954 has been an educator of the nation's mores. The edicts of the Court, by and large, lend prestige to the legitimacy of statutes and the Constitution and thus command respect and obedience on the part of the citizens.

The Courts are able to go far, probably further than either of the other two branches, in affecting the applicability of the Constitution of 1787 to contemporary society. Before the Congress would really clip the wings of the Court by either legislative or amendment action, it would have to have had numerous important reasons to do so. Since 1954, some could argue such has been the case. But the Court still stands, resolute in its position as defender of the right, as it sees the right. Thus, the only effective check on the Court seems to be judicial restraint. For even reliance on the presidential power of appointment to the Court as a means of restraint can backfire. There is no guarantee that a Justice will always be consistent or even decide cases the way the President who appointed him would like.

The judicial branch has less institutional checks than the two other branches and fewer extraconstitutional and political obstacles stand in the way of the Courts. Thus, it goes without saying that Americans have put much faith in the third branch of government. Even though the Court has fewer built-in checks upon it, the judicial is indeed "the least dangerous branch" of all.

Ten

Conclusion

I N S T U D Y I N G any phenomenon or set of relationships as vast and complex as the government of the United States—or any political system for that matter—one has a choice of procedures. One may begin with some effort to characterize the whole in broad and inclusive terms for general orientation, and then break the whole down into its component parts for more detailed analysis of its parts and interrelations. Or one can reverse the procedure, as the authors have done in this little volume. One then begins with the parts, their special characteristics, their contribution to the total operation of the system, and thereby builds toward a cumulative over-all picture. Such a process of segmental description and cumulation is not sufficient, however, in and of itself. It must still become the basis for a final effort at over-all characterization and synthesis. Such an effort is the basic purpose of this chapter.

Another way of describing this kind of synthesizing process is currently fashionable in the literature on comparative governmental institutions in political science, namely, model building. A model is a somewhat simplified representation of the thing being represented. Its purpose is to portray, more clearly than is possible through examination of the phenomenon itself, its actual form and operation. Model building is both a learning and verificational experience. One cannot build a model without learning in the process a good deal more about the thing being modeled than one knew at the outset. Furthermore, unless that learning process has been successful, that is, unless one *has* gained an accurate understanding of the thing itself in the course of construction, the model will be inaccurate and useless.

These comments on model building apply to similarly labeled efforts in the social sciences as they do to the building of architectural or mechanical models. A well-constructed model of a political system and its internal process should confirm and supplement the knowledge of the model builders (or users) about the functioning of the system, because it *does* represent reality in an accurate if somewhat simplified way. The process of building and applying the model to the study of systems should also be a process of verifying the accuracy of one's understanding of political systems generally.

This type of synthesizing process sought through model building is the concern of this section. The obvious entrée into the process is the question, What, after all, is a political system? In simplest terms it is a set of arrangements and procedures through which a community makes the various decisions necessary to ensure its own survival as an organized community, to deal with disequilibria that threaten its functioning, to allocate benefits and deprivations among its citizens when such allocation must be accomplished authoritatively, and to ensure the day-to-day management of the increasingly complex machinery for the operation of a modern industrial nation (if the community being examined resembles the United States or the Western democracies).

So far so good. But of what does this "set of arrangements and procedures" consist? In the narrowest sense it might be thought to consist largely if not entirely of the formal organs of government—executive, legislative, judicial, and administrative, plus, more or less by courtesy, political parties, pressure groups, and similar quasi-legal and extra-legal entities as discussed in the foregoing chapters. Certainly these institutions do represent, as it were, the operational "cutting edge" of the system as it discharges its various functions in a day-to-day or year-to-year sense. However, as has been stressed earlier, these elements also draw their frame of reference from the Constitution itself. The framers of the American Constitution, for example, did not merely create the standard organs of governance already listed but they contrived some rather special (and in many ways unique) arrangements for their operation and relations with each other. Hence, the process of decision-making is shaped in special ways in America that differentiate it from other democratic processes operating through apparent quite similar sets of executive and legislative organs.

Institutional and constitutional arrangements are still not the whole story as becomes quite clear when one looks more closely at institutional operation itself. The American Congress, though superficially like the British Parliament, differs fundamentally in many aspects of its operation and in the way it discharges its part of the decision-making process. These differences are by no means all traceable to differences of constitutional framework on the two sides of the Atlantic. Neither the British nor the American constitution says anything about political parties, yet the existence of parties in both countries shapes, to a large extent, the workings and contributions of their respective legislative organs and has molded them in basically different ways.

That parties should have an impact on legislative operation is hardly surprising, but why this impact should differ so sharply in these two countries is by no means as clear. Why should American parties be loose, relatively lacking in internal discipline, and therefore incapable of imposing strict discipline on legislators, whereas British parties are so much more cohesive, disciplined, and hence capable of structuring the legislative process in terms of marshaled party combat? Textbooks on comparative government have traditionally provided a series of institutional and constitutional answers to this question, but such answers are, in the last analysis, not good enough. One is forced to probe more deeply into attitudes and motivations in the minds of party members—attitudes and motivations they have derived from the whole milieu in which their respective political systems operate.

The British M.P., when elected, carries into Parliament with him not merely the awareness that the party chose him and can deny him the party label at the next election, but a deep-seated conviction that loyalty to party is of prime importance and that deference to party leadership is both necessary and legitimate. On the other hand, the American Congressman, besides his awareness that the party had much *less* to do with his election than in the case of his cousin across the sea, carries about a different set of assumptions. To him independence of thought stands higher than party loyalty in the priority scale. Whether or not to follow party leadership is a matter of choice, not of duty—choice based on policy preference, constituency concern, and indeed personal self-interest.

These underlying assumptions and attitudes, and a host of others that could have been used equally well for illustration and which might be collectively labeled the nation's *political culture,* obviously are of enormous importance in shaping the ways individuals see their roles in the system, and thus in shaping the ways in which the institutions themselves operate. In other words, identical offices in two different political communities—that is, identical in every legal-constitutional respect—are almost certain to function differently, in large part because the incumbents will bring to their offices differing culturally acquired perceptions of how they should be discharged.

This impact of a nation's political culture has only begun to be noted systematically by political scientists. Noting the work of the cultural anthropologists, it is obvious that any organized self-conscious community will, to some degree, develop a unique set of beliefs, ways of perceiving the world, of ordering priorities, and characteristic ways of behaving. Doubtless in some cases it will be possible to find historical roots for a given belief or attitude. Such a line of exploration is of little concern here, but the existence of such patterns, however difficult to trace and catalog, must be taken as a basic feature of any political system.

Intertwined with this notion of political culture is the notion of political "value" assumptions as characteristic of a society and infusing its governmental arrangements. Some students have lumped values and cultural beliefs into the one category labeled *political culture*. It is probably useful to keep the two distinct for analytical purposes. By values we mean assertions about the "oughts" of political arrangements —full popular participation "ought" to be provided for, basic freedoms of expression "ought" to be accorded to all, immunity from arbitrary punishment or detention "ought" to be the right of all, and so forth.

With values thus separately categorized, the elements in the political culture then became beliefs about the most effective way in which the system can achieve or preserve these assertions of value and conduct its business generally. For instance, Americans believe that the value of popular participation and the avoidance of tyranny can best be fostered under a constitutional scheme resting upon a federal decentralization of power and a functional separation of powers. Only thus, they assume, can overconcentration of power and its subsequent abuse be avoided. The British, who clearly share the American devotion to popular participation and abhorrence of tyranny, seek these ends by quite different means—equally sanctified by their political culture—among which are a tradition of self-restraint on the part of rulers and an emphasis on collective rather than one-man leadership.

The final major ingredient in the political system of any community, and above all of any advanced, modern nation, is the pattern of interests (as we might call it, to distinguish it from the more specific category of interest groups discussed in Chapter 3). *Pattern of interests* as a phrase casts the net widely enough to encompass any and all groupings in the society with political significance, however marginal, from the most formal and highly organized, to the least articulate, least self-conscious collections of people who share a common need, disability, or goal. Interest groups *per se* are often economic in basis, though they may have other bases as well. Stretching beyond the most tangible and visible of interests is a vast panorama of regional interests, racial and ethnic groups, classes, and categories as amorphous as all of the poor, all of the isolated aged, all of the parents or prospective parents of draftees, all of the consumers of this or that key commodity, all of the potential beneficiaries of a new medical insurance or social welfare scheme, and so forth and so on limitlessly.

These are integral parts of the political system in several

senses. The organized interests petition government regularly in quest of aid or immunity, action or inaction. They know what they want and where and how to get it. In this sense, and also in terms of their actual inclusion on advisory panels (to say nothing of the cooptation of their personnel into actual government office), they are virtually a part of the governmental structure. The less organized and the unorganized groups, the less articulate and the inarticulate, unselfconscious groups also shape the political system's operation by generating problems for solution and setting limits to politically possible solution of other problems. They are part of the pattern of interests and thus an ingredient in the overall political system.

Thus far a catalog has been made of the major elements in the political system which the model must take into account. The pieces for assembling the working model of how the system operates have, as it were, been laid out on the workbench. This operating or dynamic side of the business one might label the political *process* to distinguish it from the catalog of elements comprising the political *system*. Into the model of the political process one should be able to fit and synthesize the various elements in the American governmental structure, which were discussed in the earlier chapters of this book.

The process part of the model, for which the authors borrow some elements, with apologies, from Gabriel Almond,[1] envisions government as a two-way flow. From the groups and interests constituting the political community emanates an upward flow of demands upon government, evidences of dissatisfaction, manifestations of opposition, and so forth—in short, messages requesting the government to do or not do something. These demands are articulated in countless ways through the fabric of a free society. They take the form, as just noted, of specific petitions or requests from interest groups. These are the easiest of all for government to deal with, because they are relatively narrow and specific, usually directly or indirectly economic rather than ideological, and

---

[1] Gabriel Almond and James S. Coleman, *The Politics of The Developing Areas* (Princeton: Princeton University Press, 1960), Introduction.

hence subject to compromise and adjustment. The less-organized the interest, the more general and diffuse its demands, and by the same token, the more difficult to cope with. The least articulate and self-conscious groups tend to generate the most diffuse and difficult cues of all to interpret. Such messages consist of vague—or as with Negro ghetto riots—perhaps very powerful evidences of general dissatisfaction and unrest, which can only with great difficulty, insight, and ingenuity be translated into concrete policies.

The mass of demands upon government is channeled upward through legislators, administrators, and executive officials —and courts at times—directly, or indirectly as these officeholders glean evidence of them from news columns, letters to the editor, survey results, economic indicators, publicly and privately collected statistics, riots, and in countless other ways. The next step in the process is for the organs of government, the political parties, the legislative bodies, the various elements in the bureaucracy, the executive, and again the courts, to aggregate these demands into acceptable policy.

As has been shown, Congress in theory, and to a considerable extent in practice, is the receiving institution for these demands charged with primary responsibility for resolving them into policy decisions. As they flow into the legislative branch in the form of bills and resolutions, they are channeled to the subject matter committees where much of the actual aggregating is done. However, the Rules Committee in the House, the party leadership in both houses, and even the processes of floor consideration contribute to the final output.

Congress cannot be viewed in isolation in its discharge of this aggregative function. On the one hand it does the job too imperfectly to be able to discharge it without assistance from other organs, and on the other hand even those portions of the task which it does accomplish well are still accomplished in collaboration with other parts of the government. As to the first point, the committee structure and general decentralization of power in the Congress tend to mean that some of the broadest issues of national policy, some of the most prevalent and general demands upon government, either get less attention in Congress than they might seem to deserve, or get treated in a fashion that is more segmented and discrete than the subject matter would appear to demand.

This implied value judgment about the working of Congress in policy-making will not escape challenge from some students of the legislative process. However, most observers, whether pro- or anti-Congress, at the very least will agree that the important synthesizing impact of the President through the legislative agenda and priority list he now characteristically submits is a major factor in shaping the final legislative output. In other words, the task of aggregating the demands upon government is shared between the legislative and executive branches. Congress does much of it, but the over-all shape of the resulting program of national policy invariably bears the unmistakable stamp of the President's influence, of his scale of priorities, of his perceptions of how the cloth should be cut to accommodate the demands being articulated. The President's contribution, it will be admitted by most, also supplements that of the legislative branch by keeping under surveillance the broader national needs and demands which Congress is less well equipped to meet without White House aid.

At the other end of the scale, the bureaucracy, also the recipient of a mass of demands from its special clienteles, does a share of the aggregating job that is less often recognized. Departments and agencies act as agents in the halls of Congress and at the White House, for the coalitions of supplicant interests they have assembled. The court system too, and the Supreme Court especially, has always been the focus for changing patterns of demand for protection and intervention. In John Marshall's day the proponents of national power secured the Court as ally, as did a different pattern of interests in the Jacksonian period and corporate wealth, in turn, during the last decades of the nineteenth century and the early years of the twentieth. In the present era, minority groups and the disadvantaged generally have been making most successful use of that channel for interest articulation and aggregation which the judiciary has always represented in the American political process.

It was noted earlier that governing was actually a *two-way* flow: of demands up to government, but also of decisions and exhortations from government to groups and general citizenry. In part this latter can be viewed in the formal terms of the communication downward represented by the publication of acts of Congress in the statute books and of administrative degrees in the Federal Register. However, more than this, it is also a negotiational process. Demands are made, for example, for federal aid to elementary education or for medical care for the aged. Such demands will invariably be accompanied, as they are articulated upward, by the opposition pleas they will generate as a result of their very articulation. At this point the role of government—key congressmen, White House staffers, departmental personnel—is to draw upon all the other sources of information available in order to gauge general citizen reaction and the attitudes of other groups marginally interested. Through public statements, issued study reports, introduced bills, and in other ways, these political leaders will try out possible bases of compromise and suggested ways of aggregating the demands and objections into a pattern acceptable enough for enactment. Having made such a suggestion, they will again gather in the fruits of the upflow of reaction. Eventually, through this process of negotiation accompanied by efforts by the President and others to mold opinion into patterns that will be more receptive to the kind of compromise deemed optimal, a solution will be hammered out.

The particular interlocking pattern of institutional roles which makes up the American government almost guarantees this sort of slow maturation of compromise, this painstaking construction of a consensus as basis for action. Given a different pattern of roles, a different constitutional ethos, and a different political culture, majority supported action (or something approaching it) rather than action on the basis of consensus can be possible. Labor governments in England have nationalized the steel industry (and Tories have denationalized it, or on the second round, redenationalized it after their opponents had renationalized it!!) without having to await this slow process of accumulating support to work itself out. The differences here between the systems are not black and white, but there are differences.

This then in essence is the simple model of the political process. Presumably it fits any political system in broad outline. Any national community—even the Soviet or the Communist Chinese—generates at least muffled demands from its citizenry that must somehow be met (or effectively thwarted, often a difficult process). Legislative, executive and administrative officials all have roles to play in receiving, sifting, compromising, and negotiating these demands, though precise roles and interrelationships of roles will differ from system to system. The primary focus in this book has been on the American way of doing this political job, which has been, over the years, surprisingly effective.

Appendix

The Constitution of the United States of America

We the People of the United States, in *Order to form a more perfect Union, establish Justice, insure domestic Tranquility, provide for the common defence, promote the general Welfare, and secure the Blessings of Liberty to ourselves and our Posterity, do ordain and establish this Constitution for the United States of America.*

ARTICLE I.

SECTION 1. All legislative Powers herein granted shall be vested in a Congress of the United States, which shall consist of a Senate and House of Representatives.

[NOTE: Items which have since been amended or superseded, as identified in the footnotes, are bracketed.]

SECTION 2. The House of Representatives shall be composed of Members chosen every second Year by the People of the several States, and the Electors in each State shall have the Qualifications requisite for Electors of the most numerous Branch of the State Legislature.

No Person shall be a Representative who shall not have attained to the Age of twenty-five Years, and been seven Years a Citizen of the United States, and who shall not, when elected, be an Inhabitant of that State in which he shall be chosen.

[Representatives and direct Taxes shall be apportioned among the several States which may be included within this Union, according to their respective Numbers, which shall be determined by adding to the whole Number of free Persons, including those bound to Service for a Term of Years, and excluding Indians not taxed, three fifths of all other Persons.]* The actual Enumeration shall be made within three Years after the first Meeting of the Congress of the United States, and within every subsequent Term of ten Years, in such Manner as' they shall by Law direct. The Number of Representatives shall not exceed one for every thirty Thousand,** but each State shall have at Least one Representative; and until such enumeration shall be made, the State of New Hampshire shall be entitled to chuse three, Massachusetts eight, Rhode-Island and Providence Plantations one, Connecticut five, New-York six, New Jersey four, Pennsylvania eight, Delaware one, Maryland six, Virginia ten, North Carolina five, South Carolina five, and Georgia three.

When vacancies happen in the Representation from any State, the Executive Authority thereof shall issue Writs of Election to fill such Vacancies.

The House of Representatives shall chuse their Speaker and other Officers; and shall have the sole Power of Impeachment.

SECTION 3. The Senate of the United States shall be composed of two Senators from each State, [chosen by the Legislature thereof,]*** for six Years; and each Senator shall have one Vote.

Immediately after they shall be assembled in Consequence of the first Election, they shall be divided as equally as may be into three Classes. The Seats of the Senators of the first Class shall be vacated at the Expiration of the second Year, of the second Class at the Expiration of the fourth Year, and of the third Class at the Expiration of the sixth Year, so that one-third may be chosen every second Year; [and if Vacancies happen by Resignation, or otherwise, during the Recess of the Legislature of any State, the Executive thereof may make temporary Appointments until

---

*Changed by section 2 of the fourteenth amendment.
**Ratio in 1965 was one to over 410,000.
***Changed by section 1 of the seventeenth amendment.

the next Meeting of the Legislature, which shall then fill such Vacancies.]*

No Person shall be a Senator who shall not have attained to the Age of thirty Years, and been nine Years a Citizen of the United States, and who shall not, when elected, be an Inhabitant of that State for which he shall be chosen.

The Vice President of the United States shall be President of the Senate, but shall have no Vote, unless they be equally divided.

The Senate shall chuse their other Officers, and also a President pro tempore, in the absence of the Vice President, or when he shall exercise the Office of President of the United States.

The Senate shall have the sole Power to try all Impeachments. When sitting for that Purpose, they shall be on Oath⋅or Affirmation. When the President of the United States is tried, the Chief Justice shall preside: And no Person shall be convicted without the Concurrence of two thirds of the Members present.

Judgment in Cases of Impeachment shall not extend further than to removal from Office, and disqualification to hold and enjoy any Office of honor, Trust or Profit under the United States: but the Party convicted shall nevertheless be liable and subject to Indictment, Trial, Judgment and Punishment, according to Law.

SECTION 4. The Times, Places and Manner of holding Elections for Senators and Representatives, shall be prescribed in each State by the Legislature thereof; but the Congress may at any time by Law make or alter such Regulations, except as to the Place of Chusing Senators.

The Congress shall assemble at least once in every Year, and such Meeting shall [be on the first Monday in December,]**unless they shall by Law appoint a different Day.

SECTION 5. Each House shall be the Judge of the Elections, Returns and Qualifications of its own Members, and a Majority of each shall constitute a Quorum to do Business; but a smaller number may adjourn from day to day, and may be authorized to compel the Attendance of absent Members, in such Manner, and under such Penalties as each House may provide.

Each House may determine the Rules of its Proceedings, punish its Members for disorderly Behavior, and, with the Concurrence of two thirds, expel a Member.

Each House shall keep a Journal of its Proceedings, and from time to time publish the same, excepting such Parts as may in their Judgment require Secrecy; and the Yeas and Nays of the Members of either House on any question shall, at the Desire of one fifth of those Present, be entered on the Journal.

Neither House, during the Session of Congress, shall, without the Consent of the other, adjourn for more than

*Changed by clause 2 of the seventeenth amendment.
**Changed by section 2 of the twentieth amendment.

three days, nor to any other Place than that in which the two Houses shall be sitting.

SECTION 6. The Senators and Representatives shall receive a Compensation for their Services, to be ascertained by Law, and paid out of the Treasury of the United States. They shall in all Cases, except Treason, Felony and Breach of the Peace, be privileged from Arrest during their Attendance at the Session of their respective Houses, and in going to and returning from the same; and for any Speech or Debate in either House, they shall not be questioned in any other Place.

No Senator or Representative shall, during the Time for which he was elected, be appointed to any civil Office under the Authority of the United States, which shall have been created, or the Emoluments whereof shall have been encreased during such time; and no Person holding any Office under the United States, shall be a Member of either House during his Continuance in Office.

SECTION 7. All Bills for raising Revenue shall originate in the House of Representatives; but the Senate may propose or concur with Amendments as on other Bills.

Every Bill which shall have passed the House of Representatives and the Senate, shall, before it become a Law, be presented to the President of the United States; If he approve he shall sign it, but if not he shall return it, with his Objections to that House in which it shall have originated, who shall enter the Objections at large on their Journal, and proceed to reconsider it. If after such Reconsideration two thirds of that House shall agree to pass the Bill, it shall be sent, together with the Objections, to the other House, by which it shall likewise be reconsidered, and if approved by two thirds of that House, it shall become a Law. But in all such Cases the Votes of both Houses shall be determined by Yeas and Nays, and the Names of the Persons voting for and against the Bill shall be entered on the Journal of each House respectively. If any Bill shall not be returned by the President within ten Days (Sundays excepted) after it shall have been presented to him, the Same shall be a Law, in like Manner as if he had signed it, unless the Congress by their Adjournment prevent its Return, in which Case it shall not be a Law.

Every Order, Resolution, or Vote to which the Concurrence of the Senate and House of Representatives may be necessary (except on a question of Adjournment) shall be presented to the President of the United States; and before the Same shall take Effect, shall be approved by him, or being disapproved by him, shall be repassed by two thirds of the Senate and House of Representatives, according to the Rules and Limitations prescribed in the Case of a Bill.

SECTION 8. The Congress shall have Power To lay and collect Taxes, Duties, Imposts and Excises, to pay the Debts and provide for the common Defence and general Welfare of the United States; but all Duties, Imposts and Excises shall be uniform throughout the United States;

To borrow money on the credit of the United States;

To regulate Commerce with foreign Nations, and among the several States, and with the Indian Tribes;

To establish an uniform Rule of Naturalization, and uniform Laws on the subject of Bankruptcies throughout the United States;

To coin Money, regulate the Value thereof, and of foreign Coin, and fix the Standard of Weights and Measures;

To provide for the Punishment of counterfeiting the Securities and current Coin of the United States;

To establish Post Offices and post Roads;

To promote the Progress of Science and useful Arts, by securing for limited Times to Authors and Inventors the exclusive Right to their respective Writings and Discoveries;

To constitute Tribunals inferior to the supreme Court;

To define and punish Piracies and Felonies committed on the high Seas, and Offenses against the Law of Nations;

To declare War, grant Letters of Marque and Reprisal, and make Rules concerning Captures on Land and Water;

To raise and support Armies, but no Appropriation of Money to that Use shall be for a longer Term than two Years;

To provide and maintain a Navy;

To make Rules for the Government and Regulation of the land and naval Forces;

To provide for calling forth the Militia to execute the Laws of the Union, suppress Insurrections and repel Invasions;

To provide for organizing, arming, and disciplining the Militia, and for governing such Part of them as may be employed in the Service of the United States, reserving to the States respectively, the Appointment of the Officers, and the Authority of training the Militia according to the discipline prescribed by Congress;

To exercise exclusive Legislation in all Cases whatsoever, over such District (not exceeding ten Miles square) as may, by Cession of particular States, and the acceptance of Congress, become the Seat of the Government of the United States, and to exercise like Authority over all Places purchased by the Consent of the Legislature of the State in which the Same shall be, for the Erection of Forts, Magazines, Arsenals, dock-Yards, and other needful Buildings;—And

To make all Laws which shall be necessary and proper for carrying into Execution the foregoing Powers, and all other Powers vested by this Constitution in the Government of the United States, or in any Department or Officer thereof.

SECTION 9. The Migration or Importation of such Persons as any of the States now existing shall think proper to admit, shall not be prohibited by the Congress prior to the Year one thousand eight hundred and eight, but a tax or duty may be imposed on such Importation, not exceeding ten dollars for each Person.

The privilege of the Writ of Habeas Corpus shall not be suspended, unless when in Cases of Rebellion or Invasion the public Safety may require it.

No Bill of Attainder or ex post facto Law shall be passed.

No capitation, or other direct, Tax shall be laid, unless in Proportion to the Census or Enumeration herein before directed to be taken.*

No Tax or Duty shall be laid on Articles exported from any State.

No Preference shall be given by any Regulation of Commerce or Revenue to the Ports of one State over those of another: nor shall Vessels bound to, or from, one State, be obliged to enter, clear, or pay Duties in another.

No Money shall be drawn from the Treasury, but in Consequence of Appropriations made by Law; and a regular Statement and Account of the Receipts and Expenditures of all public Money shall be published from time to time.

No Title of Nobility shall be granted by the United States: And no Person holding any Office of Profit or Trust under them, shall, without the Consent of the Congress, accept of any present, Emolument, Office, or Title, of any kind whatever, from any King, Prince, or foreign State.

Section 10. No State shall enter into any Treaty, Alliance, or Confederation; grant Letters of Marque and Reprisal; coin Money; emit Bills of Credit; make any Thing but gold and silver Coin a Tender in Payment of Debts; pass any Bill of Attainder, ex post facto Law, or Law impairing the Obligation of Contracts, or grant any Title of Nobility.

No State shall, without the Consent of the Congress, lay any Imposts or Duties on Imports or Exports, except what may be absolutely necessary for executing its inspection Laws: and the net Produce of all Duties and Imposts, laid by any State on Imports or Exports, shall be for the Use of the Treasury of the United States; and all such Laws shall be subject to the Revision and Controul of the Congress.

No State shall, without the Consent of Congress, lay any duty of Tonnage, keep Troops, or Ships of War in time of Peace, enter into any Agreement or Compact with another State, or with a foreign Power, or engage in War, unless actually invaded, or in such imminent Danger as will not admit of delay.

ARTICLE II.

Section 1. The executive Power shall be vested in a President of the United States of America. He shall hold his Office during the Term of four Years, and, together with the Vice-President, chosen for the same Term, be elected, as follows.

Each State shall appoint, in such Manner as the Legislature thereof may direct, a Number of Electors, equal to the whole Number of Senators and Representatives to

---

* But see the sixteenth amendment.

which the State may be entitled in the Congress: but no Senator or Representative, or Person holding an Office of Trust or Profit under the United States, shall be appointed an Elector.

[The Electors shall meet in their respective States, and vote by Ballot for two persons, of whom one at least shall not be an Inhabitant of the same State with themselves. And they shall make a List of all the Persons voted for, and of the Number of Votes for each; which List they shall sign and certify, and transmit sealed to the Seat of the Government of the United States, directed to the President of the Senate. The President of the Senate shall, in the Presence of the Senate and House of Representatives, open all the Certificates, and the Votes shall then be counted. The Person having the greatest Number of Votes shall be the President, if such Number be a Majority of the whole Number of Electors appointed; and if there be more than one who have such Majority, and have an equal Number of Votes, then the House of Representatives shall immediately chuse by Ballot one of them for President; and if no Person have a Majority, then from the five highest on the List the said House shall in like Manner chuse the President. But in chusing the President, the Votes shall be taken by States, the Representation from each State having one Vote; a quorum for this Purpose shall consist of a Member or Members from two thirds of the States, and a Majority of all the States shall be necessary to a Choice. In every Case, after the Choice of the President, the Person having the greatest Number of Votes of the Electors shall be the Vice President. But if there should remain two or more who have equal Votes, the Senate shall chuse from them by Ballot the Vice-President.]*

The Congress may determine the Time of chusing the Electors, and the Day on which they shall give their Votes; which Day shall be the same throughout the United States.

No person except a natural born Citizen, or a Citizen of the United States, at the time of the Adoption of this Constitution, shall be eligible to the Office of President; neither shall any Person be eligible to that Office who shall not have attained to the Age of thirty-five Years, and been fourteen Years a Resident within the United States.

**[In Case of the Removal of the President from Office, or of his Death, Resignation, or Inability to discharge the Powers and Duties of the said Office, the same shall devolve on the Vice President, and the Congress may by Law provide for the Case of Removal, Death, Resignation or Inability, both of the President and Vice President, declaring what Officer shall then act as President, and such Officer shall act accordingly, until the Disability be removed, or a President shall be elected.]

---

*Superseded by the twelfth amendment.
**This clause has been affected by the twenty-fifth amendment.

The President shall, at stated Times, receive for his Services, a Compensation, which shall neither be encreased nor diminished during the Period for which he shall have been elected, and he shall not receive within that Period any other Emolument from the United States, or any of them.

Before he enter on the Execution of his Office, he shall take the following Oath or Affirmation:—"I do solemnly swear (or affirm) that I will faithfully execute the Office of President of the United States, and will to the best of my Ability, preserve, protect and defend the Constitution of the United States."

SECTION 2. The President shall be Commander in Chief of the Army and Navy of the United States, and of the Militia of the several States, when called into the actual Service of the United States; he may require the Opinion in writing, of the principal Officer in each of the executive Departments, upon any subject relating to the Duties of their respective Offices, and he shall have Power to Grant Reprieves and Pardons for Offenses against the United States, except in Cases of Impeachment.

He shall have Power, by and with the Advice and Consent of the Senate, to make Treaties, provided two-thirds of the Senators present concur; and he shall nominate, and by and with the Advice and Consent of the Senate, shall appoint Ambassadors, other public Ministers and Consuls, Judges of the supreme Court, and all other Officers of the United States, whose Appointments are not herein otherwise provided for, and which shall be established by Law: but the Congress may by Law vest the Appointment of such inferior Officers, as they think proper, in the President alone, in the Courts of Law, or in the Heads of Departments.

The President shall have Power to fill up all Vacancies that may happen during the Recess of the Senate, by granting Commissions which shall expire at the End of their next Session.

SECTION 3. He shall from time to time give to the Congress Information of the State of the Union, and recommend to their Consideration such Measures as he shall judge necessary and expedient; he may, on extraordinary Occasions, convene both Houses, or either of them, and in Case of Disagreement between them, with Respect to the Time of Adjournment, he may adjourn them to such Time as he shall think proper; he shall receive Ambassadors and other public Ministers; he shall take Care that the Laws be faithfully executed, and shall Commission all the Officers of the United States.

SECTION 4. The President, Vice President and all civil Officers of the United States, shall be removed from Office on Impeachment for, and Conviction of, Treason, Bribery, or other high Crimes and Misdemeanors.

ARTICLE III.

SECTION 1. The judicial Power of the United States, shall be vested in one supreme Court, and in such inferior Courts as the Congress may from time to time ordain and establish. The Judges, both of the supreme and inferior Courts, shall hold their Offices during good Behaviour, and shall, at stated Times, receive for their Services, a Compensation, which shall not be diminished during their Continuance in Office.

SECTION 2. The judicial Power shall extend to all Cases, in Law and Equity, arising under this Constitution, the Laws of the United States, and Treaties made, or which shall be made, under their Authority;—to all Cases affecting Ambassadors, other public Ministers and Consuls;—to all Cases of admiralty and maritime Jurisdiction;—to Controversies to which the United States shall be a Party;—to Controversies between two or more States;—between a State and Citizens of another State;—between Citizens of different States;—between Citizens of the same State claiming Lands under Grants of different States, and between a State, or the Citizens thereof, and foreign States, Citizens or Subjects.

In all Cases affecting Ambassadors, other public Ministers and Consuls, and those in which a State shall be Party, the supreme Court shall have original Jurisdiction. In all the other Cases before mentioned, the supreme Court shall have appellate Jurisdiction, both as to Law and Fact, with such Exceptions, and under such Regulations as the Congress shall make.

The trial of all Crimes, except in Cases of Impeachment, shall be by Jury; and such Trial shall be held in the State where the said Crimes shall have been committed; but when not committed within any State, the Trial shall be at such Place or Places as the Congress may by Law have directed.

SECTION 3. Treason against the United States, shall consist only in levying War against them, or in adhering to their Enemies, giving them Aid and Comfort. No Person shall be convicted of Treason unless on the Testimony of two Witnesses to the same overt Act, or on Confession in open Court.

The Congress shall have Power to declare the Punishment of Treason, but no Attainder of Treason shall work Corruption of Blood, or Forfeiture except during the Life of the Person attainted.

ARTICLE IV.

SECTION 1. Full Faith and Credit shall be given in each State to the public Acts, Records, and judicial Proceedings of every other State. And the Congress may by general

Laws prescribe the Manner in which such Acts, Records and Proceedings shall be proved, and the Effect thereof.

Section 2. The Citizens of each State shall be entitled to all Privileges and Immunities of Citizens in the several States.

A Person charged in any State with Treason, Felony, or other Crime, who shall flee from Justice, and be found in another State, shall on demand of the executive Authority of the State from which he fled, be delivered up, to be removed to the State having Jurisdiction of the Crime.

[No Person held to Service or Labour in one State, under the Laws thereof, escaping into another, shall, in Consequence of any Law or Regulation therein, be discharged from such Service or Labour, but shall be delivered up on Claim of the Party to whom such Service or Labour may be due.]*

Section 3. New States may be admitted by the Congress into this Union; but no new State shall be formed or erected within the Jurisdiction of any other State; nor any State be formed by the Junction of two or more States, or parts of States, without the Consent of the Legislatures of the States concerned as well as of the Congress.

The Congress shall have Power to dispose of and make all needful Rules and Regulations respecting the Territory or other Property belonging to the United States; and nothing in this Constitution shall be so construed as to Prejudice any Claims of the United States, or of any particular State.

Section 4. The United States shall guarantee to every State in this Union a Republican Form of Government, and shall protect each of them against Invasion; and on Application of the Legislature, or of the Executive (when the Legislature cannot be convened) against domestic Violence.

ARTICLE V.

The Congress, whenever two-thirds of both Houses shall deem it necessary, shall propose Amendments to this Constitution, or, on the Application of the Legislatures of two-thirds of the several States, shall call a Convention for proposing Amendments, which, in either Case, shall be valid to all Intents and Purposes, as part of this Constitution, when ratified by the Legislatures of three-fourths of the several States, or by Conventions in three-fourths thereof, as the one or the other Mode of Ratification may be proposed by the Congress: Provided that no Amendment which may be made prior to the Year One thousand eight hundred and eight shall in any Manner affect the first and fourth Clauses in the Ninth Section of the first Article; and that no State, without its Consent, shall be deprived of its equal Suffrage in the Senate.

---

*Superseded by the thirteenth amendment.

ARTICLE VI.

All Debts contracted and Engagements entered into, before the Adoption of this Constitution, shall be as valid against the United States under this Constitution, as under the Confederation.

This Constitution, and the Laws of the United States which shall be made in Pursuance thereof; and all Treaties made, or which shall be made, under the Authority of the United States, shall be the supreme Law of the Land; and the Judges in every State shall be bound thereby, any Thing in the Constitution or Laws of any State to the Contrary notwithstanding.

The Senators and Representatives before mentioned, and the Members of the several State Legislatures, and all executive and judicial Officers, both of the United States and of the several States, shall be bound by Oath or Affirmation, to support this Constitution; but no religious Test shall ever be required as a Qualification to any Office or public Trust under the United States.

ARTICLE VII.

The Ratification of the Conventions of nine States shall be sufficient for the Establishment of this Constitution between the States so ratifying the Same.

ARTICLES IN ADDITION TO, AND AMENDMENT OF, THE CONSTITUTION OF THE UNITED STATES OF AMERICA, PROPOSED BY CONGRESS, AND RATIFIED BY THE LEGISLATURES OF THE SEVERAL STATES, PURSUANT TO THE FIFTH ARTICLE OF THE ORIGINAL CONSTITUTION.*

AMENDMENT I. (1791)**

Congress shall make no law respecting an establishment of religion, or prohibiting the free exercise thereof; or abridging the freedom of speech, or of the press; or the right of the people peaceably to assemble, and to petition the Government for a redress of grievances.

AMENDMENT II. (1791)

A well regulated Militia, being necessary to the security of a free State, the right of the people to keep and bear Arms, shall not be infringed.

AMENDMENT III. (1791)

No Soldier shall, in time of peace be quartered in any house, without the consent of the Owner, nor in time of war, but in a manner to be prescribed by law.

---

*Amendment XXI was not ratified by state legislatures, but by state conventions summoned by Congress.
**Date of ratification.

AMENDMENT IV. (1791)

The right of the people to be secure in their persons, houses, papers, and effects, against unreasonable searches and seizures, shall not be violated, and no Warrants shall issue, but upon probable cause, supported by Oath or affirmation, and particularly describing the place to be searched, and the persons or things to be seized.

AMENDMENT V. (1791)

No person shall be held to answer for a capital, or otherwise infamous crime, unless on a presentment or indictment of a Grand Jury, except in cases arising in the land or naval forces, or in the Militia, when in actual service in time of War or public danger; nor shall any person be subject for the same offence to be twice put in jeopardy of life or limb; nor shall be compelled in any criminal case to be a witness against himself, nor be deprived of life, liberty, or property, without due process of law; nor shall private property be taken for public use, without just compensation.

AMENDMENT VI. (1791)

In all criminal prosecutions, the accused shall enjoy the right to a speedy and public trial, by an impartial jury of the State and district wherein the crime shall have been committed, which district shall have been previously ascertained by law, and to be informed of the nature and cause of the accusation; to be confronted with the witnesses against him; to have compulsory process for obtaining witnesses in his favor, and to have the Assistance of Counsel for his defence.

AMENDMENT VII. (1791)

In suits at common law, where the value in controversy shall exceed twenty dollars, the right of trial by jury shall be preserved, and no fact tried by a jury, shall be otherwise reexamined in any Court of the United States, than according to the rules of the common law.

AMENDMENT VIII. (1791)

Excessive bail shall not be required, nor excessive fines imposed, nor cruel and unusual punishments inflicted.

AMENDMENT IX. (1791)

The enumeration in the Constitution, of certain rights, shall not be construed to deny or disparage others retained by the people.

AMENDMENT X. (1791)

The powers not delegated to the United States by the Constitution, nor prohibited by it to the States, are reserved to the States respectively, or to the people.

AMENDMENT XI. (1795)

The Judicial power of the United States shall not be construed to extend to any suit in law or equity, commenced or prosecuted against one of the United States by Citizens of another State, or by Citizens or Subjects of any Foreign State.

AMENDMENT XII. (1804)

The Electors shall meet in their respective states and vote by ballot for President and Vice-President, one of whom, at least, shall not be an inhabitant of the same state with themselves; they shall name in their ballots the person voted for as President, and in distinct ballots the person voted for as Vice-President, and they shall make distinct lists of all persons voted for as President, and of all persons voted for as Vice-President, and of the number of votes for each, which lists they shall sign and certify, and transmit sealed to the seat of the government of the United States, directed to the President of the Senate;—The President of the Senate shall, in presence of the Senate and House of Representatives, open all the certificates and the votes shall then be counted;—The person having the greatest number of votes for President, shall be the President, if such number be a majority of the whole number of Electors appointed; and if no person have such majority, then from the persons having the highest numbers not exceeding three on the list of those voted for as President, the House of Representatives shall choose immediately, by ballot, the President. But in choosing the President, the votes shall be taken by states, the representation from each state having one vote; a quorum for this purpose shall consist of a member or members from two-thirds of the states, and a majority of all the states shall be necessary to a choice. [And if the House of Representatives shall not choose a President whenever the right of choice shall devolve upon them, before the fourth day of March next following, then the Vice-President shall act as President, as in the case of the death or other constitutional disability of the President.—]* The person having the greatest number of votes as Vice-President, shall be the Vice-President, if such number be a majority of the whole number of Electors appointed, and if no person have a majority, then from the two highest numbers on the list, the Senate shall choose the Vice-President; a quorum for the purpose shall consist of two-thirds of the whole number of Senators, and a majority of the whole number shall be necessary to a choice. But no person constitutionally ineligible to the office of President shall be eligible to that of Vice-President of the United States.

AMENDMENT XIII. (1865)

SECTION 1. Neither slavery nor involuntary servitude, except as a punishment for crime whereof the party shall have been duly convicted, shall exist within the United

---

*Superseded by section 3 of the twentieth amendment.

States, or any place subject to their jurisdiction.

SECTION 2. Congress shall have power to enforce this article by appropriate legislation.

AMENDMENT XIV. (1868)

SECTION 1. All persons born or naturalized in the United States, and subject to the jurisdiction thereof, are citizens of the United States and of the State wherein they reside. No State shall make or enforce any law which shall abridge the privileges or immunities of citizens of the United States; nor shall any State deprive any person of life, liberty, or property, without due process of law; nor deny to any person within its jurisdiction the equal protection of the laws.

SECTION 2. Representatives shall be apportioned among the several States according to their respective numbers, counting the whole number of persons in each State, excluding Indians not taxed. But when the right to vote at any election for the choice of electors for President and Vice-President of the United States, Representatives in Congress, the Executive and Judicial officers of a State, or the members of the Legislature thereof, is denied to any of the male inhabitants of such State, being twenty-one years of age, and citizens of the United States, or in any way abridged, except for participation in rebellion, or other crime, the basis of representation therein shall be reduced in the proportion which the number of such male citizens shall bear to the whole number of male citizens twenty-one years of age in such State.

SECTION 3. No person shall be a Senator or Representative in Congress, or elector of President and Vice-President, or hold any office, civil or military, under the United States, or under any State, who, having previously taken an oath, as a member of Congress, or as an officer of the United States, or as a member of any State legislature, or as an executive or judicial officer of any State, to support the Constitution of the United States, shall have engaged in insurrection or rebellion against the same, or given aid or comfort to the enemies thereof. But Congress may by a vote of two-thirds of each House, remove such disability.

SECTION 4. The validity of the public debt of the United States, authorized by law, including debts incurred for payment of pensions and bounties for services in suppressing insurrection or rebellion, shall not be questioned. But neither the United States nor any State shall assume or pay any debt or obligation incurred in aid of insurrection or rebellion against the United States, or any claim for the loss or emancipation of any slave; but all such debts, obligations and claims shall be held illegal and void.

SECTION 5. The Congress shall have power to enforce, by appropriate legislation, the provisions of this article.

AMENDMENT XV. (1870)

SECTION 1. The right of citizens of the United States to vote shall not be denied or abridged by the United States or by any State on account of race, color, or previous condition of servitude—

SECTION 2. The Congress shall have power to enforce this article by appropriate legislation.

AMENDMENT XVI. (1913)

The Congress shall have power to lay and collect taxes on incomes, from whatever source derived, without apportionment among the several States, and without regard to any census or enumeration.

AMENDMENT XVII. (1913)

The Senate of the United States shall be composed of two Senators from each State, elected by the people thereof, for six years; and each Senator shall have one vote. The electors in each State shall have the qualifications requisite for electors of the most numerous branch of the State legislatures.

When vacancies happen in the representation of any State in the Senate, the executive authority of such State shall issue writs of election to fill such vacancies: *Provided*, That the legislature of any State may empower the executive thereof to make temporary appointments until the people fill the vacancies by election as the legislature may direct.

This amendment shall not be so construed as to affect the election or term of any Senator chosen before it becomes valid as part of the Constitution.

AMENDMENT XVIII. (1919)

[SECTION 1. After one year from the ratification of this article the manufacture, sale, or transportation of intoxicating liquors within, the importation thereof into, or the exportation thereof from the United States and all territory subject to the jurisdiction thereof for beverage purposes is hereby prohibited.

[SECTION 2. The Congress and the several States shall have concurrent power to enforce this article by appropriate legislation.

[SECTION 3. This article shall be inoperative unless it shall have been ratified as an amendment to the Constitution by the legislatures of the several States, as provided in the Constitution, within seven years from the date of the submission hereof to the States by the Congress.]*

AMENDMENT XIX. (1920)

The right of citizens of the United States to vote shall not be denied or abridged by the United States or by any State on account of sex.

Congress shall have power to enforce this article by appropriate legislation.

---

*Repealed by section 1 of the twenty-first amendment.

AMENDMENT XX. (1933)

SECTION 1. The terms of the President and Vice President shall end at noon on the 20th day of January, and the terms of Senators and Representatives at noon on the 3d day of January, of the years in which such terms would have ended if this article had not been ratified; and the terms of their successors shall then begin.

SECTION 2. The Congress shall assemble at least once in every year, and such meeting shall begin at noon on the 3d day of January, unless they shall by law appoint a different day.

SECTION 3. If, at the time fixed for the beginning of the term of the President, the President elect shall have died, the Vice President elect shall become President. If a President shall not have been chosen before the time fixed for the beginning of his term, or if the President elect shall have failed to qualify, then the Vice President elect shall act as President until a President shall have qualified; and the Congress may by law provide for the case wherein neither a President elect nor a Vice President elect shall have qualified, declaring who shall then act as President, or the manner in which one who is to act shall be selected, and such person shall act accordingly until a President or Vice President shall have qualified.

SECTION 4. The Congress may by law provide for the case of the death of any of the persons from whom the House of Representatives may choose a President whenever the right of choice shall have devolved upon them, and for the case of the death of any of the persons from whom the Senate may choose a Vice President whenever the right of choice shall have devolved upon them.

SECTION 5. Sections 1 and 2 shall take effect on the 15th day of October following the ratification of this article.

SECTION 6. This article shall be inoperative unless it shall have been ratified as an amendment to the Constitution by the legislatures of three-fourths of the several States within seven years from the date of its submission.

AMENDMENT XXI. (1933)

SECTION 1. The eighteenth article of amendment to the Constitution of the United States is hereby repealed.

SECTION 2. The transportation or importation into any State, Territory, or possession of the United States for delivery or use therein of intoxicating liquors, in violation of the laws thereof, is hereby prohibited.

SECTION 3. This article shall be inoperative unless it shall have been ratified as an amendment to the Constitution by conventions in the several States, as provided in the Constitution, within seven years from the date of the submission hereof to the States by the Congress.

AMENDMENT XXII. (1951)

SECTION 1. No person shall be elected to the office of the President more than twice, and no person who has held the office of President, or acted as President, for more than two years of a term to which some other person was elected President shall be elected to the office of the President more than once. But this Article shall not apply to any person holding the office of President when this Article was proposed by the Congress, and shall not prevent any person who may be holding the office of President, or acting as President, during the term within which this Article becomes operative from holding the office of President or acting as President during the remainder of such term.

SECTION 2. This article shall be inoperative unless it shall have been ratified as an amendment to the Constitution by the legislatures of three-fourths of the several States within seven years from the date of its submission to the States by the Congress.

AMENDMENT XXIII. (1961)

SECTION 1. The District constituting the seat of Government of the United States shall appoint in such manner as the Congress may direct:

A number of electors of President and Vice President equal to the whole number of Senators and Representatives in Congress to which the District would be entitled if it were a State, but in no event more than the least populous State; they shall be in addition to those appointed by the States, but they shall be considered, for the purposes of the election of President and Vice President, to be electors appointed by a State; and they shall meet in the District and perform such duties as provided by the twelfth article of amendment.

SECTION 2. The Congress shall have power to enforce this article by appropriate legislation.

AMENDMENT XXIV. (1964)

SECTION 1. The right of citizens of the United States to vote in any primary or other election for President or Vice President, for electors for President or Vice President, or for Senator or Representative in Congress, shall not be denied or abridged by the United States or any State by reason of failure to pay any poll tax or other tax.

SECTION 2. The Congress shall have power to enforce this article by appropriate legislation.

AMENDMENT XXV. (1967)

SECTION 1. In case of the removal of the President from office or of his death or resignation, the Vice President shall become President.

SECTION 2. Whenever there is a vacancy in the office of the Vice President, the President shall nominate a Vice President who shall take office upon confirmation by a majority vote of both Houses of Congress.

SECTION 3. Whenever the President transmits to the President pro tempore of the Senate and the Speaker of the

House of Representatives his written declaration that he is
unable to discharge the powers and duties of his office,
and until he transmits to them a written declaration to the
contrary, such powers and duties shall be discharged by
the Vice President as Acting President.

Section 4. Whenever the Vice President and a majority
of either the principal officers of the executive departments
or of such other body as Congress may by law provide,
transmit to the President pro tempore of the Senate and the
Speaker of the House of Representatives their written
declaration that the President is unable to discharge the
powers and duties of his office, the Vice President shall
immediately assume the powers and duties of the office as
Acting President.

Thereafter, when the President transmits to the President
pro tempore of the Senate and the Speaker of the House of
Representatives his written declaration that no inability
exists, he shall resume the powers and duties of his office
unless the Vice President and a majority of either the
principal officers of the executive department or of such
other body as Congress may by law provide, transmit
within four days to the President pro tempore of the Senate
and the Speaker of the House of Representatives
their written declaration that the President is unable to
discharge the powers and duties of his office. Thereupon
Congress shall decide the issue, assembling within forty-
eight hours for that purpose if not in session. If the Congress,
within twenty-one days after receipt of the latter written
declaration, or, if Congress is not in session, within twenty-
one days after Congress is required to assemble, determines
by two-thirds vote of both Houses that the President is
unable to discharge the powers and duties of his office, the
Vice President shall continue to discharge the same as
Acting President; otherwise, the President shall resume the
powers and duties of his office.

AMENDMENT XXVI. (1971)

Section 1. The right of citizens of the United States, who
are eighteen years of age or older, to vote shall not be denied
or abridged by the United States or by any State on account
of age.

Section 2. The Congress shall have power to enforce this
article by appropriate legislation.